START YOUR OWN

AT-HOME

CHILD CARE

BUSINESS

START YOUR OWN

AT-HOME

CHILD CARE

BUSINESS

Patricia C. Gallagher

Doubleday

NEW YORK   LONDON   TORONTO   SYDNEY   AUCKLAND

*To my wonderful husband John
To my beautiful children:
Robin, Katelyn, and Kristen
To my loving parents and my family for their
enthusiastic support*

Published by Doubleday, a division of Bantam Doubleday
Dell Publishing Group, Inc., 666 Fifth Avenue, New York, New
York 10103.

Doubleday and the portrayal of an anchor with a dolphin are
trademarks of Doubleday, a division of Bantam Doubleday
Dell Publishing Group, Inc.

The first aid section on pages 103–5 is reprinted with the
permission of the American Academy of Pediatrics, © 1989.

Library of Congress Cataloging-in-Publication Data
Gallagher, Patricia C.
Start your own at-home child care business.
Rev. ed. of: Child care and you. 1987.
Bibliography: p.
1. Day care centers—United States.   I. Gallagher,
Patricia C.   Child care and you.   II. Title.
HV854.G35   1989   362.7′12′068   89-1562
ISBN 0-385-24896-2
ISBN 0-385-24582-3 (pbk.)

This book is a revised and expanded edition of *Child Care
and You*, originally published by Gallagher, Jordan & Asso-
ciates in 1987.

All Rights Reserved
Printed in the United States of America
Book design by Chris Welch
June 1989
First Edition
BG

ACKNOWLEDGMENTS

So many experienced child care providers have enthusiastically shared their ideas with me during workshops, interviews, and friendly conversations.

I would especially like to thank Sandra Gellert and Maria Otto for their dedication to establishing family day care as a profession of status and honor. The Child Care Law Center, San Francisco, has paved the way for providers involved with zoning issues. Child Care Solutions and Metro Day Care Systems, information and referral services in my home state, have helped countless providers to manage their business through educational workshops.

Susan Gordon, Pam Faix, Kathy Reed, Carol Fountain, Missy Ridpath, Margaret Machemer, Carol Gubitosa, and Deborah Sims have all shared practical ideas about child care with me.

Peter Manakos, director of the Lansdale Library, and Marion Peck of the Montgomery County library have offered encouragement and helpful suggestions that are greatly appreciated.

Rachel Klayman, my editor, has been wonderful. She has the natural ability to put herself in the role of a potential child care provider and posed all of the right questions. I am grateful for her dedication to this book.

Last, but certainly not least, to my friend, Susannah Thomer, who has typed and retyped many versions of this book. Her sense of humor and "unofficial editor" interest helped to make the technical aspects of completing this book a lot of fun.

To all of my assistants who have helped me in my child care programs over the years, especially Marianne, Alice, Diane, and Dot, I offer my gratitude.

Preface

There was a time when a successful career was vitally important to me. I was a woman born in the early fifties, college-educated in the sixties, and married in the mid-seventies. The media had devoted a great deal of attention to the recognition, high salaries, and impressive credentials women could expect in the modern business world. But what about motherhood? Smiles, hugs, kisses, and the thrill of teaching my toddlers has given me a sense of satisfaction I never experienced in the workplace.

Like many other women of my generation, I delayed the decision about whether to have a child until my thirties. My husband and I even wondered what a life without children would be like. Would we be able to enjoy vicariously the excitement of watching our nieces and nephews dyeing Easter eggs or waiting for Santa?

My "moment of truth" came about as I returned from a business trip to St. Louis. On the return flight I was seated next to a woman who was an obstetrician. She asked my age and whether I had any children. She said at my age I had no time to waste. It was that chance conversation which caused a change in my life.

Almost a year later to the day Robin Leigh arrived.

Robin was a delight, and within eighteen months she had a sister, Katelyn. We "struck gold" again! I guess you could say that I have adapted to motherhood because we now have a third little girl, Kristen Janine.

But there was one major shortcoming. When I left the corporate world we became a single-income family, although we wanted to continue to live the lifestyle of a working husband and wife. Faced with this dilemma, I sought to assess my strengths and weaknesses with the thought of launching my own business.

I felt there were three criteria that would make such a business worthwhile. It had to be profitable, emotionally satisfying, and home-based so that I could be with my children.

It's important to mention that I returned to my career after my first baby. John and I juggled careers, housework, my evening MBA program, and parenthood! We were both realistic enough to know that we could not expect such smooth sailing with two babies and a similar schedule. It was my decision to give up the "glamor" of getting up at 6 A.M., sitting in traffic jams, worrying about job performance, and returning home exhausted at 6 P.M.

I had worked for a major corporation for four and a half years when I received the wonderful news that I was expecting my first child. Several women in my department had recently had babies and it all seemed so exciting. They were the center of attention, and everyone was constantly asking them how they felt, when they were due, were they coming back to work, how soon, were they going to bottle-feed or nurse? Then just a few days before their scheduled leave of absence a luncheon was held in their honor, and they were given lots of beautiful baby items. The luncheon, of course, was a surprise.

In May of 1982 it was my turn. I told a few people that I was expecting and of course swore them to secrecy so they wouldn't tell anyone—yet. It was always crucial to tell your manager at the right time that you were leaving, especially for me since, as an account representative, I wanted to be sure that any sales I was working on would be credited to me.

For that reason I told my manager that I would be back on the job within three months. "Please don't give my accounts to anyone else. I'm coming back!" I told him. I did return within twelve weeks, but as I look back I really wonder how I did it. How could I have left my precious "bundle of joy" in someone else's care?

At the time it was not a difficult decision; I had seen so many others return to work that I assumed I would do the same. But the decision did cost me something. I lost fourteen months of nurturing, loving, and spending full days with my baby. Yes, I made a respectable amount of money and it did help our family afford what many consider luxuries, but I now wish that I had spent more time with Robin. All of my neighbors sent their children to nursery school but when Robin was of preschool age I decided not to do so. I needed time to catch up. There are many women like me who are opting to put their careers on the back burner and are interested in providing a child care service for working parents.

I wrote this book to give practical information to the woman who wants to supplement her family's income by starting a child care program in her own home. Such a program is a service offered to working parents whose children you watch on a regular basis. The ideas contained here will also have wide appeal to others who are interested in helping children to learn and develop through creative activities. Preschool teachers, volunteers for church baby-sitting services, baby-sitters, day care aides, and grandparents may also find the activities, safety tips, and playroom suggestions extremely beneficial. Even if you do not wish to begin a full-time child care program, you might enjoy offering a "mother's day out" program in your home once a week.

I made a career change from teaching to corporate life in the late seventies. Now that I am home with my own children, I appreciate my varied academic and occupational experiences because they have enabled me to create a satisfying job for myself while enjoying the role of full-time mother and wife.

And you can too! Though our backgrounds may not be the same, don't sell yourself short. By simply following my suggestions and using your natural creativity, you will be on your way to supplementing your family's income.

CONTENTS

AUTHOR'S NOTE

Although the children in your care will be
both boys and girls, I have chosen to use the
pronoun "he" when referring to children so
that this book will read more smoothly. Since
most caregivers are women, I have used
"she" when referring to the caregiver.

Introduction

This book is a guide for those who would like to start a child care program in their home or apartment. Such a program can be profitable and enjoyable provided you have a plan.

If you simply follow the steps and the daily plans outlined in this book, you should have no problem. Probably one of the greatest advantages of this business is that it requires little cash outlay.

In addition, by working from your home, you will note savings in expenses that are usually incurred when you work outside the home. Gas, daily lunches, contributing to office collections, and wardrobe expenses are reduced. For me, there was also the very valuable benefit of totally eliminating my own child care expense.

The child care business gives you almost immediate profit because you are paid on a regular basis. The start-up costs are minimal since many of you will be able to use what you already have in your home. Although you may need baby equipment, toys, and some other supplies, you will be pleasantly surprised to find that your friends and relatives have lots of used items that they would be glad to pass on to help you get started in your new venture. When the word gets around that you enjoy caring for children, the inquiry calls will start very quickly. I also found that my day care parents passed used equipment on to me after their child outgrew the need for a walker, swing, or portable cribs.

There are many other intangible benefits to being a day care provider. My own children had plenty of playmates and I was glad that I could be with Robin and Katelyn to share their small triumphs throughout the day. A friend whose own children are in elementary school has found that the children in her care help fulfill her need for love and affection throughout the day. And Estelle, my wonderful neighbor who offered to care for my daughter Robin, enjoyed our "little bird" because she knew that she was helping a baby to get off to a good start in life. She devoted herself to Robin as if my daughter were one of her own children.

All of us have something special within ourselves that we can offer children. I hope that you will see the home day care business as a way to grow in many directions. You will discover that you have many talents and abilities you never knew you possessed. It is wonderful to be considered a child care professional and to operate your own highly valued business. You will gain confidence as you meet and get to know many different types of people.

If your background includes baby-sitting, teaching, nursing, mothering, or any position that has included working with children, you are probably highly qualified. Of course, the most important credential is a love of children. You will discover techniques for reaching each child in your care as you gain experience. The simple ideas for keeping children entertained with interesting crafts, games, songs, and educational activities will make the hours fly by. The activities do not require special equipment or expensive supplies, only items that most of us have on hand. If not, substitutes are easily found.

Good luck with your new, extremely rewarding venture!

In this book I will refer to various statutes and regulations and comment upon common childhood illnesses and injuries. Of course, this book is not a substitute for legal or medical advice. You should consult all the applicable laws and regulations in your state before you set up your at-home child care business. Further, in all matters relating to a child's health, particularly in respect to any symptoms which may require diagnosis or medical attention, the parents and the child's physician should be consulted first.

OFF TO A
GOOD START

Examining Your Motives
for This Business

Do you love children? Do you need to earn money? Or is it some combination of the two?

Many people think that taking care of children is an easy way to earn money. They reason that, since they are at home with their own children, they might as well take in a few more. Although it might sound easy at first, ask anyone who is caring for children and they will tell you that it is not that simple. It has its good points and bad ones like any other job. As any mother knows, some days run more smoothly than others. This is, after all, a job, not just baby-sitting for a couple of hours at night when the child is sleeping. As a provider of child care, you should be able to love children other than your own. Mothers and fathers all over the country are looking for a loving caregiver for their children.

Some people just love children and don't need the money they earn from child care to buy their groceries and pay their bills.

Such people are very fortunate and rare but they do exist. I know, because Estelle, the woman who cared for my child, was very patient about our payments and very casual about the number of hours for which we owed her. At the end of the week we would say, "How many hours did you work?" and she would reply, "Oh, about seventeen!" My husband and I knew that she was doing us a favor, since Robin was usually there at least three full days a week, or twenty-four hours. Estelle's children were grown and I knew she was sensitive to the financial situation of a young family with two working parents. She gave us many breaks about paying and offered many extra services. On many occasions, while she cooked for her own family, she made extra food for us so that we had something already prepared when we got home. This type of child care arrangement is ideal, almost like having a fairy godmother.

If you are in this to make money, however, you must plan to run your home like a business. From the outset, you must be organized so that your clients know that this is your chosen profession and that the income you earn is as important to you as the money they receive from their employers. For example, since the parents are probably paid for holidays such as Christmas and Thanksgiving or when they call in sick, these same benefits should apply to you.

When you meet with parents on the initial visit, you must go into detail about policies. Many people use a contract of some type. In this book you will find a description of the major points you will want to mention in your contractual agreement with parents.

Your style of child care may be somewhere between the two approaches I've described. Caregivers who are "strictly business" may state in their contract that parents must pay for the whole week whether their children come or not. Other providers may feel that the parents should pay only for the days that a child attends. The policies of your day care program must reflect your own personal style. It may interest you to know, though, that as I talk to people around the country conflicts about payment are the number one problem.

Assessing Your Aptitude as a
Day Care Provider

First I want to dispel the myth that the child care business is an easy way to make money. The only people who could really believe that have never done it themselves. They are akin to the father who thinks that his wife has it easy all day at home with the kids. His opportunity to understand her many challenging roles comes when his wife is hospitalized or takes on part-time work and it is his turn. This same man finds himself praising his wife and saying, "I really have to give you credit—I don't know how you do it all!"

The questions that follow will heighten your awareness of what is required of someone who opens her home and hopefully her heart to a group of children. Try to be honest with yourself as you ask yourself these questions.

- Are you healthy and energetic?
- Do you have a great deal of patience?
- Are you tolerant of different types of people?
- Do you enjoy children other than your own?
- How do you handle emergency situations?
- How do you feel about wear and tear on your furniture?
- Can you stand a messy house?
- Can you provide a warm environment that will make a child feel welcome?
- Can you tolerate marks on your walls and daily spills on your floors?
- Are you self-controlled?
- Do you want the responsibility of caring for someone else's children?
- How does your family feel about this venture?
- Can you modify your home to make it conducive to the care of young children?
- Are you interested in reading about new trends in child rearing and child development?

- Can you understand the day care family well enough not to try to take the place of the parent or parents?
- Are you dependable?
- Are you flexible in your dealings with other people?
- Are you sensitive to other people's feelings?
- Do you react in a mature fashion in stressful situations?
- Children need continuity and love. Can you offer them this kind of security for a year?
- Do you have references? (By this, I mean people who know you well and will attest to your character and competence.)

When I first decided to offer a day care program, I enthusiastically related my plans to a good friend, who had five children under the age of nine. She, too, had a teaching background and loved children. I knew that she had held various part-time jobs over the years in order to supplement the family income, so I felt that this would be a perfect business for her too. I was shocked when her facial expression conveyed that this was the last type of job she would be interested in. Although she would be extremely competent and would have passed any suitability test, she wanted to branch out in areas not related to children. At that stage of her life it was important to her to pursue her interests in landscaping and in learning computer programming. Perhaps when her own children are grown, she may see this business as a way to utilize all of those valuable years spent living with and loving children.

Another example comes to mind of an acquaintance who is very competent but, at present, not suited for this home-based opportunity. She and her husband recently separated and she needs an income. Because the marital difficulty stemmed from domestic violence, she fears her husband will cause a scene while she is providing day care. The environment is not a stable one for her or for children. She has all the qualities of a loving caregiver but the timing isn't right.

In a recent workshop that I offered, one woman spoke of how difficult she has found the day care business. During the discussion that followed, we examined why she was unhappy. It was not her decision to start a day care program. Her husband felt strongly that mothers with small children should not work outside of the home, and it was he who decided that she should offer a day care program. She foolishly agreed to do this for three years.

This is not the kind of business you should start by default. I hope by asking yourself the questions listed earlier, you will get a realistic picture of what is important.

I can honestly say that I love caring for children in my home but you have to answer truthfully when you ask yourself, "Am I suited for this profession?"

Self-employment Versus Agency Affiliation

Now that you have assessed your aptitude, it's time to decide whether you would like to operate as an independent day care provider or be affiliated with an agency.

Many people who elect to care for children in their homes start their businesses entirely on their own. They call about licensing or registration, procure insurance coverage, purchase all of the necessary supplies, childproof their homes, advertise for clients, and proceed independently. This type of day care arrangement allows you to be self-employed and responsible for all aspects of organization and operation.

Agency affiliation is another way to start. Agencies contract with day care providers to care for children of parents who would not otherwise be able to afford the weekly fee.

Many religious organizations, welfare groups, and community associations recruit suitable child care providers for parents. They work with you in all aspects of setting up your business. They often provide orientation and regular supervision. They usually collect the fee from the parent or parents and pay you a fixed amount per child. They provide helpful hints about the best way to handle discipline, sibling rivalry, and other difficult issues. Ideas for providing age-appropriate activities are usually included as part of the program.

There are many advantages to this sort of arrangement: the

sponsoring organization may provide arts and craft supplies, baby equipment, toys, books, and other necessary start-up equipment. They also provide the children you will be caring for, which means you are spared the trouble of advertising. The agency usually provides substitute care in case of your illness, and may also offer free insurance or assistance in locating low-cost coverage.

One drawback from a financial standpoint is that you may have to take a certain number of "subsidized" children. In a nonexclusive type of agreement, you may take subsidized children as well as others.

Of course, by affiliating with an agency, you lose some control over the way you operate your business. In a sense, you are working for the agency. Before making the final decision about agency affiliation versus self-employment, find out more about the benefits of each by calling your state licensing office. They will be happy to give you the name of the agency that is responsible for recruiting subsidized day care providers. The agency in turn will explain its program to you. You may also want to talk to providers who have worked independently and those who have worked under the auspices of an agency. Find out the pros and cons from their personal experiences.

Since caring for children through an agency may be partially supported by state or federal budgets, you may find there are additional regulations you must adhere to. Some mothers have told me they think it is a good idea to begin family day care by working for an agency. You can benefit from the guidance you'll receive and probably save yourself some costly mistakes and unnecessary frustration. This is the reason why franchises are so popular in the business world. You do not want to reinvent the wheel.

Professional Contacts

My advice would be to go through the proper channels and comply with all requirements so that you can say with pride that you are a professional child care provider.

- Contact whatever agency in your state or city is involved with children to learn of specific safety, education, and health requirements that are applicable when caring for children in your home. Most states require licensing or registration, although specific requirements vary from state to state. Even after the state approves, your town or county may have additional requirements for you to follow. They may be more specific about health, sanitation, fire, nutrition, and safety. No matter how many children the licensing bureau permits you to care for, you must consider your personal limits. Six children may be manageable for one person but very frustrating for you. Make sure you comply with those regulations. Parents will be more willing to leave a child in your care if you are state-approved or state-licensed.

My advice would be to contact the licensing bureau in your state (see Appendix A). There is often confusion about whether you need to be registered, licensed, or certified when caring for children in your home. In some states it is voluntary and in others mandatory. And in a few states there is no regulation at all. So that you are fully aware of what is required in your state, call or write and ask for a complete application package for home-based family child care. The packet will probably include a copy of your state's regulations, an application form, a survey about your home, and a form for your doctor to fill out about your health (see Appendix D for sample forms). In addition, there may be forms to fill out stating that you have not been convicted of child abuse or neglect of children. Owing to the case overload of many licensing departments, you may never be visited for a site approval, and you will probably receive by mail your certificate to operate.

Because so much legislation concerning family day care is pending, be sure that you understand what is *currently* required. You will probably be surprised to learn that the regulations are minimal, and you will likely have no problem with compliance. The regulations are meant to serve as minimum standards for health and safety, but it is really up to the parents to monitor the care that their children receive. In some states the providers are instructed to give a copy of the rules and regulations to the day care parents. If the parents note that the provider is not in compliance with the day care standards, they are advised to notify the licensing department so that an inquiry visit can be made.

Licensing and registration are intended to protect you and the children in your care by providing a framework of safe conditions. The state licensing representative may schedule an appointment with you or just pop in unannounced. In either case, it is helpful to know the general criteria by which your suitability as a caregiver will be measured. Use the following checklist to evaluate your environment and temperament before you are actually visited. Do not panic if you are found to be in noncompliance with some of the safety standards. You will probably be given a period of time to fix a faulty smoke alarm or to clear some clutter that has been noted as a fire hazard.

■ Contact the United States Department of Agriculture (USDA) Child Care Food Program in your area. The federal government provides funds to regulated caregivers for reimbursement of some of the money that they spend on food for children. To find out if you meet the requirements, contact your licensing representative and ask for the name of a sponsoring agency for the USDA Child Care Food Program.

The Child Care Food Program (CCFP) will send a monitor to your home to make sure your kitchen is clean and your stove and refrigerator are operable. If you decide to serve the children meals and snacks, they will reimburse you a fixed amount. Certain paperwork is required if you elect to participate. For example, you will have to submit meal plans for approval before the sponsoring agency will send a monthly check. You will also have to complete a monthly report that tells how many children you are serving and what you are feeding them. The payments that you receive are tax-free, unless you spend less than what you receive in reimbursement.

The monitor will visit your home periodically to review your food-handling operations and observe how you comply with the meal-planning and record-keeping policies. You are under no obligation to serve meals or to participate in this program but many providers feel this is an additional service that they can offer to parents. Some providers form groups that buy food in bulk and take advantage of quantity discounts. They also discuss

DAY CARE HOME EVALUATION

Name of Day Care Mother: _____ Date _____

Address of Day Care Mother: _____

Key: Write appropriate word to describe facility and performance: Excellent, Good, Improving, Needs Improvement.

I. Physical Characteristics of the Day Care Home

A. Inside Space: Full Use   Partial Use
   1. Sufficient for licensed capacity   _____
   2. Space arrangement and play area   _____
   3. Lends itself to children's activities (uncluttered)   _____
   4. Cleanliness   _____
   5. Safety precautions   _____
   6. Lighting   _____
   7. Ventilation   _____
   8. General appearance of home   _____

B. Outside Area
   1. Fence   _____
   2. Space for play activities   _____
   3. Protected area (sun and/or rain)   _____
   4. Mowed and cleaned   _____
   5. Safety precautions   _____

C. Equipment (excluding toys)
   1. Nap facilities   _____
   2. Meal service   _____
   3. Special equipment (playpens, potty chairs, etc.)   _____

Comments: (Use back if necessary)

II. Work with Children

A. Methods of Working with Children

    1. Sensitivity to child's feelings   _____

    2. Awareness of child's progress or lack of progress   _____

    3. Accepts child as is   _____

    4. Positive approach to children   _____

    5. Sets limits which are realistic and appropriate   _____

    6. Consistent in following limits   _____

    7. Suitable methods to help child accept limits   _____

    8. Enjoys humorous incidents with children   _____

    9. Reasonable expectations and goals suitable to child   _____

   10. Treats children with respect   _____

   11. Assists child in gaining self-confidence   _____

   12. Plans personal life so as not to interfere with child care   _____

Comments:

B. Activities and Play Equipment

    1. Plans suitable and stimulating activities for children   _____

    2. Provides adequate play equipment   _____

    3. Helps child learn proper use and care of equipment   _____

    4. Supervises play adequately   _____

    5. Provides for active and quiet play   _____

    6. Participates in training program   _____

Comments:

C. Meals and Snacks

    1. Served on time   _____

2. Attractive and appetizing _____

3. Well balanced _____

4. Handling of problem eaters _____

5. Size of serving suited to child's needs _____

Comments:

D. Nap or Rest Arrangement

1. Regular _____

2. Well scheduled _____

3. Duration suitable to child's needs _____

Comments:

III. Day Care Mother

A. Personal Qualities of Day Care Mother

1. Friendly, warm _____

2. General appearance and appropriateness of dress _____

3. Speech and voice: clear and well modulated _____

4. Tact and courtesy toward parents: tolerant and considerate of others _____

5. Displays a sense of humor _____

6. Dependable _____

7. Self-confident _____

8. Enthusiastic about working with children _____

9. Demonstrates a desire to learn _____

10. Profits by suggestions _____

11. Avoids personal involvement with parents _____

12. Maintains good personal hygiene _____

Comments:

IV. Maintenance of Health Standards

A. With Children
  1. Prompt reporting of illnesses and accidents _____

  2. Awareness of child's daily health status _____

  3. Use of appropriate methods in handling sick children until professional guidance is secured _____

  4. Use of good judgment in discussing child's illness with parents _____

  5. Follows professional advice _____

  6. Keeps emergency phone numbers readily available _____

Comments:

B. With Day Care Home Family:
  1. Day care mother's physical health is adequate for child care _____

  2. Day care mother's mental health is adequate for child care _____

  3. Maintains health standards as set forth in state standards for a day care license _____

Comments: Counselor _____

Nurse _____

Educational Consultant _____

This evaluation has been reviewed by me.

Signed _____

Date _____

meal and snack recipes, thus reducing time spent in food planning.

- Call your *insurance agent* to inquire about additional insurance coverage. Despite precautions, accidents do happen, so you should be prepared by purchasing liability and accident insurance. Accident insurance is much easier to find and is less costly than liability insurance.

Much has been written about the difficulty of finding insurance coverage for day care. I would recommend asking your homeowner's insurance agent first. Do not say that you are opening a day care center in your home, rather that you are thinking about caring for a few children in your home. (State the number of children.) Insurance agents may become very nervous at the prospect of a large claim someday.

You may need a special policy because all standard homeowner's policies exclude business pursuits. I, personally, would not care for children without having adequate day care insurance. If day care coverage is not available from your own agent at an affordable cost, try calling other agencies. I would use as a ballpark figure about $50 to $75 per child per year. If you are receiving estimates that are much beyond those figures, continue to shop around. Talk to other day care providers in your area and ask where they obtained their coverage. Also ask your state licensing representatives what guidance their department can give you in this very important area. If you have a local day care association, request its assistance. It may have a group insurance policy that is available to its members.

Insurance companies fear the lawsuits that may result from child abuse or neglect charges. They are also concerned, to a lesser degree, about accidents that may occur in a day care home. Of course, the best insurance is a watchful eye and a childproof home.

Ask about placing a rider on your existing homeowner's policy which covers claims related to children. Ask if there are any exclusions that would limit your coverage under certain conditions specified in the policy, for example, a pool on your property, more than three children in your care, a pit bull, or other situations the insurance company would consider high risk.

As you read through the insurance policy, be sure you understand the limits to the coverage and the exclusions. Do not make the assumption that just because you have insurance you are totally insured no matter what happens. You should also be aware of the many types of insurance coverage available within a policy description. Inquire about inclusion of protection for claims brought against you for child abuse; coverage for dispensing medication, slander, alienation of affection; and coverage for field trips, product liability, and transportation.

It is important to attend to all the details about licensing in order to become insured. Most insurance companies will require that you fulfill all of the health and safety requirements and that you have a professional attitude about caring for children. A valid license or registration certificate confirming that you meet the minimal standards set forth by your state regulations will probably have to be filed with the insurance company. Applying for a license partially demonstrates that you are committed to professionalism.

What can go wrong? What if a child falls down the stairs and breaks a leg? The parents may try to sue you for the expenses not covered by their own insurance. It is important to remember that coverage varies not only from company to company but also from region to region. Some companies will cover an entire home; others require you to take out a separate policy for the day care children. Understand your policy clearly. Do not assume that an ordinary household liability policy will insure children in your care. Ask whether the policy covers the following:

- bodily injury that occurs accidentally;
- accidental damage to property of another;
- expense of emergency medical care at time of accident;
- legal cost of defending against suit by injured parties;
- transporting children in the car. Is this coverage included as a rider on your existing homeowner's policy?

It's also important to ask the following questions:

- If you are renting an apartment, do you need tenant's insurance?

- Is there a limit to the coverage, such as $100,000 per child or is it $100,000 per accident?
- Are others insured, such as you (the family day care provider) your spouse, relatives who reside with you, helpers, and substitute providers?

To differentiate between the two main types of coverage available, keep in mind that accident or medical insurance covers the hospital and doctor's bills if a child falls and breaks his arm. Since liability begins with the letter "L" it is easy for me to connect liability insurance with securing protection from lawsuits.

You might also check with the parents to see if they carry any insurance on the child so that you can plan your own insurance needs. Be certain both you and the child's parents understand the insurance coverage, that each of you understands exactly when and where the children are covered: en route to and from the day care home, in the home or yard, or on neighborhood excursions.

Some experienced providers have told me that they have the parent sign a waiver or "hold harmless agreement" absolving them of any responsibility should any injury or damage occur. The lawyers I consulted told me that this type of statement would probably not hold up in court although it may act as a deterrent to a parent who wants to sue over something minor.

If you are currently working for a company that provides health benefits, you may wonder how to go about obtaining health insurance for yourself once you start your own business. Obtaining major medical insurance on your own is expensive, so many people who are in business for themselves join an organization that provides group coverage. As a member, you might be able to protect yourself and your family with a comprehensive health insurance plan. (Do not confuse this type of insurance with protecting the children. This policy is to pay for *your* medical and hospital expenses, prescription drugs and medicines if you become sick and need radiation, X rays, home health care, etc.).

Liability and accident insurance information may be obtained by writing to the National Association for Family Day Care, 815 15th Street NW, Suite 928, Washington, D.C. 20005 (202-347-3356).

This is an association of various individuals, associations, and agencies that support the concept of family day care. Their mission is to promote quality child care and enhance the professionalism of family day care providers. It is a large network and offers many advantages to its members. Newsletters, conferences, and well-informed providers can offer assistance regarding child care concerns you may have.

- Save all receipts so that an *accountant* can review your records at tax time. Some of the costs of taking care of children in your home are deductible. Since the Internal Revenue Service (IRS) considers day care in the home a business, in most cases you will need to follow the regulations for filing an income tax return. Don't let this intimidate you because it can work to your advantage. You incur so many expenses that you will be able to make this business even more profitable if you keep accurate records and take appropriate deductions.

I find that the easiest way for me to keep track of the money I spend is to use a notebook to record the money coming in (income) and going out (expenses). I also have a calendar with large blocks that I use to mark attendance each day. The parents can sign in and out so that you have accurate records of the number of hours that you watched each child. At the end of the week you can transfer the totals to a notebook which lists each child and the amount paid per week or month. I use an accordion-type folder to store receipts which I categorize by expenditures as in the following example:

Household Expenses

toilet paper
paper towels
napkins
cleaning supplies
soap
paper plates
light bulbs
trash bags

Education

classes
workshops
textbooks

Supplies

playpens
walkers
swings
towels
sheets
pillows
cribs

Printing

business cards
flyers

parent newsletter
brochures
parent agreement
sign-in sheets
miscellaneous forms

Groceries

food

Fees

lawyer
accountant
insurance premium

Dues and Fees

membership dues to day
 care association

Car Expenses

mileage to drive to store,
 workshops, field trips;
 gas, oil, repairs;
 insurance (keep a log
 of miles driven and
 destination)

Assistant Provider

occasional person
   needed to fill in or
   assist

Repairs

a child put crayons in
   our dryer
screen door smashed in

Toys

games
puzzles
blocks
riding toys
books
educational guides

Travel

attendance at day care
   conferences and
   meetings

Entertainment

holiday celebration
gifts for children

Subscriptions

women's magazines
children's magazines
newsletters

Utilities

percentage of heat,
   lighting, electricity,
   water

Record Keeping

calculator
rubber bands
filing cabinet/folders
pens, pencils
stapler
bank charges
check printing costs
notebooks

Advertising

newspaper ads to recruit
   children
cost of supplies for flyers

Arts and Crafts	*Miscellaneous*
crayons	VCR
paint	record player
tape	cassette recorder
construction paper	
scissors	
glue	
marking pens	
paste	

Be conscious of all of the things you buy. Save every receipt. If you buy items at a garage sale, ask the person to list the items and amount paid. If you have made a major purchase and did not save the receipt, simply cut a picture of it from a toy catalog that lists the retail price. As you proceed with your business, you will make many purchases, and you will need to document in your records how these items are related to your work. When you return from the grocery store, circle in red the day care items you purchased or buy your groceries using two separate shopping carts so that the checkout person gives you separate receipts for your purchases. You could also just take your day care-related groceries to the checkout counter first and pay for them with a separate check.

I can't overstress the advantages of keeping good records. At the end of the month, evaluate your financial situation. Make sure you are not spending more money on food and supplies than you are making. You may find out that you are not charging enough or that you are overspending.

In addition to federal and state taxes, you also are required to pay another tax. The Social Security tax is the tax that entitles you to social security benefits. If you worked for a corporation, it would be paying part of this tax and deducting the rest from your paycheck, but since you work from your home, you will be wholly responsible for this tax. If you are confused by any tax information, you can call your local IRS agency for assistance. Ask your licensing bureau if there are any special tax workshops for day care providers. In my home state of Pennsylvania, the local information and referral services offer tax help workshops free of charge to home child care providers.

You may also find it useful to order some materials from Resources for Child Caring, Inc., a nonprofit organization (see Appendix B). Of particular relevance is a guidebook called *Basic Guide to Record Keeping and Taxes* which explains step by step how to fill out tax forms. I was surprised to find there were many deductions I did not know about. Another booklet, titled "Annual Update for Preparing Your Federal Income Tax Return," is revised each year. This booklet is invaluable because it brings you up to date on the rapidly changing tax laws. These publications are available from Resources for Child Caring, Inc.

My personal feeling is that, although you are certainly capable of filing the proper forms, it might be advantageous to review your income tax return with a tax professional before mailing it to the IRS. Don't go to just any accountant but attempt to find one who has experience with the day care business. There are also many free publications that are applicable to the provider. At your request, the IRS will mail you tax publications such as

Your Federal Income Tax—Takes you through each part of tax return, explaining the laws (Forms 1040, 1040A).

Tax Guide for Small Business—Describes Federal tax laws (Forms 1040, Schedule C).

Employer Tax Guide—Tells employers about their tax responsibilities for their employees, explains requirements for withholding, reporting, and paying taxes (Forms 940, 941).

Credit for Child and Dependent Care Expenses.

Business Use of Your Home—Shows how you can deduct the use of part of your home as a business expense (Forms 1040, Schedule C).

Record Keeping for a Small Business—Shows you how to keep records to ensure that you pay only what you owe.

It normally takes about three weeks for the publications to arrive. They do not change drastically from year to year.

■ Contact your family *lawyer* to check on any local or state requirements that apply to child care in the home. The advice of a lawyer tends to be expensive. If you are lucky enough to be related to one, try to have all of your questions answered. The most common problem requiring the expertise of an attorney is zoning. In some states, in order to obtain a license, you must notify your township police or zoning board of your intent. Some people have launched a full-fledged business only to receive a call notifying them that their neighborhood is not zoned for child care. If you have a day care association, you might call and ask for suggestions about how to handle this potential problem.

Of course you could also call the zoning board anonymously and ask questions. The downside of this suggestion is that you may be alerting them to your business, which could put you out of business. You could also pretend you are considering moving into the area from out of state and are just calling for information about home businesses—specifically home child care.

One woman I know was told by the state licensing department that, in order to be approved, she had to notify the police or zoning board. She overcame this obstacle by taking a very casual approach. She simply dialed the local police, identified herself by name, and said, "I baby-sit for a few children in my home and I wanted you to know where I live in case of an emergency. Thank you very much." The conversation was short and simple. I don't know whether it really fulfilled her obligation but she is still operating two years later.

An acquaintance of mine bought a lovely home in a residential neighborhood. The house was perfect because it had a separate area which was perfect for a mini-day care center. The state representative approved everything, but she found that the neighbors weren't too excited. She applied for a variance, paid money to a surveyor to draw up a blueprint, familiarized herself with all of the data pertaining to safety ordinances, but in the end she was unsuccessful. Every cloud has a silver lining. Although this particular opportunity did not work out, she is quite happy now in a high-paying nursing career.

One woman recently told me that she called her local township office to inform them she was considering child care in her home. She was told that she would have to pay a $300 nonrefundable application fee. (Zoning varies from one location to another. Check out your own township's current zoning laws and procedures for obtaining a variance.) She told me that she just hung up the phone and decided to proceed without becoming involved with the red tape. This is probably a good time to mention that the majority of day care homes are not licensed. Caregivers often do not want to tackle potential zoning problems. They may be concerned that they could be closed down because their area is not zoned appropriately.

There are two schools of thought about the zoning issue. Some people are willing to just start up their business and, if there is a problem with zoning, deal with it at that time. Other people prefer to do everything by the book. They prefer to examine all aspects of day care red tape *before* beginning. It is important to remember that you may be approved by your state licensing representative but, if a neighbor lodges a complaint, you may have to go through a local approval process.

This is probably a good time to mention that, if your neighbor who shares your driveway does not like your dog, your children, or you, then with almost absolute certainty you can expect that he or she will not welcome additional noise, excess traffic, or any inconvenience related to your home business. This is the type of person who is likely to complain to the zoning board.

On the other hand, you are providing a very valuable service. Your neighbors may be very excited to know that someone like you will be able to help them with their day care needs.

If you decide you would like to pursue a variance to a zoning ordinance because you have been notified that neighbors have complained, you must be prepared to spend some money and time. See if you can find anyone else who has been through a variance hearing who can advise you.

Basically, the procedure would be something like this. An application fee is usually charged to you. You must attend the hearing armed with "ammunition" as to why your home is suitable for the child care business. Expect to see some neighbors who live close by. Hopefully, they will be on your side but don't count on it. Bring your own team of well-wishers.

When I first decided to provide care, my target starting date was the day after Labor Day. On July 31, I placed copies of my advertising flyer in all my neighbors' mailboxes. (I later found out that it is against postal regulations to put anything in a mailbox, but it's fine to leave flyers underneath people's doors.) I notified all the residents of my plans for two reasons. First, I wanted my neighbors to know of my intent to operate a day care business so I could help them with their day care needs. But more important, if anyone had any objections, I wanted to know before I actually started. Fortunately, I had wonderful neighbors and I never experienced any problems.

If you anticipate that some of the older people in your area may object to traffic congestion or parking problems, you can assure them that the parents will not all be coming at the same time. If they are concerned about the excessive noise in your backyard, you can certainly appease them. Explain that you are planning activities around your sandbox and will be taking the children for walks around the yard looking for leaves and acorns. It will not be as noisy as a school recess yard!

In this chapter, I've tried to give you the "cement" that will hold the foundation of your child care business together. Now it's time to add to that mix the fine art of advertising your service to the public.

ADVERTISING
YOUR
BUSINESS

When I decided to offer child care in my home I typed very neat index cards and spent an evening posting them all over town. Then I came home and waited to be deluged with phone calls. Whenever I had to go out, I was excited about coming home, anticipating that my husband would have a million phone messages for me. Well, the response to my cards was less than overwhelming. I received no calls.

My friend, a working mother, explained why she felt that this first marketing strategy was faulty. Mothers with young children are attracted to signs that are bright and creative. Their eyes focus on a piece of construction paper with cutouts of mothers and babies holding balloons or just smiling together as they enjoy some happy activity. Having grasped the concept, I spent several evenings getting phase two of my advertising campaign off the ground. I took down the index cards, which were a bit too businesslike, and replaced them with mini-posters featuring pictures cut out of a Sears catalog. With colorful marking pens, I filled in the details of my program. My friend was right! My business took a dramatic turn for the better.

The following suggestions should help you get off to a good start:

- Tell as many friends and neighbors as you can about your child care program. When I began, I composed a letter explaining my interest in caring for children in my home. I outlined my background and listed some of the activities that I planned to do with the children. I gave this neatly typed letter to all of my friends, acquaintances, and neighbors.

  Even people who did not have children received my new business announcement. I reasoned that everybody comes in contact with parents who need child care. I hoped that people who knew me would recommend my service.

  Be sure to have someone proofread your advertisement or letter. You want it to create a favorable impression. To enhance the appearance of the letter, you can copy it on colored paper, available at a quick print shop. They may also have clip-art—decals or logos usually not protected by copyright. You are free to use them for your promotional pieces. (See sample ad on page 265 for example of clip-art.) You can also use clip-art to decorate your business card, flyer, or parent agreement.

- Design a colorful flyer. Shape the ad to suit your program and your credentials. Make a pocket out of construction paper to hold your flyers. Decorate the construction paper with cutouts from magazines—pictures of mothers and children. Post your flyers in supermarkets, churches, community bulletin boards, pediatricians' offices, and wherever parents congregate.

  In addition, I always had some flyers in my pocketbook so I could pass them out to mothers I met at the playground, birthday parties, or fast-food restaurants.

  Whenever I posted my signs I made sure that my appearance was clean and neat. People always seem to be curious when you are placing something on a bulletin board. I noticed that, when I was finished tacking or taping, someone always came over to see what I was attaching. I wanted people to know I cared about all aspects of my business and they could assume that my home, my children, and my own personal appearance reflected the quality program that I offered.

Recently I taught an orientation class for new day care providers. I remarked that, if Robin and Katelyn had ice cream all over their outfits, I would not take them with me to hang up flyers. One woman strongly disagreed and felt that the ice cream could also be interpreted as "Oh, what a nice mother—she took her kids to the farm to buy ice cream cones." The most important thing is to follow your own instincts about creating a good impression.

Another idea is to cut a poster board into four pieces. Decorate each one. Take a piece of thin wire, hook about ten small pieces of paper to the wire, and attach it to the bottom of the cardboard. On each paper write a brief description of your program. That way, an interested mother can tear off a piece of paper that gives her more information than a phone number.

I don't know what happens to flyers and advertisements that are placed on bulletin boards, but they do seem to disappear. You will probably have to keep replacing them. (There are some markets that have a two-week limit.) If your ad does stay on the board, it sometimes becomes weatherbeaten. Make sure your ad looks fresh and neat because it is a reflection of your business. A sample ad is shown.

Are You Looking for Child Care?
I will provide a "day of fun" (games, stories, educational activities) for your child while you work or go to school. Safe, loving atmosphere—small group—state-approved.

■ Advertise in your local newspaper. If your newspaper has inexpensive advertising rates, this may be one way to use your investment capital wisely. Again, modify the ad to suit your credentials and your program. It is advisable to list two phone numbers—one as an alternative since you will not always be at home to take a call. I used my parents' number and they would tell callers that I would return the call shortly. You could also purchase an answering machine, which is a tax-deductible business expense. You will not want to miss important calls when you go out for the evening. In addition, there may be times during the day when it is not convenient for you to absent yourself to answer the phone.

When you actually sit down to design your advertisement, you may wonder what to say. Perhaps some of the words and phrases listed below will help. Since you are offering a program that will provide a day free of worry for working parents, you want to convey that you are a loving and responsible adult. Experiment by combining some of the following words and phrases.

loving mother	state-approved	licensed
experienced mother	large play yard	trails for nature walks
lots of TLC	arts and crafts activities	mother who loves mothering
enclosed yard	reasonable rates	energetic mother
mature mother	comforts of home	reliable
responsible	dependable	fun times for your child
plenty of toys	healthy home environment	well equipped for fun
individual attention	limited group size	three years experience
family atmosphere	nonsmoker	meals served as needed

■ Give your program a name such as: "Lots of Love and Laughter," "Home Away from Home," "Miss Carol's Play Group," "Cuddly Bear Day Care," "Happy Times Day Care." I would use this name for the homemade signs that you post around your neighborhood. However, if you are planning to establish a checking or savings account for your business, the easiest way to do it is to put it in your own name, not in the name of your program. The same is true for credit card accounts. If you are married, it's best to keep the business's credit card in your name and the family card in joint names.

- Mention a major thoroughfare or landmark that will describe to parents the general vicinity of your child care program. For example: "Located near Route 422 bypass," "King of Prussia area," "Near Suburban Hospital," or "Convenient to Maple Road School." If you live in an area that is not very well known, you want to be sure that prospective customers know that you are conveniently located near their home, workplace, or en route to work. One provider wasted a lot of money by repeatedly placing a very general ad. It said "Philadelphia area," rather than "Close to City Hall."

- There are many child care information and referral services in operation throughout the United States. Some are for profit and are owned by individuals. Others are nonprofit and provide services free of charge or at a very minimal cost. The purpose is to match parents needing providers with available day care centers and day care homes. The list is shared so that the parents may use the names as a starting point in their search for child care. If you are going to *provide* care, you will want to call the information and referral service and ask to have your name included. This is free advertising for you. The names on the list are not necessarily *quality* child care providers, however. It is merely a compilation of names. The parents must carefully screen, evaluate, scrutinize, and check references.

  Ask the information and referral service to inform you of any workshops, classes, or newsletters that would help you in your efforts to enhance the quality of care you provide for the children.

- If you produce an advertisement like the one shown on p. 31, be sure to mount it on a piece of colored construction paper so that it is more noticeable on a community bulletin board. You don't want your sign to get lost in the blizzard of ads for bazaars, bicycles, flea markets, skates, and apartment rentals.

- Color in the picture with colored markers to give it a little pizzazz. Your sign has to be noticed before people can call you.

- If you have the tear-off for your phone number, be sure to cut the paper so that people can easily take the number without ripping the whole paper. Also, clip off one or two of the tear-off phone numbers *before* you post your flyer. People will feel that your service is popular and in demand. When they notice that "others" have also taken notice of your program, they will be more likely to take a number for themselves.

- Don't just put your phone number on the tear-off portion. Add a few words about the service such as "Baby-sitting" or "Child Care" or the name of your program. Sometimes people will clip your number and not remember whether the number was for a garage sale, used bicycle, or a day care provider.

- Don't put too much information on your sign. You want to have the opportunity to *share* your ideas with people when they call you for additional information. (Notice that I didn't specify price or age group on my sample flyer.)

Responding to Telephone Inquiries

A first impression is lasting and the way you answer the phone can either make or break "the sale." If you have children, now might be a good time to teach them telephone manners. Explain to them you are running a business and they can help you to succeed by putting their best foot forward. (Your husband is included here too!)

A happy, confident "hello" will start your conversation off on the right foot. From that point on, the suggestions outlined here will serve as a cheat sheet if you place them next to the phone.

- Introduce yourself in a friendly, pleasant, self-assured manner.
- Explain that you have a safe, organized play group for children in your home.
- Explain that you love children very much and that your home is a happy place for children to spend their day.
- Be sure that you state your credentials and experience— nurse, teacher, mother, Girl Scout leader, and so on. If you have had training in first aid, mention that too.
- Emphasize that your program is not just playtime but a somewhat structured day following a schedule of activities including stories, games, educational activities, and free play.
- Inform your caller that children may bring their own lunches or you will provide lunch.
- Explain that snacks are provided in the morning and afternoon.
- State your fee and what is included.
- Arrange for both the parent or parents and child to visit you and tour your home before the day the child is to join the program. This will make everyone more comfortable.
- Thank the parent for calling. Say you enjoyed talking to her or him and that you will look forward to a meeting soon.

Keep in mind that people love to talk about themselves, so be sure to ask the caller's name and the name of the child. Ask questions to show you are interested in learning about the child's particular needs. People are flattered when you mention their name frequently during the conversation. For example, you could say, "I've really enjoyed talking to you, Mary. I'll look forward to meeting you and Josh next Tuesday at 4 P.M."

If someone calls at an inappropriate time, such as when you are in a hurry or there are four screaming kids in the background, I recommend that you say, "Mrs. Harris, I appreciate your call but I am just on my way out. May I call you back sometime this evening? When would be a convenient time for you?" Then, when all is peaceful and you can talk without interruption or distraction, you should call the potential customer back.

Occasionally parents will make an appointment and not show up. Of course, common courtesy dictates that they should call you and postpone or cancel but sometimes they just never arrive.

When parents call you initially, they may want to come over and observe during the day while you have children at your home. Although this seems like a good idea, there can be complications. For one thing, you will not really be able to sit down and devote your time to the prospective newcomer. Your own children often act up at this time and your house might look as if a bomb hit it. Although all of these things may be totally acceptable once someone gets to know you, their first impression may not be favorable. My suggestion is to be very candid and say, "I would love for you to come over and meet me when I have my group of children here but I'll tell you what has worked out well for other parents. The *first* time that I meet with parents, it is better if they can visit in the evening. Would it be possible for you to come over Monday or Tuesday evening? At night, I have plenty of time to sit down and talk to you and I can really explain what we do here. You can also meet my husband, John, and Josh can play with Robin and Katelyn. Then the next time you come you're more than welcome to observe or drop in at *any* time."

Because so much has been written about providers who do not have an "open door policy," some parents may feel that, if they cannot come in and meet you at any time, you must be "hiding something." To that type of parent you could say, "I'd love to have you come over. How about Monday at 1 P.M.? Most of the children are napping at that time and I'll be able to talk to you while they are asleep." Many parents are just shopping around and are calling random names from a list, inquiring about hours, price, and programs. You do not want your home to have a steady stream of "lookers" because that is not fair to you or the children. The parents could be gently told that one of the reasons that you prefer an initial meeting to take place at night is because you like to devote all of your attention to the children and, when you have guests, it is hard to keep an eye on everything that is going on. This should reflect positively on you because the parents will know that the children are your number one concern and you are not interested in promoting your business while you are caring for children.

Of course, all these suggestions depend on the number and ages of the children in your care. If you are caring for one infant and a three year old, there is no reason not to invite the parent over for tea in the morning while the baby is in the playpen and the preschooler is playing with blocks. However, if you are responsible for five frisky five year olds, you might be better off scheduling an evening visit.

I have done it both ways and my personal opinion is that it is much better to have the parents come over after hours. There are many people who currently care for children whose approach would be the opposite because they feel that evenings and weekends belong to their own families. They do not want to conduct interviews during their personal family time. It might be a good idea to talk to other caregivers and ask for their suggestions.

Measuring Up
to Parents' Standards

When parents call you in response to your advertisement, you may feel they are giving you the third degree as they begin to ask you a series of questions. So that you are not defensive in your responses to them, you should understand they are looking for the most responsible and loving person. You may very well be that person but, at this point, you are still a stranger to them.

In recent years the media have informed parents about some very horrible things that have happened to children while under someone else's care. It's no wonder that parents are wary. Child care in America is very much in the public eye.

Many television shows and women's magazines have addressed the topic of "Who Is Watching the Children?" or produced shows with titles like "Day Care Nightmares." For this reason, parents are becoming better educated about evaluating child care providers and selecting quality programs. Checklists have been developed to encourage parents to compare the answers of prospective providers in order to make an informed decision.

When I first began looking for a baby-sitter for Robin, I visited the home of a provider who was very highly regarded. I met with her on two separate occasions. Although I was satisfied for the most part, there was one thing that made me very uncomfortable. She had a teenage daughter who was very sassy. On each occasion mother and daughter argued in a heated fashion. I did not select this woman. I felt that the tension-filled environment was not desirable for an infant, at least not for my daughter.

At another home, the woman was very kind and seemed like the nice grandmotherly type I had hoped to find. There were a few things, though, that made me very nervous. A fan was placed on a bureau to cool the hot summer air and a bottle of pills was next to the bathroom sink. Since I genuinely liked the lady, I thought I should be honest with her and express my concerns. Surely she would agree that a houseful of kids, a fan, and medicine made a dangerous combination. She explained that she just taught the children not to touch and that she did not believe in rearranging her whole house. A red flag went up for me and I knew that Robin was never going to spend any time at this house.

I asked another experienced caregiver where the children napped. She said that they all rested with "Pop-Pop" in the queen-size bed. You do not want to do anything that could be interpreted as poor judgment, no matter how innocent it appears to you.

The point of this last anecdote is to help you understand that people will not only want to know about you but will also judge the family members who might be home during the day. You may think that's unfair, but it's best to be prepared.

I have related a few of my experiences so that you can read between the lines when people ask you questions. If they ask about your ideas on discipline, it may be an indication that they have had a bad experience with someone else.

A few mothers were not at ease with some things in my home that seemed perfectly safe to me. There was a stream in the very back of my property which troubled one mother. It was so far back that I had never even been near it because of the thick brush and prickly bushes. She was worried sick that her child might be in danger. I didn't pressure her in any way to see my point of view. She would never have a moment's peace if she went to work and worried. She perceived the stream as dangerous and I respected that because I know that what is considered safe by one parent's standards is quite unsafe by another's.

One mother did not like the expandable safety gate that I used to separate the kitchen from the dining room. She had read that this type of gate was dangerous because children had died in accidents when their heads became lodged in the crisscrossed bars. I, too, was aware of that possible danger but the children in my care were never left unattended. I knew that she had no cause to worry.

Many times, people will ask you if you are licensed. Although licensing or registration is required in some states, licensing alone does not ensure quality care. Parents may lull themselves into a false sense of security by assuming that a licensed or registered home means that the caregiver is exceptionally well qualified. In many states it is just a matter of filing paperwork, and certainly both good and bad people are capable of doing that. In my home state, if you are caring for three children or fewer you do not have to apply for any type of licensing. Therefore, if I were asked whether I were licensed I would explain that a small-scale day care program is not obligated to be licensed in the state of Pennsylvania.

In their search for the person who best meets their needs, parents will probably be using questions similar to the ones that I have listed. They will probably be judging you by the following criteria:

Is the caregiver licensed or registered?
How many children are being cared for?
How long has she been caring for children?
Is her home child-oriented (bright, cheerful, colorful)?

Do you like the caregiver?

Is the caregiver warm and loving?

Does the caregiver inspire your confidence?

Do the other children look happy?

Will the caregiver teach as you would at home?

Is the caregiver enthusiastic?

What is her method of discipline?

If she has children of her own, do they seem well adjusted?

How does her family feel about her caring for other children?

Will there be older teenagers or adults in the house while the children are there? Do you feel comfortable about that?

Will the caregiver honor your special requests?

Could the caregiver handle emergency situations?

What activities are planned?

Are you satisfied with the napping arrangements?

Is the dining area sanitary?

Are emergency numbers posted next to the phone?

Are parental visits welcome?

Is inside play space adequate?

Is the house childproof?

Does the house appear to be in good repair?

Is outdoor play area safe and away from traffic, streams, and construction sites?

It is likely that parents will also ask for recent references.

Parent/Child
Preliminary Visit

Always remember that parents are preparing to leave their most valued possession in your care. When I was planning to return to work after my first baby was born, I had a difficult time locating a good provider. ("Provider" and "caregiver" seem like such cold words and "baby-sitter" just isn't respectable enough for such a quality profession. However, these seem to be the titles that are used most frequently in the field.) The most important thing to me was that I had to genuinely like the person and trust her completely. My own personal situation was like a dream because Estelle was wonderful in every way. However, there were a few months when I had to depend on people I did not know very well to care for my child. At times like that I found myself less productive on the job because I was anxious about the kind of care my baby was receiving. Because of the publicity about child care horrors, I was pretty particular about selecting a caregiver for my child. Sometimes, though, parents are in desperate need of care and aren't as vigilant as they should be. During your conversations with the parents, you want to let them know the following facts:

- You love children.
- Their children will not be sitting in front of television all day. "Sesame Street" and other children's programs are okay for part of the day.
- You plan your day—it is not playtime all day.
- You don't want children who are sick to come. (Parents appreciate this consideration.) In my policy statement, I define sick as fever, vomiting, and contagious diseases.
- Their child will have your attention, your approval, kind words, and plenty of smiles.
- Your program offers chances for active and quiet play *and* that the child has the opportunity to play alone as well as with other children in a group.
- Your program is free from pressure and competitiveness.
- Your home is a happy place to visit.
- You understand that children have a short attention span, learn slowly, and need clear, simple directions.
- You will cuddle a child who is frightened or uneasy.
- You are responsible and trustworthy.

Most children walk in rather timidly when they meet you for the first time. Of course, this depends on their age and whether they have been exposed to other baby-sitters or have attended nursery school. It is probably best not to fuss too much over a child when he first comes in. Be extremely cordial to the parent. Offer coffee, tea, or a cold soda to the parent and apple juice to the child. Let the child come around on his own. Leave a few toys scattered around the room that will probably catch and hold his attention. While you converse with the parent the child must be shown by your words and manner that you are a loving person. You want to convey that this is a place to play with other children and with lots of nice toys. There are pictures to paint and blocks to build.

After about fifteen minutes sitting on the couch getting to know the parents, I offer to give them a tour of my home. If the child is willing, I take him by the hand and say, "Let's go see our playroom. Here is our record player, our books, crayons, and paints." The mini-tour shows the rooms that I plan to use and I give the parents and child a brief idea of what I plan to do in each room. Sometimes I even describe one of the sample activities to give them a better picture of the daily routine.

Parents like to know about the projects you do with the children, and I hang the daily works of art on the refrigerator, cabinets, or the wall so they can see that the children are playing and learning while at my house. I also tape large cardboard cutouts of numbers, shapes, and letters on doors and walls. I explain to parents that mine is not a rigidly structured learning program but that frequently during the day I ask, "Can anyone see a four?" or "How many red squares can you see?"

One home that I visited when I was looking for child care particularly impressed me because I saw all of the children's art projects displayed prominently. A small child-size table was set up in the playroom with two little teddy bears comfortably seated on plastic chairs. It looked as if a tea party was about to begin!

As you are showing your home, be sure to point out all of the safety precautions that you have taken. For example, I would say, "As you can see, I have safety latches on all of my kitchen doors and cabinets," "My medicine cabinet is locked," "This is the cabinet where I keep all of my cleaning supplies. You can see it is completely out of reach of children." Implement the room-by-room safety tips I list in Chapter 5. Make a point of telling the parent about the extra effort you make to assure the children save the names "Mom," "Dad," and "Grandmom," for members of the family. This is a very sensitive issue, so be sure to mention it.

ESTABLISHING
THE
GROUND
RULES

In my discussions with other providers, the biggest problems seem to be conflicts with the parents, not with the children. In order to minimize misunderstandings in the future, I review my policies with the parents before we establish a friendly relationship. I show them a copy of my Day Care Policy Sheet, which enables me to discuss important issues concerning fees, hours, and day-to-day policies.

As we go over the policy together, I ask them if they have any questions. I really want both of us to understand the arrangement. Some providers call it a contract, but it is not really a legal document and could not be enforced. Besides, I like the parents to feel that this is not a big business but that I am a mother who loves children and enjoys providing a service. You need not worry that people will take advantage of you if you are reasonable and firm.

I have heard of parents who did not pick their children up by the designated closing time. The provider's solution was to charge a late fee. I feel that you must set certain hours and stick to them. If someone needs a sitter at 6:30 A.M. and your hours begin at 7:30 A.M., do not be too anxious to extend your hours of operation. You need time for yourself and your family. Parents know that my hours are from 7 A.M. until 5:30 P.M. If they are not there at closing time, I have their permission in writing to call someone whom they have authorized to pick up their child if they are delayed. They provide two alternates who are permitted to pick up the child. In the evening I have plenty to do and need to know that by five-thirty my own family time will begin.

Setting Your Fee

Some people find it difficult to explain their fee policy when they are first starting out. It is easier if you go over the important points by using a Day Care Policy Sheet. Don't be shy when it comes to discussing money. You have to be mindful that this is a business and you are being paid for the valuable service you are providing.

Most providers care for children because they need the income. You should be clear about your payment policy from the beginning. Of course, don't forget the human element. We all have weeks when we are a little short in our checking account but, if you are counting on this money, don't feel bad about asking for it. Ask the parents to have their cash or check in an envelope with their child's name on it. Occasionally, you may take the children on a special outing (zoo, museum, play) or you may need to ask for an additional dollar here or there. Explain this up front so there will be no confusion later on.

To avoid misunderstandings with parents, think about the following potential problems before you compose your policy sheet:

- What will your fee be and how many hours are included for that amount?

- How much notice is expected when a parent decides to withdraw the child from day care (e.g., two weeks)?
- What is your charge for any additional time?
- Will you charge different rates for infants, preschoolers, school-age children?
- What is the schedule and method of payment?
- Will you charge if child is absent? (Some caregivers charge a minimal fee such as $4.00 for such absences.)
- What is your policy for late pickup?
- Will you charge for holidays or vacations?
- Do you have a discount fee for siblings?
- Are breakfast, lunch, or snacks included in fee?
- What would you like the parents to bring? (You may tell them that each child should bring personal drinking cup, scissors, paste, crayons, diapers, extra set of clothes, or formula).
- Inform parents that they should have a backup child care system in the event that you are sick or must attend to a family emergency. (Remember that at times *your* children may get sick).
- Inform the parents of your vacation schedule so they have adequate time to make alternate arrangements.
- Collect a $5.00 deposit to be credited toward the first time the child attends your program.

If the parents wish to hire you, you can then provide them with a Day Care Policy Sheet and an Enrollment Letter which explains your child care arrangements. (Sample provided next page.) Some caregivers prefer to write the Day Care Policy Sheet as a contract which both provider and parents sign. This method serves to explain what is important to you. The sample form that follows may be useful to you.

Be sure to establish an open channel of communication between you and the parents. If you really feel that you will not be able to get along with the prospective family, this is the time to say so. Your values, beliefs, and cultures may be so different that you might not be able to handle the situation. It is best for the child if you say so now so he does not go from one child care

D A Y   C A R E   P O L I C Y   S H E E T

The weekly fee is _____

The fee is payable on _____, and it includes the following services:

_____

_____

You may bring your child to my home at _____ and pick him up no later than _____.

A fee of _____ per hour will be charged for any additional time.

You will need to furnish the following items of clothing:

_____ _____ _____ _____

The following people, and only these people, will be permitted to pick up the child in case the parent cannot:

NAME _____

ADDRESS _____

PHONE NUMBER _____

RELATION TO FAMILY _____

NAME _____

ADDRESS _____

PHONE NUMBER _____

RELATION TO FAMILY _____

My absent policy is _____

My sick policy is _____

My vacation schedule is _____

My holiday schedule is _____

Enrollment Letter

Dear Parents:

Thank you for your interest in enrolling your child in my program. I hope I can provide all of the love and attention you could possibly want for your child. All of the children I care for are treated as my own, and I hope that everyone feels like part of the family.

The reason I began providing day care in my home is because I really enjoy working with little children and I wanted to supplement our family's income. As I explained to you, I've found it best if everyone is aware of some of the policies that have helped to make our program satisfactory for all.

I have prepared the attached agreement, which includes the areas that are most important to me. I hope that you will be comfortable talking to me about any area with which you feel you will not be able to comply. Because I have my own family to consider, it is important that all of the parents respect my hours of operation, sick policy, and need for prompt payment of the weekly fee.

It is also important that we are in agreement about my policies regarding vacations, holidays, and other absences. I would also appreciate your advising me of any important changes in your family life which may affect your little one's adjustment to day care.

Again, thank you for allowing me to care for your child. You can be assured that I will do my best to provide an interesting day for your child so that you can have peace of mind while you are not present.

Sincerely,

Jane Doe

situation to another. You might want to write into your policy sheet that you have a two-week trial or adjustment period. If it does not work out for either side, there will be no hard feelings and other arrangements can be found (easier said than done!).

I took a casual approach when it came to the adjustment period. I said, "I hope that everything works out but if you have any problems, please don't hesitate to let me know. And if I feel that things are not going well here, would you mind if I told you?" How could anyone not say, "That's fine"? There have been only two occasions when I felt that it would be best for all if other arrangements were made. One little girl was used to being cared for by her grandmother. She really missed her. She cried for the better part of the day even though we had tried a gradual approach before she actually started full time. Her crying was really unsettling to the other children because they felt that there must be something to cry about, and at times we had a whole chorus of crying kids. My assistant and I discussed it. We felt that it wasn't fair to anyone that Natalie should require so much attention. Although her mother felt that we should "Just let her cry until she accepts it," we felt that it would be better if her mother looked for someone who could come to Natalie's home as her grandmother had done. I know that I would never want my youngest daughter Kristen to cry that much at someone else's home.

Eric was a very active four year old. Most of the children in my home were much younger. He teased and taunted them regularly. We gave him lots of love and individual attention but he still did not seem to blend with the rest of the group. Everything would be fine until Eric bounced into the room. We felt that it was a matter of poor placement. When he first joined our group he was two years old, but now that he was older, wiser, and more boisterous, he needed a new environment that included children who were closer to his age. He had outgrown our group. His parents understood that he needed more room to run and play and that he would be challenged by a preschool curriculum that would prepare him for kindergarten the following year. A transition was made. I know that it was a good move for everyone.

There is a saying that "Some people make you happy when they come and others make you happy when they go." I especially loved Christopher and his mother. Cyndi was one of the nicest mothers. I always enjoyed talking to her in the morning. Because she was changing her work location, she would no longer be able to use our day care program. I can still feel the lump in my throat when I think of the sadness I felt on Christopher's last day with us. Some children find a special place in your heart and you really miss them when they move on. I hope the parents realize that we feel like a family during the day and that we want people to keep in touch and come back for a visit.

At the initial meeting, the parents may want to leave specific instructions about their child (schedule, feedings, ointment applied, etc.) while the caregiver feels that she must care for the child as she sees fit. With a large group of children she may not be able to attend to the parents' directions for each individual child. Remember that the parents are interviewing you but you are also screening them. You do not want every child you meet to join your program. Nor do you want every parent. In a sense, you have to be selective. You may want to tell the parent who has very specific instructions that you would like to accommodate her wishes, however you do not have time to provide that kind of attention for her child. She will have to continue looking for day care because you will not be able to meet her needs. This type of problem often breeds resentment and is not good for either party. Once again, it is important to keep the lines of communication open with the parents and discuss problems as they come up.

Crash Course in Family
Day Care Benefits

You may wonder, "What can I offer the children?" Here is a crash course in the benefits of your family day care business. Besides love, security, friendship, respect, good nutrition, and a safe environment, you will be giving the children opportunities for creative and exploratory play. Some of the other points that you want to include when talking with the parents are that you offer

- informally organized playing and learning in a new setting.
- new playmates, new experiences.
- learning to socialize in a group situation.
- fun learning through games—outlet for creative expression.
- opportunity to develop large and small motor skills.
- chance to grow in self-esteem.
- nursery-type activities.
- good foundation for entering school.
- to the parents, a day free of worry about child care arrangements while at work, at school, or pursuing vital activities.

Application for Day Care

The following application covers physical and emotional information about the children in your care. You may want to go through with a yellow marker and highlight the questions *you* would like the parents to answer. I think the questions indicate you really want to know their child's needs, and it is also an excellent way to facilitate a discussion about nap time, toilet training, discipline, and eating habits. For example, I would ask the parents if they wanted me to save what was left over from the child's unfinished sandwich and lunch box contents or did they want me to encourage the child to eat everything on his plate. I would also ask what they wanted me to do if their little one seemed fussy. Was there a favorite blanket, toy, or song that would help to calm him down? By just talking about the areas that are mentioned on the application form, I found that the parents and I learned a great deal about each other. This discussion also helped us to find out if we were miles apart in our early childhood rearing philosophies. I can honestly say that the parents and children I care for are wonderful. There is mutual respect and we work together for our common goal of loving and caring for the children.

Application Forms (usually provided by state or county child care agency)

Make sure that the application form is completely filled out and that there is no question in your mind that you understand special instructions or unusual situations indicated. Make notes of your own concerning special needs that you have noticed during the preadmission interview.

The state licensing office should be able to provide you with an adequate supply of admission forms. If forms are not available, you could duplicate the following sample.

APPLICATION FOR DAY CARE

Family Name _____ Mother _____ Father _____

Address _____ Tel. _____ Marital Status _____
Children for whom placement is requested:

Name _____ Nickname _____

Birth Date _____

Mother's Employer _____

Address _____ Tel. _____
Work hours:
Number of days:
Father's Employer _____

Address _____ Tel. _____
Work Hours:
Number of days:
In emergency call _____ Tel. _____

Relationship _____

Who will call for child? _____

Means of Transportation _____

Other members of household (including children not under care):

1. _____

2. _____

Has child had previous day care placement? _____

Reason for requesting placement _____

Age of child when mother returned to work _____

Doctor or clinic used _____

Address _____ Tel. _____

DEVELOPMENTAL HISTORY

Personal History

Type of Birth: Normal _____ Premature _____

Any complications? _____

Age child began sitting ____ Crawling ____ Walking ____

Is child a good climber? ____ Does child fall easily? _____

Age child began talking ____ Does child speak in

words? ____ Or sentences? ____

Does child have any difficulties in speaking? ____

Other language ____

Special words to describe child's needs _____

Health

What arrangements can you make for child's care during

illness? _____

Doctor's name _____

Address _____ Tel. _____

What communicable diseases has child had?

Measles (Big Red) ____ Measles (3-day) ____

Mumps ____ Chicken pox ____ Whooping cough ____

Other ____ Any serious illness or hospitalization? _____

Hospital preferred _____

Any physical disabilities? ____ Any known allergies

(asthma, hay fever)? ___ Insect bites, medicines, etc. ___

How many colds has your child had this past year? ___

How does the child react to an elevated
temperature? _____

Special instructions if child becomes ill _____

Are any medications given regularly? ___
Eating
Is child usually hungry at mealtime? ___ Between
meals? ___

What are child's favorite foods? _____

What foods are refused? _____

What eating problems does child have? _____

Any food allergies? ___ Does child eat with spoon? ___

Fork? ___ Hands? ___
Toilet Habits
Can child be relied upon to indicate his bathroom
wishes? ___

What word is used for urination? _____ For bowel
movement? _____

Does the child need to go more frequently than usual
for his age? ___

Is child frightened of the bathroom? ___ Does child
have accidents? ___

How does child react to them? ___ Does child need
help with toileting? ___

Was the child easy or difficult to train? _____

Record Keeping

Daily Records

In a notebook, you should log the names of the children who attend each day. This will come in handy when there is an outbreak of flu, chicken pox, or some other illness that is catching. You will know at a glance who might have been exposed.

Jot down notes about each child on a daily basis. Parents like to know how a child ate, slept, and any amusing or amazing things that he accomplished.

Note any minor accidents, how long the child slept, eating patterns, and any special needs that you may have noticed.

See page 56 for a sample sign-in sheet. Parent should fill this out each morning when they drop off the child. In this way you will know at a glance if there are any special instructions for the day.

Permanent Records

In a file box, drawer, or cardboard box you must store the forms supplied by the regulating agency. Be sure that the parents have completed the application consent and emergency forms accurately and that they are kept up to date. Parents should remember to tell you if their address or their telephone number at work changes. Be sure that all records are dated, clear, concise, accurate, and up to date. All records should be treated as confidential and information should not be shown to outsiders. Label a section in your file for major categories such as grocery receipts, utility bills, large purchases, repair bills, USDA Child Care Food Program receipts, tax information, and so on.

Activity File

So that you have a record of directions for specific activities, keep samples of the crafts that you have made or some good recipes, activity pages, and general interest articles about children. Someday when you have nothing special planned, you can save your sanity by looking in your box of past successes for some tried and true ideas.

Time Off for You

Since you will have informed parents about your vacation schedule in your "Day Care Policy Sheet," there should be no surprises if you are closed for the last week in August. Be sure parents understand that you will also be taking time off to celebrate certain religious or secular holidays. My days off include Christmas, New Year's Day, Easter, Thanksgiving, Memorial Day, Labor Day, the Fourth of July, and the day following each of those holidays.

Inevitably, there will be times when you have a doctor's appointment that cannot be conveniently rescheduled, or when you don't want to miss an activity at your own child's school. Canceling day care is not the only option. Sometimes relatives are willing to help in a pinch. For example, my sister and mother occasionally help me out as substitutes. There are also times when my husband comes home from work for a few hours to watch the children.

Suppose you have to rely on a substitute who is not a relative. I usually search for substitute caregivers by placing an ad in the newspaper. Colleges, high schools, and women's organizations are other potential sources of substitute caregivers. In any case, it's important that you find out about a caregiver's background before deciding to allow her to care for children in your home.

I ask prospective caregivers to fill out an application, and I interview them in my home and visit them in their homes whenever possible. To put them at ease, I explain that I have information about child care and my daily routine that I would like to share with them. State regulations often require that each person who works with you must have a clean bill of health and criminal clearance.

I would also suggest that you arrange for the prospective care-

SAMPLE SIGN-IN SHEET

CHILD'S NAME	PHONE # WHERE PARENTS CAN BE REACHED TODAY	MAY YOUR CHILD GO FOR A WALK?	ANY SPECIAL INSTRUCTIONS?	TIME NOW	WHAT TIME DO YOU EXPECT TO RETURN?
1.					
2.					
3.					
4.					
5.					
6.					
7.					
8.					

9.	10.	11.	12.	13.	14.	15.	16.	17.	18.	19.	20.

giver to work with you on several occasions. You can offer her on-the-job training with pay. During the training period, jot down notes about how you feel she relates to children. Ideally, she should demonstrate common sense, empathy, and patience, and take a positive approach in her dealings with children. Be sure, too, that she understands any special instructions you specify in writing.

If you find that working five days a week does not allow you sufficient time for your own needs, you might want to consider my friend Eleanor's solution. She provides child care only four days a week and reserves Fridays for herself. A four-day program allows her time to do her own housework, to run errands, and to volunteer as a "lunch mother" at her daughter's school. In addition, some of the parents are able to arrange for a relative to spend Fridays with their children, thereby reducing their child care expenses.

There are many other possible ways to structure a part-time child care program. For example, I know of two licensed caregivers who are close friends and who take turns caring for the same group of six children. Since neither of them wants to be committed to providing full-time care, Mary cares for the children during the first and third weeks of the month, and Fran runs the program during the second and fourth weeks. They are both present at the initial meeting with parents.

Everyone involved benefits from this innovative arrangement. Mary and Fran can rely on each other as backup caregivers. The children enjoy a change of pace and a different selection of toys when they visit the two separate homes. And, if either Mary or Fran gets sick, the parents do not have to look for a substitute caregiver at the last minute; they already have a standby caregiver who knows their children well.

PREPARATION

FOR THE

CHILDREN

Setting the Stage

By now you may be wondering how much space is necessary for a home child care business. The minimum amount of space required varies from state to state. I have seen home day care programs operating in apartments, mobile homes, and in all sorts of houses—large and small. Most standards suggest only that there be "adequate" room for sleeping, playing, and eating. You will probably try several arrangements before you discover one that meets the needs of all the children in your care.

The key is to organize the space available to you so that it is functional, comfortable, and easy to keep reasonably neat. Imagine the sequence of events in the average day to get a better idea of what your needs will be. For example, when children arrive you will probably want to have coat hooks for jackets, space for boots and umbrellas, and a shelf for diaper bags. It's also a good idea to have cardboard boxes labeled with each child's name for miscellaneous belongings. A sign-in sheet like the one on page 56 should be placed in a convenient spot so that parents can record the time when they arrive, as well as any special instructions for the day. If you find that you need more play space, try rearranging your furniture.

When I started my business, I moved my kitchen table against the wall to create more space and hung a large blackboard on the wall of my laundry room. I then set aside special areas for homemaking, dress-up activities, and playing with blocks. I stored coloring books, crayons, art supplies, and games with small pieces in a closet, and used our hallway, kitchen, family room, and bathroom as the primary day care areas. (Fortunately, our room arrangement allows me to keep the children in view at all times.) When I started out, my outside play area did not have expensive equipment, only riding toys, a tent, and a sandbox. Before you invest in a lot of new furniture or equipment, see what you can improvise with what you already own.

As you arrange and rearrange your home, it may be helpful to keep the following requirements in mind.

Planning for Infants

- Diapering, feeding, sleeping area
- Safe play area away from older children

Planning for Toddlers

- Diapering, feeding, sleeping area
- Safe play area with blocks, books, and toys
- Quiet area for individual play
- Group play area for simple arts and crafts activities

Planning for Preschoolers

- Feeding and rest area
- Safe play area with a variety of stimulating activities to choose from

- Adequate outdoor space for running, jumping, and riding toys

Planning for School-Age Children

- Quiet area to unwind and do homework
- Outdoor space to exercise and play

Some caregivers allow children to play throughout their homes while others prefer to specify day care areas and keep other areas off limits. Whatever you decide, I advise you to place anything that is valuable or breakable well out of reach. To keep blocks, dolls, clothes, and games from littering your floor, use boxes and crates.

Basic Start-up Equipment

The following materials are not essential to begin a child care program, but you may want to keep your eyes open for bargains at flea markets or moving sales. Bear in mind the age of the children in your care when buying or borrowing toys.

Equipment and Supplies for Infants and Toddlers	Toys for Preschoolers and School-Age Children	Equipment for All Age Groups
■ Twin stroller to calm two fussy babies at one time (Check your thrift shop.)	■ Trucks and cars ■ Toy kitchen furniture ■ Dishes, pots ■ Dolls ■ Carriage	■ Boxes for each child's personal belongings ■ Clothes hamper for soiled clothes

Equipment and Supplies for Infants and Toddlers

- Safety gates
- Playpen
- Portable cribs
- Rocking chair
- High chair
- Baby walker
- Cribs, sheets, crib bumpers. (No pillows for infants.)
- Blankets, towels, washcloths, bibs
- Mobiles
- Music box
- Changing table
- Floating bath toys
- Blocks
- Pull toys
- Dress-me doll
- Clutch balls
- Doll carriage and doll bed
- Kiddie car
- Scooter
- Crib mobiles
- Cuddly toys
- Play telephone
- Dairy wagon
- Texture ball
- Squeeze toys
- Nesting and stacking toys

Toys for Preschoolers and School-Age Children

- Toy crib
- Puzzles
- Doctor kit
- Blackboard and chalk
- Record player, tape recorder, records or tapes
- Blanket tent
- Indoor slide
- Climbing toys
- Small tables and chairs
- Riding toys
- Tumbling mat
- Wheelbarrow
- Plastic shopping cart
- Playhouse
- Blocks
- Wooden toys
- Books
- Soap bubbles
- Musical instruments
- Play telephone
- Beanbags
- Rocking horse
- Tires
- Paints, clay, paper, crayons, paste, scissors
- Old wallets,

Equipment for All Age Groups

- Carpet squares to sit on or play with

Equipment and Supplies for Infants and Toddlers	*Toys for Preschoolers and School-Age Children*	*Equipment for All Age Groups*
■ Rocking horse ■ Simple puzzles ■ Plastic dishpan, measuring cups, and measuring spoons	keys ■ Play money ■ Used envelopes ■ Empty food boxes, washed containers ■ Boots ■ Old garden hose (can be used to play firefighter) ■ Commercial toys such as Tinker Toys, Legos, and Lincoln Logs ■ Jump rope ■ Sandbox, pails, and shovels ■ Chalk (for use in playing hopscotch) ■ Balls suitable for kickball, wiffle ball, and basketball	

Let your friends know that you would like to receive any extra toys they come across during spring cleaning. Make it clear that you don't want or need objects unless they have all of the pieces and are in good working order. Believe it or not, you do not want to have too many toys. Too much clutter will only lead to confusion for both the children and you.

Some libraries and child care organizations have toy lending libraries. My local library allowed me to borrow puzzles, small toys, books, cassette tapes, and videotapes for children.

As I walk through shopping malls and grocery stores I always note anything I think a store owner might want to discard and ask him to save it for my child care program. With a little imagination, a large box can easily be transformed into a gasoline pump or a drive-through car wash. Don't feel bad if some shopkeepers are not very helpful or generous. It never hurts to ask. I have gotten many free supplies.

Understanding Your Role as Caregiver

As a concerned caregiver, you should be knowledgeable about the development of children and should expect to wear many different hats. You will be many things to the children in your care:

- You should care for their physical health as if you were a *physician*.
- You should look for ways to stimulate their intellectual growth as if you were a *professor* of early childhood development.
- You should plan nutritious snacks and lunches as if you were a *dietitian*.
- You should observe their behavior as if you were a *child psychologist*.
- You must love them and respect them in good times and bad, in sickness and in health, as if you were their *parent*.

You can help foster a successful, happy, and confident child simply by

- showing enthusiasm and excitement when the child accomplishes something.
- teaching the child while "playing" by talking about what you are doing and what he is doing.

- avoiding the "hands off, he'll do it when he's ready" philosophy.
- demonstrating a loving and accepting attitude.
- taking a positive approach. Instead of saying, "Don't touch," say, "Please handle it gently." You might say "You need to . . ." instead of "I say that you have to . . ."
- asking questions about familiar experiences and situations and discussing what you see and hear.
- complimenting a child's drawing by saying, "Tell me about it," not, "What is it?"

In the days and weeks before the start of your child care program you will want to read as much as you can about the characteristics and interests of each age group. You may also want to consult physicians, nurses, parents, psychologists, and nursing mothers' groups. They will probably be happy to share their knowledge with you.

Even if you've already successfully raised your own family, it doesn't hurt to brush up on what to expect from those terrible twos and mercurial threes. In the pages that follow, you will find some basic information about infants, toddlers, preschoolers, and school-age children.

Infants

Researchers tell us that the first years of life are the most critical for a child. As a caregiver, you will have many wonderful opportunities to introduce infants to the world around them. As you go through the day, always remember that a baby who is treated with tenderness and affection has the best chance of growing up to be a loving child. A child who feels confident that his needs will be met—whether he is hungry, wet, uncomfortable, or lonely—will be better able to trust in future relationships. Here are a few guidelines to keep in mind:

- Start off the day with adequate amounts of nutritious food.
- Give infants opportunities to use all their senses.

- While you are bathing a child, give him lots of opportunities to splash. Fill containers with water and, if you are in an especially playful mood, add a few drops of food coloring to the water.
- Let the baby know that he is special to you. Even as an adult, you know how it feels to miss a loved one. The baby is sure to miss his mother or father. Do all that you can to make the day care experience a happy one.
- And don't forget—smile often. Studies have shown that when babies look at an adult face a smile is the first thing they notice.

Coping with Crying Babies

Some infants cry when they are dropped off, some when they are picked up, and some cry all day. Your job is to be patient, supportive, and understanding at all times—in other words, a superwoman. Always be ready to offer extra cuddling.

Sometimes swaddling a crying baby can help. When my daughter Robin was a newborn, she always managed to wiggle over to the corner of the crib. My mother explained that she was trying to be close to something like her mother's body. Since that security was not available, the side of the crib became a substitute. She suggested that I wrap Robin in a blanket so that her arms and legs were kept secure. I noticed with my second child that, from the beginning, she was rarely fretful because she had the comfort and security of a wrapped blanket.

If a baby is crying, you should check the basics. Is he hungry, wet, afraid, or tired? You should also make sure that an open pin is not sticking into his body. I remember the day when we took Robin to a family party. She was fussier than she had ever been in her entire eight-month life span. When we got home we discovered the reason for her constant howling—a straight pin on her new dress had been poking her all day long. Of course, my husband and I felt awful.

Another time we noticed that one of her toes was terribly swollen. As we examined it closely, we saw that a very thin piece of thread was wrapped several times around the toe, restricting the circulation. We surmised that it must have been a loose thread from one of her socks—but how long it had been bothering her, we'll never know.

Developmental Milestones

Children develop at different rates. Some walk early, some begin much later. Parents are very sensitive about how quickly their children achieve certain developmental milestones. You should try to bite your tongue when you are about to say something that may cause a child's parents pain. No parent wants to hear: "I'm really surprised that your baby isn't crawling, walking, or talking by this age." You may have had a child of your own or a very dear nephew who reached these same milestones early, but I can tell you from personal experience that when someone makes a comparison it hurts your feelings.

Recently a woman who cares for babies told me of a particularly "slow" eighteen month old she was caring for. I asked her what seemed to be the problem. She said the child wasn't talking very clearly. At the time of the conversation, I had my own one-and-a-half-year-old daughter with me. I happened to think that my daughter Kristen was quite advanced for her age (a mother's pride, of course!), and she wasn't talking very clearly either. This particular provider recalled that her own child was reciting poetry at this stage. Perhaps her child was exceptionally bright, or perhaps the intervening years had caused her to glorify her child's earliest accomplishments. At any rate, I assured her that the little girl she was taking care of was doing just fine for her age.

The developmental chart that follows should give you a general idea of what you might expect from a child at a certain chronological age. Since every baby is unique, please do not use this chart to form a judgment about a child's intelligence or to determine whether a child is normal. As you review the chart, be aware that children who were born prematurely take awhile to catch up and may develop at a slower rate.

Coordination

Using hands and eyes

Characteristics:	Most babies first do this between:
Follows an object with eyes for a short distance	Birth and 6 weeks
Follows with eyes from one side all the way to the other side of head	2 months and 4 months
Brings hands together in front of body	6 weeks and 3½ months
Grasps a rattle placed in fingers	2½ months and 4½ months
Passes a toy from one hand to the other	5 months and 7½ months
Grasps a small object (like a raisin) off a flat surface	5 months and 8 months
Picks up a small object using thumb and finger	7 months and 10 months
Brings together two toys held in hands	7 months and 12 months
Scribbles with a pencil or crayon	12 months and 24 months

Using ears and voice

Pays attention to sounds	Birth and 6 weeks
Makes vocal sounds other than crying	Birth and 6 weeks
Laughs	6 weeks and 3½ months
Squeals	6 weeks and 4½ months
Turns toward your voice	4 months and 8 months
Says "Dada" or "Mama"	6 months and 10 months

Uses "Dada" or "Mama"
to mean one specific   10 months and 14
person   months
Imitates the speech
sounds you make   6 months and 11 months

Behaving with People

Looks at your face   Birth and 1 month
Smiles when you smile
or play with him   Birth and 2 months
Smiles by self   6 weeks and 5 months
Pulls back when you pull
a toy from his hand   4 months and 10 months
Tries to get a toy that is
out of reach   5 months and 9 months
Feeds crackers to self   5 months and 8 months
Drinks from a cup by   10 months and 16
self   months
Uses a spoon, spills little   13 months and 24
    months
Plays peekaboo   6 months and 10 months
Plays pat-a-cake   7 months and 13 months
Plays with a ball on the   10 months and 16
floor   months

Infant Activities

Did you know that babies can get bored too? It is best to give them a few toys at a time and later replace some of them with different ones to provide variety. Babies have differing personalities, and you should tailor activities to suit a baby's interests.

Some activities are enjoyed universally by babies. Laugh with the baby as you dress, bathe, and feed him; make up nonsense rhymes as you count fingers and toes, name body parts, hold the baby on your lap, and read aloud. Even before a baby understands language, it is beneficial to talk and to count fingers and toes while dressing a baby.

It really isn't necessary to spend a lot of money on toys for infants. Babies will enjoy learning about different textures by touching wet grass, the rough bark of a tree, or an animal's soft fur. They are also easily amused by kitchen toys such as plastic scoops, measuring cups, ice cube trays, mixing bowls, and pots and pans. Be sure to remove from plastic bottles caps or lids that could be swallowed.

Toddlers

The word *toddler* usually refers to a child between one and two-and-a-half years old. Toddlers are not quite in the infamous terrible twos stage, but they are well on their way!

The toddler is constantly trying out new skills and testing the limits set by adults. Caregivers have described children of this age as loving, frustrating, challenging, funny, and charming. This period can be very wearing for the caregiver. Hearing a child say "No!" a hundred times a day is no pleasure. It is important to understand that "No" reflects a child's growing need for independence. I once asked an experienced mother what I could do about my daughter Kristen's pattern of negativity. She said, "Wait until she outgrows it." That bit of common sense is really the answer.

Children of this age sometimes suck their thumbs or fingers. The pediatrician I spoke to said not to worry about this habit. I was under the impression that it meant that the child was insecure and in need of more love and affection. Although that may be true in some cases, many toddlers like to suck their thumbs simply because it is comfortable for them. This is also the age when security blankets, favorite stuffed animals, and other more unusual objects become important to a child. Once again, this stage will pass and is harmless.

As any parent of a child this age knows, this is the period when you may have to start thinking about discipline. By discipline I mean teaching the child that there are boundaries of acceptable behavior. A firm "No" may be enough to teach a toddler not to pull a lamp cord. One of my children once had a temper tantrum in a library, and I was asked to leave. I was embarrassed, but I learned a valuable lesson. My expectations for her were too high. How could I possibly expect a baby not to want to babble and run around in such a colorful place? Experts say that when a child has a tantrum you should do your best to ignore it and follow it up with a warm and loving activity. It isn't any more pleasant for the child to kick and scream than it is for you to witness it.

When I first began my program I interviewed many potential assistants. I felt very fortunate when Ellen, who was studying early childhood development, accepted my offer to work part time. She worked only one day and called me that evening to give me two weeks' notice. This was not really a surprise to me because I already had certain misgivings about her. As I observed her playing a game of hide-and-seek with two year olds in the backyard, I heard her telling them to hide anywhere in the yard while she closed her eyes and counted to ten. At this point I felt compelled to join the game. Good judgment should have told her that two year olds cannot be allowed to run around helter skelter while an adult's eyes are closed. As the mother of a toddler, I can assure you that you can never take your eyes off a child of this age.

Let me describe my daughter Kristen as an example of an active toddler. Kristen's daily activities seem to consist of saying "No!" ripping up pieces of paper (I think they are supposed to be tickets), flushing the toilet, and pulling things out of the kitchen cabinet and hiding in it. Other activities include carrying a pocketbook stuffed with her treasures, dumping food from her high chair tray when she is finished, pulling things out of drawers, scribbling on paper, and crying for every toy that her sister has. She is also interested in games like "What does a cow say?" "Where's Kristen?" "Touch your nose." "Bring Mommy a diaper." And "Ring-Around-a-Rosy."

She is beginning to be able to sit still for a story and loves to point to animals, flowers, and other familiar things pictured in books and magazines. She will sit in her high chair and color a picture while listening to a record.

At present she has a very limited vocabulary but that doesn't fool me. She knows all that is going on but just isn't verbal yet. I know that children develop language skills at different rates. To encourage her to talk, I praise her when she says "candy," "doggie," or "shoe." She can do simple tasks such as putting the doll in the toy box and can get her jacket when it is time to leave.

She cries occasionally when I leave her with a baby-sitter but I know that it only lasts for about thirty seconds, so I make a quick exit. When my husband and I talk to our children, we try to use descriptive words such as "Katelyn built a tower with her *red* Legos." Whenever possible, you should emphasize texture words like "hard," "soft," "scratchy," and "smooth."

Kristen's favorite toys at this point are an old purse, hats of all shapes and sizes, a lunch box, clothespins, a shoe box, and oatmeal cartons filled with safe odds and ends. She also enjoys playing with washable dolls, puzzles, a playhouse, blocks, a sliding board, a doll carriage, a doll bed, and a tricycle. You might ask parents to bring some equipment for their own children such as a wagon or kiddie car.

Recently a doctor said that a toddler's favorite toy is his mother. As a caregiver, you may come in a close second. You may be surprised at how easily a child is entertained and stimulated by your enthusiasm, laughter, and affection.

Toddler Learning Development

This is the time when you can start to teach children to do simple tasks. They can imitate you as you open and close your hands, touch your head, or jump up and down. At this stage they will be starting to talk and will be encouraged by your praise of their efforts. As you go around the house, point out concepts like big, little, up, down, in, out, open, close, and begin to introduce them to colors and shapes.

Toddlers learn from old standards like "Mary Had a Little Lamb" and "Ring-Around-a-Rosy." You can teach size relationships by placing small boxes or metal cans inside larger ones. Playgrounds have a wonderful appeal for this age group—especially dirt, sand, and water. But the most important aspect of a toddler's development is the person who is with him for the better part of the day. Your enthusiasm and interest are the key factors that will foster growth in his thinking, playing, motor development, and social interactions. It is sometimes difficult for providers to realize that this age group has a very short attention span and has not yet mastered sharing or cooperation. Following directions in a game like Simon Says is really beyond their level.

Preschoolers

Children are usually considered preschoolers when they are between two and a half and six years of age. Children of this age are real delights but they are also very sensitive. They are easily frustrated and need to feel comfortable coming to you for a loving pat when their feelings have been hurt or if there is a conflict over toys. Teach the children in your care to ask for help and be ready to step in when "taking turns" and "playing by the rules" just aren't working out.

Children of this age may say things they don't mean. For example, a child who declares, "I hate you," may just be mimicking something he heard an older sibling say. Preschoolers also seem to be very concerned with "best friend" status. You will probably encounter crying and sadness because a child has threatened another child, "I'm not going to be your best friend anymore." Another trauma for a preschooler might occur when a friend says, "I'm not going to invite you to my birthday party." Luckily, these crises—which usually involve much shrieking and wailing—pass in a matter of minutes. However, you will need a great deal of patience. Nerves of steel may be adequate!

Every once in a while you will meet a child who is exceptional. Jed was only three years old when I first met him, but he taught me quite a bit about children. His parents were both psychologists and had raised a boy who endeared himself to virtually everyone. On the first day he came to our home we went for a walk. He picked up some leaves and said, "Look at this *beautiful green* and *brown* leaf." As he drank his milk he commented, "It's *fresh* and *cold* and *white*." Using descriptive adjectives as you talk about everyday things is a great way to expand a child's vocabulary. When my ten-month-old daughter would crawl into a castle of blocks or interfere unintentionally, it was always Jed who would explain to the others, "She's only a baby—zero years old. She doesn't understand yet."

But it was Jed's way of handling preschool problems that was really an eye-opener. Most children whined and complained or cried when someone took their favorite toys, but Jed would just come up to me and say calmly, "Miss Trisha, I have a problem. Can you please help me?" He would then explain the situation concerning his uncooperative or rowdy playmates. His parents must have taught him to talk things over and not to get upset. He had faith that adults would help him. He was really a beautiful child in every way. I feel fortunate that I had the opportunity to learn important lessons from Jed—a little boy who was extremely sweet, loving, and wise beyond his years.

Preschool Learning Development

Even though most parents will tell you that they don't want to push their children academically, I have found that most of them want the children to learn while they are at your home. Parents seem to take pride in the fact that Johnny can count and knows shapes and colors.

You can help stimulate preschoolers to learn in a number of ways. Point out similarities and differences in everyday objects. In your conversations, talk about things in sequence so that they understand what you mean by "the day before yesterday," "today," and "tomorrow." Children can learn a great deal by playing games such as Bingo, cards, and putting together puzzles that do not contain too many pieces.

Free play is also important for children of this age. They enjoy playing in crates, in the sandbox, or on swing sets without too much adult direction. If you observe them playing, you will notice that they are starting to learn how to share and take turns. However, they will still come to you for help zipping their coats or refereeing a dispute over a favorite toy. When you announce, "It's time to make a craft or listen to a story," preschoolers want to be assured that there will still be plenty of time to continue their own creative games later.

Once seated at the table, they take pride in their work as they mold clay and use crayons, paste, and scissors. This is also the stage when children enjoy dressing up as mothers, fathers, nurses, doctors, and firefighters, and this kind of role playing is important to their development.

Homemade Toys for Preschoolers

You may want to keep a box of clothes for dress-up play, or put some hooks inside a closet door to hang the clothes on. For dress-up materials give them a curtain or sheet for a king's robe; a lady's fancy half slip for a queen's gown; a variety of hats (lady's, fireman's, workman's, serviceman's); discarded men's neckties and jackets; purses and wallets, complete with toy money, coupons cut from magazines, or poker chips. They may also enjoy playing with empty food boxes and washed plastic milk cartons. An empty box that has been taped shut can be transformed into a store, restaurant, or kitchen.

School-Age Children

A good friend of mine, Maureen, offers an after-school program. During the day she cares for her own two children and a baby, but after school she is responsible for several older children. The parents who hired her realize that when school-age children are home alone they can become involved in dangerous situations. By offering an after-school program, you are providing a valuable service for the parents as well as the children.

Maureen's main goal is to provide a pleasant, relaxed environment for the kids who come after school. She greets each child with a hug, a bright smile, and a kiss and tells them how glad she is to see them. Remembering how her mother used to greet her, she realizes the importance of asking them about their day. A tasty snack is always on the table. Some children at this age feel funny about needing a caregiver so she tries to give them space to unwind and relax.

I asked Maureen to suggest a few activities that had worked well for her, and she named the following:

- Allow the older children to coach the younger ones by teaching them games and helping them with homework or other projects.
- Teach the children sewing or embroidery.
- Help children to assemble model cars, boats, or planes.
- Provide opportunities for woodworking with simple tools, often a popular activity.
- Plant apple, orange, or grapefruit seeds in your yard.
- Make a terrarium in a mayonnaise jar. Put a piece of charcoal on the bottom. Add a layer of gravel, then a layer of dirt. Put some seeds in the jar and replace the lid. The plants will never need to be watered.
- Provide table games and jigsaw puzzles.
- Encourage some of the children to stage a play for the others. (Give them a shopping bag with about five articles in it such as a flashlight, dish, telephone, raincoat, and brush. The skit should incorporate these items.)
- Make available sports equipment such as bats and balls, a basketball, and a soft football.
- Supply paints, clay, crayons, paper, and chalk.
- Camp in the backyard by setting up a tent. Practice zipping, unzipping, reading a compass, making knots. (A Boy Scout Handbook may come in handy.)
- Let the children become part of family traditions by helping you plan and prepare for celebrations. They can help you select a Thanksgiving turkey and Christmas tree, make Halloween costumes and Valentine's Day cards, dye Easter

eggs or make matzo ball soup for Passover. Talk about other holidays like St. Patrick's Day and Martin Luther King Day.

- Simple recipes can teach children many skills in the kitchen so teach them basic kitchen safety rules as well as how to cut, grind, grate, beat, stir, mash, measure, pour, strain, squeeze, wash, and peel. They will learn about foods, following directions, and telling time.
- Let the children plant seeds. Fill half a paper cup with dirt, push a couple of seeds into the dirt about ¼ inch deep. Dampen soil and place in a well-lighted room. Explain how seeds germinate.
- Borrow foreign-language cassettes from the library.
- Provide opportunities for collecting coins, stamps, bottles, bugs, shells, butterflies, pictures of birds, or rocks. Consider the interests of the children in your group and build on that interest.
- Teach basic card games such as Old Maid, War, gin rummy, and poker.

Because children of this age are under pressure during the school day, it's a good idea to give them some freedom when they are with you. We know what it is like to be under stress and children experience stress too. Perhaps getting a head start on their homework or watching television is all they need to do. When planning how much independence a child will have at your home, discuss the situation with the parent in the child's presence.

School-age children need to know that you trust and like them. Try to be very positive and take advantage of any opportunities to praise them. Children of this age like to feel important, so don't forget that they can be great helpers.

Choosing the Right Age Group for You

When I first considered what age children I wanted to care for, I thought that infants would be best for me. My sister Joann was planning to help me and she had a baby who was eight months old. Robin was eighteen months old and Katelyn was three months old. We imagined a perfect little nursery filled with happy infants—an idyllic Mother Goose Land.

We decided to try occasional baby-sitting first and let parents know that we were available to watch their infants for a few hours while they went shopping or ran errands. Thank goodness, we didn't make a commitment to any parent for full-time day care.

The first morning that four little ones arrived, we learned that infant day care was not for us. Joann's baby wanted special attention, and I found that Robin wasn't too excited about my fussing over other babies. When the mothers returned and remarked how clean and happy all of the children looked, Joann and I gave each other a knowing look. We were both thinking of the hours when we wondered how we would get through a morning with our "gaggle of squawking geese."

Later, when I decided to start a program on a larger scale, I knew that I wanted to care for children two years or older. In that way, I wouldn't be torn between meeting the needs of babies and my own two children. I also knew that I wanted more of a nursery school environment. However, I did not require the children in my care to be toilet trained, and many of them were still in diapers.

In order to determine which age group would be best for you, think about the children you enjoy most. Some people just love babies. However, before taking the plunge and accepting a houseful of infants, remember that your state licensing group has established a limit as to how many children in each age group can be cared for in the home. Infants are a great deal of work, both physically and emotionally. In addition to worrying about what and how often to feed them, you will be dealing with multiple sleeping and diapering schedules (not to mention multiple parents). You want to be sure that you will have the time and energy left over to play with the babies. Since the first year of a child's life is so crucial to later development, you want to offer more than an assembly-line style of child care.

Since many mothers today return to work when their babies

are still very young, you may find that you receive a lot of inquiries about infant care. Since you can charge more money to care for an infant, it may be tempting financially to accept several babies into your program. Keep in mind, though, that many new mothers will expect you to provide highly individual care for their babies. In a large group, that is simply not possible. I believe that two infants is the optimal number because you can take them for walks in a double stroller and feed them one at a time. Babies need the warmth of a loving person feeding them as opposed to someone propping up a bottle.

On the other hand, suppose initially you decide, "Infants are not for me." You may face a situation that will cause you to reconsider. Suppose you care for a charming two year old whose mother is now expecting her second child. She plans to return to work in six months and really wants both her children to be together. In this instance, if you like the family, you might agree to try the baby.

Expanding Your Knowledge of Child Care

As a professional, you may wish to learn more about early childhood development and current trends in child care. The easiest way to contact organizations that can help is by telephone. Simply identify yourself in a friendly, confident manner, explain that you care for children in your home, and ask if they offer any services that could help you. Here are a few suggestions:

- Libraries provide magazines, videotapes, and books on child care. Borrow training videos and watch them while the children are napping or in the evening. Videotapes on discipline, first aid, crafts, running a small business, and other child care-related issues are very good sources of information, especially if you are unable to attend classes or workshops.
- Enroll in courses at community colleges, universities, and continuing education centers.

- Child care conventions are offered on a state and national level and will keep you informed of the latest trends and issues in child care.
- Subscribe to newsletters for family day care providers (see Appendix B).
- Take advantage of training sessions offered by the Red Cross, mental health agencies, and child care bureaus.
- Join associations of providers, advocates, and lobbyists who have up-to-date information about USDA Child Care Food Programs, legal issues, and tax laws that affect caregivers (see Appendix B).
- Call the National Association for the Education of Young Children (NAEYC) at 1-800-424-2460 and ask for the Information Services Group.
- The local Community Coordinated Child Care Council, also known as the 4-C Group, can be very helpful to family day care providers. Ask your local social service group whether the 4-Cs operate in your county.

HEALTH AND SAFETY

Childproofing Your Home

Childproofing your home can save you from tragedy. Share the room-by-room lists in this chapter with the significant people in your life. A large number of accidents occur in the homes of grandparents who are not accustomed to many of these precautions.

When I began my program, I thought that my home was completely childproof. Yet on several occasions I discovered safety hazards that I had overlooked. For example, we had a deck that was elevated about six feet above the ground. My husband and I thought that this would be a great place for the children to ride their tricycles when the ground below was too wet after a heavy rainstorm. We were concerned about children falling through the rails, so we enclosed the deck with a chicken-wire fence. We didn't realize that the children would be able to stand on the seats of their riding toys and lean over the railing. Upon discovering this hazard, we removed all the patio furniture and riding toys and used the deck only for activities such as building blocks and reading stories.

One way to check for safety hazards is to get down on your hands and knees as if you were a crawling baby. From this perspective, you will notice many unsafe situations you might otherwise overlook.

The lists that follow will take you through your house or apartment room by room. You alone know the ages and maturity of the children in your care. Use the information as a starting point but make your own decisions about health and safety based on your good judgment and on your knowledge of children.

Kitchen

- Use ant spray rather than ant traps on the kitchen floor.
- Tablecloths can be grabbed by curious hands and pulled down. Why not use place mats?
- Waxed floors can be slippery.
- Always use a safety strap when a baby is in the high chair.
- Wipe up a spill immediately or cover it with newspaper until you have the time to get to it.
- If your home is older, was lead-free paint used on the woodwork? Children have been poisoned by eating chips of paint with high lead levels.
- If you decide to throw away a refrigerator, be sure to take the door off. Children have suffocated when they were closed inside and could not open the door.
- If possible, remove the handles from your stove when not in use.
- Don't store goodies in cabinets above the range. Children have climbed on stoves and their clothes have caught on fire.
- Do not throw dry cleaning plastic bags into the trash can. A child could pull one out and suffocate.
- Lock up all cleaning and exterminating supplies (child-resistant caps are not 100 percent safe).
- Turn pot handles away from curious hands on the stove.

- Keep sharp knives and utensils out of reach.
- Never put a knife into a toaster.
- Keep matches in a metal container that is out of the reach of children.
- Electric fans and kerosene heaters should be nowhere near the hands of children.
- These common items have the potential to be harmful: balloons, coins, seeds, grapes, shells, toys with loosely attached ribbons, wheels, pieces of broken toys, hot dogs, popcorn, beans, screws, hard candies, buttons, pins, carrots, tacks.
- Wear an apron with large pockets so you can pick up broken toys, small pieces, and loose pennies that might be dangerous.
- The U.S. Food and Drug Administration has advised that rubber pacifiers and bottle nipples should be boiled five to six times—each time in fresh water—before they are used for the first time. The FDA urges parents to take this precaution because some nipples and pacifiers on the market contain levels of nitrosamines (carcinogens) well above the new recommended level of ten parts per billion.

Bedroom

- Make sure nightclothes are made of fire-retardant materials.
- Put away perfumes, shaving cream, men's cologne, and cosmetics, which can be lethal if swallowed.
- Get rid of mothballs, which can be poisonous.
- Toddlers have suffocated in closets. It is important to know where they are at all times. (This is a good reason to check on them frequently during nap time.)
- Baby powder can be dangerous if inhaled by a baby.
- Toys with pompoms, pins, buttons, or wheels are hazardous and should be removed from crib or playpen.
- Keep crib away from window and drapery cords, which could cause strangulation.

- Move crib away from electrical outlets.
- Never leave blankets or towels hanging over the crib.
- Crib slats must have a maximum space between slats of 2⅜ inches. The Consumer Product Safety Commission has issued warnings about the danger of older cribs which do not meet this criterion.
- Make sure there are no holes in the child's mattress or pad where stuffing might be exposed. Make sure that the edging is sewn securely on blankets.
- Peek in on a sleeping child regularly. Remove barrettes when a child naps.
- Pillows and stuffed animals in a crib can cause suffocation or may be used as "stepping-stones."
- Make sure that screens are secure so a child does not fall out of a window.

Living Room

- If you have a gun collection, lock it away! A day care home is no place for such things. Always store firearms unloaded. (It's hard to believe, but five hundred children a year are killed by firearms kept around the house.)
- Put chain locks up high on the doors because most children can turn knobs.
- Remove anything that is fragile.
- Put tables with sharp corners in another room temporarily.
- Always lock doors. Doors left ajar are dangerous even for a crawling baby.
- Repair any worn or exposed wires on lamp or appliance cords. Cover electrical outlets so children cannot insert any objects.
- Keep combustible materials like clothing, curtains, and paper away from lamps.
- Tie a bell to each door so that you are always aware of a child's comings and goings.

Bathroom

- Store electric curlers and hair dryer out of reach when not in use. (Do not leave plugged in on counter next to sink.)
- Flush away all old medicines. Even aspirin is dangerous.
- If possible, reduce the temperature of your hot water heater so that a child cannot scald himself. Run cool water first. Add hot water.
- Never turn an appliance on when standing on a wet floor. Teach children not to touch appliances with wet hands.
- Keep toilet lids closed. Believe it or not, children have drowned in the toilet when they leaned over and couldn't pull themselves back out.
- Never leave a child alone in a bathtub.

Stairways

- Install safety gates at the top and bottom of stairs when a baby starts to crawl.
- Never leave things which could be tripped over on steps.

Outside Area

- Don't assume that window screens will prevent a child from falling through. During hot summer months, when houses of all types have open windows, a child can also fall from a window in a two-story suburban house. Keep cribs away from windows and, if you have to have air, open the window only 4 or 5 inches. Use window guards to prevent an active child from playing with the screen.
- When picnicking outdoors, cover food that is not being eaten.
- Be alert for poisonous berries which may look attractive to youngsters. Know your poisonous plants. For example, a lily of the valley is a beautiful plant but it can cause irregular

heartbeat and mental confusion; castor beans can be fatal; certain bulbs like hyacinth and daffodil can cause diarrhea and vomiting, as will common privet; daphne, rhododendron, azaleas, and especially oleander can be fatal.

- Keep your shed locked and install childproof locks on your gate if your yard is enclosed.
- Do not plant shrubs which draw bees. Remove a wasp's nest if attached to side of house.
- If you have a standard backyard swing set, then it more than likely has open links. Hair can become tangled in the links or fingers can be cut if a child tries to grasp the chain when falling. To remedy this problem, buy some hose (similar to garden hose) and slip a 3- to 4-foot length over each chain before hanging the swings. Take another piece of the same type of hose, slit it along one side, and slip it onto the edges of the swing seat—then a wild flying swing will not hurt an innocent passerby.
- Lock up garden tools, fertilizers, and insect sprays.
- Do not allow young children to play outside unless an adult is present.
- Adults must be present even if a baby pool is used (put fresh water in pool each day). Try a sprinkler!
- A fenced yard is best for a group of children.
- Make sure that the yard is free of debris like rusty nails, glass, sharp cans, or bottles.
- Supervise jump-rope activities.
- Sandboxes should be covered when not in use. (Cats are attracted to them as litter boxes.)
- Make sure all outdoor equipment is safe and in good repair.
- Sprinkle salt over icy areas on the pavements near your house.
- Repair any loose boards or protruding nails.
- Remind children to be alert at all times. Instruct them to stay away from electrical facilities. It's dangerous and illegal to climb electrical towers.
- Never fly a kite or model airplane on rainy days. Wet strings are good conductors of electricity.
- Fly a kite away from electrical wires, TV, CB, or radio

antennas. Electricity could go right down the string to you. Use wood and paper in your kite.

- Choose a wide-open area when flying a kite. Avoid busy streets and highways. Keep away from fallen wires.
- If a kite or model airplane gets snagged in a power line, don't pull the string or climb the power pole. Leave the kite or model airplane there and call the electric company for help.
- If a child wants to climb a tree, make sure it is away from power lines. Never allow a child to climb utility poles, substation fences, or transmission towers.
- Build tree houses only in trees that have no electrical wires running through or near them.
- If you have an aboveground deck, be sure to put chicken wire around the sides to prevent children from falling. Remove chairs, tables, or toys that children could stand on.

Cautions About Medicine

- Medicines should not be left in your purse.
- Even so-called childproof caps can sometimes be opened by children.
- Do not give empty medicine containers to children to be used as toys.
- Never bribe a child to take medicine. Do not refer to pills as candy.

Safety Notes
for the Playroom

When Robin was born a friend gave her some baby toys made by a very reputable toy manufacturer. I put them in her crib during the first few months because I thought she would enjoy touching them and looking at the bright colors. When I entered her room one time I was alarmed to see that one of these toys was wrapped around her neck. I was very upset and was ready to call the Consumer Product Safety Council to report this very unsafe product. I thought that it should be recalled immediately.

My sister-in-law, who is a specialist at a children's hospital, gently told me that I had given Robin a toy that was not age-appropriate. The package clearly stated that this toy was not recommended for children under eighteen months of age. It looked like a baby toy but it was not meant for infants. It was my mistake because I was not aware of the importance of reading labels.

Once an experienced mother asked me at what age I removed rattles from cribs and playpens. I didn't know that there was any reason to do so. She explained that one of her children once broke the handle off a rattle, exposing sharp edges, and removed the small beads inside. Another friend told me that her son had managed to find a tiny rip in the seam on the playpen pad and had chewed the foam stuffing. She glanced over to see him with something in his mouth. Luckily she was right there or he might have choked on it.

Don't take any chances. If something doesn't look safe to you, it probably isn't. Don't count on toy manufacturers to make products that are safe for all children. Their motive is profit, so you must act as the true monitor of toy safety.

Are you aware of the following safety notes for your playroom?

- Toys must be durable and able to withstand heavy usage.
- Toys must be easily cleaned.
- Toys with ribbons, cords, or strings which could become undone could cause strangulation. Also beware of stuffed animals and toys with small buttons, bells, tiny wheels, string, eyes, and ears which could be swallowed.
- Toys should be made of material that will not crack or break to expose sharp edges, points, nails, or pins.
- Avoid dart games and the like which could cause eye injuries.
- Toys that are made with toxic paint may still show up as hand-me-downs or at garage sales.
- Avoid toy boxes with lids. Use a laundry basket or an open box to store toys.

- Balloons are not safe for young children. Be especially careful of the broken pieces which may fall to the floor after they pop. A child may try to eat them and choke.
- Read labels. Toys are clearly marked for age groups. Take advantage of the rigorous testing that precedes these age-range determinations. An injury could occur if a baby swallows a small piece from a toy that was intended for an older child.
- Look for the words *flame retardant* or *flame resistant* on toys made of fabric.
- Keep toys for older and younger children separate. Explain that it is dangerous for a baby to have more sophisticated toys.

Did you know that approximately one hundred thousand children have toy-related accidents each year? The U.S. Consumer Product Safety Council says the primary cause is misuse of toys, not faulty toy design. However, choosing toys wisely and supervising children closely is still the best way to prevent accidents.

If a product bears the symbol or name of any of the following organizations, it is an indication that it is probably safe.

- Good Housekeeping Seal of Approval
- American Academy of Pediatrics
- National Safety Council
- Underwriters Laboratory (which verifies that materials used in all new toys are safe)

Report complaints about unsafe toys to the United States Consumer Product Safety Commission at 1-800-638-2772.

Planning for Emergencies

You must take the responsibility of caring for other people's children very seriously. In any emergency, the most important consideration is a child's well-being, so don't hesitate to call the rescue squad. Seconds can be valuable. Be prepared by posting emergency numbers next to every phone in the house. If any of your neighbors is a doctor or nurse, you may want to keep their phone numbers handy as well. It is also a good idea to keep each parent's work telephone number next to the phone.

I would not begin caring for children without taking a first aid course, which is usually offered by a local hospital or by the Red Cross. You should be familiar with basic medical treatment and how to administer CPR. Having been trained in these procedures will give you confidence if you ever need to administer medical treatment.

What if a toddler fell down the steps? What would you do if you had three other little children depending on you? Think about your options. You could put everyone in your car and drive to the hospital, call all the parents and ask them to pick up their children immediately, call the injured child's parents and ask them to come get their child, or call an ambulance. In all cases, notify the parent of the injured child *immediately*. If necessary, have a responsible friend or neighbor stay with the other children. You could arrange for a neighbor to come in and help you a few times so that, in case of such an emergency, she will be familiar with the children and your routine. There is nothing like being prepared. Of course you would pay her for her help.

Even if you have your own children, you'll have to consider the well-being of *all* the children in your care. A little boy I was caring for once pushed my daughter Robin, causing her to bang her head on the sharp corner of the television. Although it wasn't a life-or-death situation, if it had been someone else's child I would have immediately called the parents and taken the child to the medical center for stitches. Instead, I held compresses on Robin's cut throughout the day and kept watching the clock, waiting for pickup time so that I could rush her to a doctor's office. By the time we arrived she was feeling fine . . . so fine that she hid under the doctor's desk and would not come out. The doctor didn't charge us his usual fee but determined (from a distance!) that had we come earlier he would have given her a few stitches.

Fortunately, the emergencies I have had to deal with were

limited to a child who was stung by a bee and a little boy, Steven, who put a stone into his nose. In Steven's case, our first thought was to ask him to try to blow the stone out. We hesitated because we were afraid that he might inhale and we could have a more serious situation on our hands. We decided to call his mother, who was only a few minutes away. Luckily, he followed her instruction to blow and it worked. Mission accomplished.

Pinched fingers, scraped knees, splinters, and small cuts occur regularly, so you will want to have first aid supplies readily available. Since accidents will not be limited to one part of your house, you should have first aid kits in at least two locations.

There are other emergency situations that may arise. You may be called to school for a serious problem with your own child or you could develop a painful toothache. These examples may seem highly unlikely but my point is that you should be prepared to leave on short notice if necessary.

When I was pregnant with my third child I worried about the possibility of accidentally falling and not being able to get up. What would I do with all the children and what would they do with me? Since "an ounce of prevention is worth a pound of cure," we role-played some possible accidents. If I couldn't get to the telephone, the older children knew they should dial 0 and say, "I need help." They were told to explain what had happened and not to hang up the phone. The operator would be able to trace the location of the call so that the rescue squad could come. We also pretended that I was attending an injured child. We acted out the scene of Katelyn falling off a sliding board. One of the children had to run and get the bandages.

As a game, I also showed them pictures of potentially hazardous situations that I had cut out of magazines. We discussed bicycle safety rules and looking both ways before crossing the street. We also pretended to find things on the ground outside and I cautioned the children not to put anything in their mouths without first showing it to an adult. A fire drill may seem a bit extreme to you, but it is a potential emergency situation that deserves consideration.

You could also teach the older children to dial the phone number of a neighbor. Let them practice dialing and explaining the situation on a toy phone. You could ask a neighbor if you could allow some of the children to make a "trial call" just in case you are ever in distress. I also instructed Robin and Katelyn, in a real emergency, to run to two neighbors' houses. These types of practice drills can be expanded to include "Never Talk to Strangers" and "What to Do If You Are Lost."

Common Childhood Illnesses and Injuries

The information provided below is only meant to give you an overview of some of the common illnesses and injuries that young children experience. It is not meant to be all inclusive and should not be interpreted as substitute for calling the parent and doctor. In all cases, contact the parent immediately and seek medical advice for emergencies, symptoms of illness, or anything that you see as potentially jeopardizing a child's mental or physical health.

The following descriptions by Dr. Susan S. Aronson, Clinical Professor of Pediatrics at Hahnemann University, may help you know what to expect from illnesses and injuries of young children.

In general, children are usually irritable and more demanding and need more attention when they are ill than when they are well. Early childhood health problems can make caregivers feel that the children in their care "get everything that walks past the front door." On average, preschool children have six to eight upper respiratory infections per year. That means some have two or three, while others have ten to twelve. But take heart, these childhood illnesses build the child's immunity. Children outgrow the tendency to get many types of illness. Ear infections, for example, become less frequent as the ear structures become larger.

Abdominal Pain

Abdominal pain is one of the most frequent complaints of children. Although there are a few serious problems which are associated with this symptom, usually abdominal pain comes from such simple things as a virus, muscle soreness from coughing, constipation, stress, or a urinary tract infection. A severe pain which interferes with the child's normal activity or one which is located in one specific spot is more worrisome than one which comes and goes or one which is more diffusely felt over the abdomen. Asking a child to use one "pointer" finger to show you where it hurts will often reveal the more generalized discomfort of minor illness by seeing the child draw a circle around the navel. For children with severe, persistent abdominal pain or pain located in a single spot to which the child can point repeatedly, have the parent consult a physician. A doctor's help is also needed if there are other symptoms of serious illness such as a temperature of 105 degrees or over, fever for two or more days over 100 degrees, refusal to eat or drink anything for a day, failure to urinate or pain on urinating, difficulty breathing, or a recent blow to the abdomen. In general, avoid giving laxatives, enemas, or medicine unless prescribed by a physician, or making a big issue out of bowel movements or toilet training. Frequent small amounts of room-temperature fluids like water, tea, gelatin, soda, diluted apple juice, grape juice, or chicken broth may make the child feel better.

Allergy

There are a variety of ways in which children react to particular substances such as pollen, foods, dust, drugs, or insect stings, depending on their body sensitivity and the route the substances can be breathed in, touched, swallowed, or injected. Symptoms of allergy depend on which tissues are exposed and reacting. They can include itchy eyes, runny nose, difficulty breathing, swelling, hives, or other itchy rash. The best way to manage an allergy is to avoid the substance which causes the allergy. If this is impossible, antiallergy medicines (e.g., antihistamines) may help.

Anemia

Anemia is a condition in which a child doesn't have enough iron-containing hemoglobin in his blood. The usual cause is iron deficiency resulting from inadequate intake of iron during infancy, preschool, or adolescence to keep up with rapid growth during these periods. Children who are anemic often have an increased susceptibility to infection, developmental slowness, and irritability. Anemia has causes other than iron deficiency, but these are uncommon in childhood. Anemia must be diagnosed and treated by a health professional.

Asthma

The symptoms of asthma can range from mild wheezing to severe shortness of breath. Wheezing is distinguished from obstruction of the nose by the fact that in asthma it takes longer to get air out of the body than to draw it into the body. Asthma attacks are related to allergy, infection, emotional stress, or some combination of the three in people who are predisposed (genetically) to wheeze. When this problem happens for the first time, the child needs to be assessed by a doctor so medicine can be prescribed to relieve the symptoms. Care must be taken to identify a child who wheezes because a small object stuck in a child's windpipe may also cause wheezing.

Bites

Children often bite in anger or frustration. Otherwise tame and loving pets may also bite if they are taunted. When the skin is broken by teeth, many bacteria are introduced into the wound.

Immediate vigorous washing with soap and water followed by thorough rinsing with running water helps to prevent infection. Be sure to notify authorities of animal bites if the animal is not known to have been vaccinated against rabies.

Insect bites are very common. Stingers should be removed promptly before swelling around them makes removal more difficult. Honeybee stingers can be removed most easily by gently pulling or scraping with a fingernail in a direction parallel to the skin. Some doctors recommend a quick application of a paste of meat tenderizer and water to help break down the venom if it has not already become too dispersed in the tissue. For itching and swelling, application of cold packs or cold water helps.

Bumps and bruises

When a blunt injury causes some damage to underlying tissues, there is accumulation of tissue fluid and/or blood under the skin. A bruise is a collection of blood under the skin. Swelling is caused by fluid leaking from blood and lymph vessels into the tissues. To minimize the amount of fluid accumulation, apply pressure, cold water, or cold packs and elevate the affected part. Wringer, bike spoke, and other crush injuries need a doctor's attention as they can be more serious than they appear at first.

Burns

Even minor burns are quite painful. Rapid application of cold water helps to remove heat from the tissues and stop further injury. Blisters are sterile dressings over a burn and should *not* be broken. More severe burns need a doctor's attention. Household plastic wrap or aluminum foil make good dressings over burns until medical help is obtained. Ointments and creams should not be used unless prescribed by a doctor.

Colds

Colds are caused by viruses which the body must overcome by itself. Antibiotics do not help unless there is a bacterial infection. Cold medications generally do more harm than good by making secretions dry, thick, and harder for the child to get out of his system. Young children, especially those under five years of age, get many colds whether they stay at home or are in a child care situation.

The worst part of a cold lasts two to three days, but symptoms may last for several weeks. Most colds bring sneezing, a runny nose, and watery eyes, but little or no fever. These same symptoms may precede other illnesses such as chicken pox or measles. An infant with a congested nose may have trouble sucking and be greatly helped by removal of mucus with an aspirator. Coughing from a cold may cause vomiting. Remember to encourage the child to drink lots of liquids when he has a cold.

Unfortunately, young children sometimes develop other illnesses from a simple cold. It is important to watch for a severe sore throat, a sharp rise in temperature, difficulty breathing, pain in the ear or back of the neck, or a persistent chest cough. These symptoms may indicate that an infection requiring medical treatment has developed. It is especially important to watch for the symptoms of an ear infection. Young children often pull or rub their ears when coming down with an earache. An untreated ear infection can sometimes lead to hearing loss or more serious illness. Children with ear pain or persistent tugging at the ear should always be examined. Colds can be spread from a few days before the first symptoms appear until the child stops sneezing and coughing. They are spread by touching surfaces wet with the virus (usually hands) more than by sneezing and coughing directly.

In any upper respiratory infection (or cold) the mucous membranes of the nose become swollen and pour out extra amounts of mucus. This mucus normally runs out and is pushed forward by the lining of the inner nose. During a cold the nose may become blocked and the mucus can run down the throat, where it is swallowed when the child is awake. During the sleeping hours this mucus runs down the throat and causes the gurgling sound so common to infants with colds. This sound does not mean pneumonia.

When the nose is blocked, the child breathes through the mouth. This air is much drier than air normally coming through the nose and the mucus becomes thick and sticky, causing the child to cough, "rattle," and have difficulty breathing. Humidifiers help to keep mucus thin so it doesn't block the child's airway. Cool mist ultrasonic humidifiers are best.

Be certain the child cannot reach the nozzle of the hot water vaporizer or a severe burn can result. There is no danger of this when a cold water vaporizer is used. Do not place a child with a high fever in a hot steam tent. A cold mist vaporizer should be used. The cool dampness will help to bring the temperature down. Be sure to clean a cold mist vaporizer with diluted bleach water (one tablespoon to one quart of water) after a week or two of use to clean out the mold that grows in the moist machine parts. Or follow the instructions that come with the machine to clean it.

Diaper rash

Diaper rash is the result of an irritation of the skin by wetness and rubbing of the diaper or contact with stool which is aggravated by the breakdown of urine by the bacteria on the skin.

There are three ways to treat the irritation:

1. Reduce the irritation itself:
   - Leave baby without diaper and plastic pants. (Use cloth diapers without plastic pants or use oversized diapers allowed to hang away from the child's bottom. Change the diaper more often to keep urine and stool off the skin and the skin dry and cool.)
   - Put baby in cool sitz baths (at least 15 minutes gives time for deep cooling and contraction of blood vessels).

- Cool compresses can be used if cool baths are not available.
2. Make it hard for the bacteria on the skin to grow:
    - Put vinegar (2 to 3 tablespoons) in bath water or in cool compress water. Vinegar is a mild acid which helps to prevent bacteria growth. Bathing also cuts down the need for rubbing the child's sore bottom to clean it.
    - To make the urine more acid (which reduces bacterial growth), feed a child acid fruit juice. Cranberry juice is good for this purpose. Citrus juice is less effective.
    - Bacteria do not grow well in diluted urine—give enough liquids to make the child's urine look like water. Diluted urine will not have a less yellow color.
3. Stools contain broken-down bile, which is like a detergent and is irritating, so change a child promptly and wash well.
    - With a small infant, bottom cleaning can easily be done over the sink. Do not run water from the tap directly onto an infant's skin. Use your hand to cup the water and put it on the baby. Be sure that a sudden surge of hot water from the tap cannot scald the child.
    - To avoid rubbing the skin, pat dry.

Earache

Earaches almost always mean that a doctor's attention is needed. The most common problem is backup of mucus or swelling and closure of the eustachian tube, stopping air movement into the middle ear. Having the child "sniff" the mist from a vaporizer sometimes unblocks the tiny eustachian tube through which air moves up to the middle ear from the back of the nose and throat. Chewing gum also sometimes helps. Because the doctor must look in the ear to identify the problem, put nothing in the ear. If vaporizer and chewing gum don't help in an hour or so, check and treat the child for fever and arrange for the child to see a doctor.

Fever

Fever is usually the result of an infection, but the height of the fever does not indicate the seriousness of the infection. The child's temperature can be measured with a thermometer to see if it is going up or down. Normal temperatures vary from 97.5 to 100 degrees, with a tendency for temperature to increase in the afternoon and evening.

Children tend to be irritable and sleepy and often refuse to eat or drink when they have a fever. If the cause of the fever is a shot or simple infection, treat the fever to make the child more comfortable and better able to drink, and to reduce excess fluid loss through evaporation from the child's overheated body. Offer small amounts of liquids at frequent intervals. Citrus juices and milk will tend to upset the child's stomach, so avoid them. Clear liquids like flat soda, gelatin, chicken broth, apple juice, or grape juice are best. If the fever is 102 degrees or more, acetaminophen may be given in a dose of 6 mg. per pound of body weight.

When the child's temperature is over 102 degrees, tub baths with plain lukewarm water may be used to help bring it down. The water should be comfortably warm to prevent the child from shivering, which raises the body temperature. It takes 30 to 40 minutes in the tub to lose enough heat into the water to bring the temperature down. Adding a few floating toys may make the experience more pleasant.

Remember, a fever is often an indication of an infection. Ear pain or unexplained fevers should be discussed with a doctor or nurse. No harm will result from taking the child outdoors with a fever; it may even help to cool him off. Minimize the amount of clothing on a child with a fever. Blankets and sweaters are not needed indoors.

Lice

Lice are bloodsucking insects that live on humans. Scalp lice are usually first noticed as itchy red pimples where the hair meets the back of the neck. Since the insects are only 2 to 4 millimeters long, they are not easy to see. The eggs (nits) are tiny pearly white to gray egg-shaped objects that stick tightly to the hair shaft. Lice are transmitted by direct contact with an infected person or indirectly through clothing, headgear, and combs. Treatment consists of using a special rinse or shampoo. The most effective treatment is a product called NIX, available by doctor's prescription. Any lice treatment should be followed by careful combing to remove all the nit shells. Some doctors recommend using a solution of equal parts of vinegar and water to help loosen the nit shells from the hair shaft before combing. Clothing and bedding should be washed in detergent, rinsed in very hot water, and run through the dryer to kill both lice and eggs. Other members of the child's family or group should be checked carefully. Objects that can't be washed should be put in tightly sealed plastic bags for two weeks during which newly hatched lice will die. Children with lice are contagious until the nits and lice are no longer present, usually after one treatment with NIX or two treatments a week to ten days apart with other chemicals. The chemicals used to treat lice are pesticides and should not be overused.

Nosebleed

Nosebleeds start from injury to the lining membrane of the nose. Dry air, a cold, being hit in the nose, and picking at the nose are all ways in which the lining membrane can be injured. Once injured, a clot or scab often forms and is itself irritating. When the child picks at the scab or hits the nose the bleeding may start all over again. To stop a nosebleed, first have the child blow his nose thoroughly to completely clean out old blood and mucus. Immediately place your finger and thumb across the nose at the place in the nose where the bone ends and the softer, more flexible cartilage begins and squeeze the nostrils closed for five minutes by the clock. Don't peek. Cold cloths on the back of the neck don't help. Do not tilt the head back because the blood will run down the back of the child's throat, which may cause him to feel nauseated later. Few nosebleeds will continue after firm pressure is applied in this way.

Pinkeye

Also known as conjunctivitis, this inflammation of the membrane covering the inside of the eyelids and the white of the eyeballs occurs primarily in summer and early autumn. The causes for pinkeye symptoms are infection, allergies, colds, irritation from smog or chemicals, or foreign object in the eye. Its symptoms are red, irritated, tearing eyes, swollen lids, painful and itchy eyes, and a mucus discharge that makes the eyelashes sticky. The child may have trouble opening his eyes after sleeping. You can remove this discharge with a wet cotton ball, wiping from the inner to the outer corner of the eye. The eyes can be soothed by rinsing them with a boiled saltwater solution (¼ teaspoon salt to 1 cup water) and by applying warm compresses to the eyes four or more times a day. Wash your hands carefully after treating infected eyes.

Children under five years are most susceptible to infections. Conjunctivitis is transmitted by contact with discharges from the eyes or upper respiratory tract of infected persons, through contaminated fingers, clothing, or other articles. It is very contagious as long as the infection is active. To prevent infection, encourage frequent handwashing.

If the eye discharge is pronounced, drops and ointment should be obtained from the doctor to put in the eye. Children with active eye discharge should be excluded from child care unless they are known to have a noninfectious form of conjunctivitis. Usually a child with infectious conjunctivitis who has been treated for twenty-four hours with antibiotic drops and/or ointment can return to the group.

Teething

Children's first teeth come in any time between three months
and one year. Some children have minor pain and irritability
with teething, others may even run a temperature of 100 degrees.
Temperatures above 100 degrees, persistent diarrhea, and runny
nose are probably *not* due to teething. Cold pacifiers and teething
rings do help, as does acetaminophen.

Ticks

Ticks are insects that feed on animal blood. They are common
in wooded areas and are often found on pets and young children. They attach themselves to the skin when they are empty,
looking like black or brown 1-millimeter dots with legs when
they crawl. When full, they are usually bluish in color and the
size and shape of a large kernel of corn. A gentle tug with a
tweezers placed close to the tick's head or with fingers protected
by tissue or a rubber glove can then be used to remove the insect.
Care should be taken to inspect children regularly to discover
ticks before they have a chance to feed and so as not to crush
the tick's body on removal. Ticks spread several diseases, including Rocky Mountain spotted fever, and Lyme disease, in-
fecting the person during their feedings. An infected tick's body
will be loaded with the disease.

Communicable Diseases

Chicken pox. Incubation period: 11–21 days. Symptoms: slight
fever, pink bumps that develop tiny blisters, then scab over.
Communicable from day before rash until all blisters are dry.

Measles. Vaccine preventable from 15 months of age. Incubation period: 10–14 days. Symptoms: runny nose, cough, red eyes,
fever; rash develops on third or fourth day. Communicable during stage of cold symptoms until five days after rash appears.

Mumps. Vaccine preventable from 15 months of age. Incubation period: 14–21 days. Symptoms: fever, swelling, and tenderness of salivary glands at angle of jaw in front of ears, under tongue. Communicable from day before onset of symptoms until swelling has disappeared.

Rubella. Vaccine preventable from 15 months of age. Incubation period: 14–21 days. Symptoms: fever, swollen glands, especially in back of neck, rash appearing about two days later. Communicable one week before rash and at least four days after.

Haemophilus influenzae type b. Vaccine preventable from eighteen months of age. Incubation period: a few days. Symptoms: child may have mild coldlike symptoms rapidly progressing to fever, stiff neck, severe croup, difficulty beathing, and becoming gravely ill. Requires antibiotics.

First Aid

Convulsions:

Protect the child from injury.
Lie on side with head lower than hips.
Put nothing in the mouth.

Fainting:

Keep in flat position and raise legs.
Turn head to the side.
Do *not* give anything by mouth.
Call your doctor.

Fractures:

If an injured part is very painful, swollen, deformed, or if motion causes pain, suspect a fracture.
A fractured part should not be moved until it has been splinted.
Call a physician or ambulance.
Do *not* move a child who may have a neck or back injury, as this may cause paralysis.
Wait for help to arrive.

Sprains:

Apply a cold compress and elevate the injured arm or leg.
If you suspect a fracture (see above), call your doctor.

Head Injuries:

Seek immediate medical assistance for any of the following:

- Unconsciousness or drowsiness
- Convulsions
- Inability to move any body part
- Oozing of blood or watery fluid from the ears or nose
- Severe or persistent headache
- Head injury in any child less than 1 year old

If there are no symptoms, you may let your child sleep, but
awaken every 1 to 2 hours and make sure the child can recognize
you.

Poisons:

If a child is unconscious, becoming drowsy, having convulsions,
or having trouble breathing, call an emergency ambulance.

- Swallowed poisons. Any nonfood substance is a potential
  poison. Call the Poison Center immediately. Do not induce
  vomiting except on professional advice. The Poison Center
  will give you instructions for use of syrup of Ipecac.
- Fumes, Gases, or Smoke. Protect yourself first. Get the vic-
  tim into fresh air. Call the fire department. If the child is
  not breathing, start CPR and continue until help arrives.
- Skin Exposure. If acids, lye, pesticides, or any potentially
  poisonous substance comes in contact with a child's skin,
  brush off dry material gently. Wash skin with large quantities of soap and water. Remove contaminated clothing.
  Wear rubber gloves if possible. Call the Poison Center for
  further advice.
- Eye Exposure. If any substance is splashed in the eye, flush

with water for at least 15 minutes. Call the Poison Center for further advice.

Coping with Stress

Taking care of a group of young children can be very trying, especially if you also have a family of your own. There will be days when you will just want to crawl under the covers and go back to sleep. I remember one especially difficult day. A two-liter bottle of soda spilled on the floor at eight in the morning, my daughter had a high fever and needed a prescription medicine, my car wouldn't start, and it was pouring rain. That might not sound too awful, but keep in mind that I was also responsible for a large group of active children. Another day care provider had told me about days when she felt like going into her bedroom and locking the door, but until that day I couldn't really understand what she meant.

It's perfectly natural to have bad days when you feel more anxious or overwhelmed than usual. Even though you do not leave the house to go to work, you *are* working, and almost any job can be stressful. Although some people may blithely call you a "baby-sitter," you know that you rarely sit down unless it is to tie a child's shoelaces.

You will know the difference between a bad day and a day when you are not in control of your emotions. Parents and other caregivers experience the same feelings you do, and there are groups available to help. Give the children an activity to keep them busy and call a neighbor, a friend, or a crisis line set up to assist people who are under a great deal of stress.

Caring for children, even your own, requires patience, stamina, creativity, and resourcefulness. There will be times when you say to yourself, "I need a break." You must be in good physical health just to keep up with kids. I often hear people say, "Where do children get their energy?" I don't know the answer to that question, but I can assure you that they have plenty of it! Remember to follow a well-balanced diet and drink plenty of fluids. A friend of mine who was caring for children in her home complained that she was always exhausted. She said she didn't have time to eat and was living on snack foods. That was precisely why she wasn't functioning effectively. If you can, plan some quiet activities for the children during the day so that you can rest on the couch or relax with a book or magazine.

Perhaps you need to reexamine your daily routine. When you follow a plan, the day will go more smoothly. I do not recommend that you undertake major housecleaning or sewing projects while you are caring for children. You will find yourself getting very frustrated and will probably get upset with the kids. Be realistic about what you can accomplish during the day. The children are your main priority. It's not a good idea to attempt to make a Halloween costume for the Girl Scout party with a houseful of preschoolers or a colicky baby.

There are lots of ways to reduce stress. Running, walking, or working in your garden will help to fight those uptight feelings. Talk to a friend or relative and share your feelings with them. If you know that the cause of the pressure is a child you just can't handle, consider asking the parents to make other child care arrangements. In the evening, find time for yourself. Write letters, take an exercise class, or just go out and have fun. Make lists of what you want to accomplish each day so that you have a general plan to follow. Read books about getting along with people. You'll find that there are many simple techniques for dealing with difficult parents, a difficult husband, or difficult children.

If you have children of your own, there may be times when your own family will have to take top priority. Don't ignore signs of stress such as upset stomach, mood swings, headaches, aggressive reactions, and confused behavior. Take stock of your own personal situation and know when to quit. It is best to take a break from child care when your limits have been taxed.

There are other situations that may require you to take some time off. Perhaps you or someone in your family has had serious surgery, a relative needs you, or you feel that your own children need your full-time attention. At first, your family may have supported your venture, but later you may find that no one else helps out with the household responsibilities or that the family resents having extra people in your home. You may also find that caring for children is more demanding than you had anticipated, or that it is not as lucrative as you first thought and you need to earn more money to support your family.

A friend, Karen, had some difficulties in her personal life. Her husband had quit his job and was home most of the day. He wasn't used to being with lots of children and was under a great deal of stress because of the job loss. They were having financial problems and one of their children was ill. The whole situation was physically and emotionally draining. Karen asked my advice about whether to continue her child care program. I had been in her home and felt that there was too much tension in their family life and that she should take a "mental health break." The most important thing to recognize is that, when stress does occur, it should be dealt with right away.

Preventing Child Abuse

An adorable little boy was once enrolled in our program. He had some special needs and, after a trial period, we felt it would be best for him to go to a school that would be better equipped to deal with his problems. I explained to his mother that, although we loved him, it would be best if she could find another arrangement in which he would receive more individual attention. She was disappointed but understood our situation. The next morning a friend of hers arrived at my door. She explained that the little boy's father had a "mean streak" and had thrown the child across the room. He misunderstood our request and thought we had "expelled" his child for bad behavior. At that point we decided to keep him in our program because we knew he was well cared for while he was with us. After that we were constantly on the alert for any possible signs of child abuse, including

- Bruises or burns not adequately explained by the parent
- Repeated injuries
- Unusual sexual behavior
- Parent and child who show no affection for each other

- Parents under the influence of drugs or alcohol
- An unkempt appearance or other signs of neglect

Use your own good judgment because the preceding signs are by no means *proof* of abuse.

As this story illustrates, some children are safer in day care than with their own families. Abusive parents are not necessarily evil people. They need immediate help in order to cope with overwhelming feelings of anger, fear, and frustration. If you see or suspect child abuse, you have a moral and (in some states) legal obligation to notify authorities such as the local Child Protective Services. Never allow a child's well-being to be jeopardized because of a reluctance to get involved.

If you are ever afraid of what you might do to a child, remember that you are not alone. There are many people who feel the same way. Ask yourself the following questions:

- Do you sometimes feel troubled or nervous and have no one to talk to?
- Do you feel down in the dumps?
- Do you sometimes feel the urge to hurt a child just because you're angry with yourself—or someone else?
- Do you sometimes feel unable to cope with the responsibilities of adulthood?

If you can answer yes to any of these questions, it's time to seek help. People who have abused or are afraid they may abuse a child have found help in groups like Parents Anonymous (1-800-421-0353, Pacific Time, California). Members of Parents Anonymous meet regularly to share their feelings and frustrations. Seeking support for yourself could help you to be a more loving and attentive caregiver.

READY,
SET, GO

A Child's First Day
at Your Home

The first few days are an adjustment for everyone. It helps to invite the new child and his parent or parents over for a couple of visits before they join your program. In that way you will get a feel as to what the child will be like, and your home will be familiar to the child. It is best not to add more than one child at a time.

One of the first questions parents ask is, "What would you like my child to call you?" I ask the children to call me "Miss Trisha," but you may prefer to be called Mrs., Aunt, simply by your first name, or some other variation. As I said earlier, just be sure to reserve "Mommy" and any special terms of endearment for a child's parent.

Occasionally the children may slip and call you "Mommy." This is not one of those cute things you want to tell a child's mother. My situation was the reverse. Robin and Katelyn were accustomed to hearing the day care children call me Miss Trisha.

They sometimes called me Miss Trisha too! There was a little pain in my heart at night when I would read them a story and they would slip and call me Miss Trisha instead of Mommy.

Saying Goodbye

New parents often ask, "Should I just sneak out or should I say goodbye?" The correct answer is probably that the parent should explain to the child she is going to work, the store, or to church, and add, "I'll be back at five o'clock." Parents can also say, "After you wake up from your nap, I'll be back to pick you up" or "You'll know I am coming when the big hand is on the twelve and the little hand is on the five." A child will be less anxious if he knows when to expect his mother and if he knows what the schedule will be in day care.

Examine some of the hidden reasons behind a child's fear of unfamiliar settings. By understanding a child's perspective, you will be better able to help the child enter the new situation with confidence. It is not fair to say that he has nothing to fear; children have their own worries. The child may wonder:

- What if my mom doesn't come back?
- What if no one wants to play with me?
- What if I have to sleep in a dark room?
- What if I never go home again?

You will find that allowing a child to bring a security blanket, favorite toy, or a picture of his mom and dad will help ease the separation. In a couple of situations, I have asked the mother to leave an empty pocketbook and her sweater. When one little boy, Michael, became anxious about his mother's disappearance, I pointed to the familiar objects and calmly reassured him that she was on her way back to pick up her sweet little boy, her pocketbook, and her sweater.

When you meet parents, you may also want to suggest that they tell their child a "day care story." To help her child approach this strange situation with confidence, his mother could make up a story about a child who goes to stay at a "friend's" house while his mother is working. By hearing about what happens at the day care home in advance, the child will know what to expect and the adjustment should be smoother.

Sometimes a child who adjusted quite well for the first few days will announce, "I'm not coming here anymore." The novelty of new toys and new playmates may have eased the initial adjustment. However, when he realizes that a day is a long time to spend without his mother, it's normal for him to go through a phase when he says, "This place is not for me!"

Some crying is normal for a young child encountering a new routine. Lots of tender loving care will help make the child feel secure and at home. If you have a friend or relative who can help you when a new child is starting, your day will go more smoothly.

In my experience, it is best not to pick up a child until he gives signs that he is ready. Give him time to adjust to the new situation. If all goes well, it won't be long before the child warms to you. If he has visited with his mother on several occasions before the first "real day," you'll have a head start.

My friend Terry was once caring for a boy named Evan. Evan started screaming as soon as he and his mother reached Terry's front door. He knew that this routine meant separation. Terry remained calm and placed a cookie and a plastic cup filled with juice within his view. She then went about her business as usual. Evan sized the situation up and eventually went over to eat the snack, which served as a distraction. After that he was fine.

Free Play Versus Structured Activities

I have found that everyone functions best with a schedule. A schedule does not have to be rigid but you should have a general idea of the blocks of time in your day and of how much time you plan to devote to free play, adult-guided activities, outdoor time, naps, meals, and snacks.

Little children love to play. You will be amazed at how the

simplest activity fascinates them. Since I strongly believe that having fun is part of learning, I give the children in my care plenty of time for good old-fashioned play. They run, jump, and laugh about things that grownups have long forgotten were funny.

However, children also need to have some structured activity during the long hours they spend in your home, and I have included many suggested activities in Chapters 8 and 10.

It is important to carefully balance free play, structured activities, and quiet activities. When you have a group of energetic youngsters in a room, the noise can sometimes be earsplitting. Children need to know that they can get away from it all and enjoy some independent time—at least for a little while. They need their own space, perhaps a corner of the room where they can just cuddle up with a favorite blanket.

As you rearrange your home for day care, remember that it is important to create separate play areas so as to encourage children to express themselves. One area of the room may have a child-size shatterproof mirror and a dress-up box. Another area of the room may contain games and puzzles that allow a child the means to test new skills and abilities. A child's playful explorations are his way of learning about life.

When working with children, you must prepare but also realize that "kids will be kids" and that some of your best-laid plans will have to be reorganized when something unanticipated happens. For example, our group was all set to visit the local pumpkin farm when my assistant's son had a biking accident that required a trip to the emergency room instead. Fortunately, he was okay and the children were pacified with a few extra cookies and a promise that we would visit the farm the following day.

One way of planning your day would be to think about what you would want your own child to do if he were with a day care provider. From this vantage point, it was easy for me to plan activities. Use the daily activity plans in Chapter 8 as a guide. Since your program's hours of operation may be different than mine, modify the schedule to suit your situation.

You probably have a special interest or hobby that you will want to include in your day. One friend especially enjoys music and she plays the piano and has sing-alongs more frequently than other caregivers I know. I especially love reading to children, so whenever we have a lull or I need a way to calm down a houseful of spirited children, I opt to read aloud a nice soothing "bedtime" story.

Please keep in mind that all times are approximate and will very much depend on the number of children being cared for, their ages and, (believe it or not) the weather. Ask any schoolteacher and she will be quick to tell you how rainy days affect children. Weather permitting, children need fresh air and a chance to enjoy swings, the sandbox, or just the autumn leaves.

Planning Meals
and Snacks

Nutrition is an important part of a child's development. It is tempting to take shortcuts when serving food to children but day care providers have a responsibility to serve balanced meals and healthy snacks. Upon request, the U.S. Department of Agriculture will send you sample meal plans which may be helpful.

There are so many disturbing new discoveries about what's healthy and what's not that it is easy to be confused about eating properly. We often learn that food we were taught was good for us is now considered dangerous to our health. You probably already know that it's best to go easy on eggs, yogurt, and foods containing red dyes that may be carcinogenic. As for snacks, you can't go wrong with fresh fruit, dried fruit, raw vegetables, crackers, and cheese. Be aware that many fruit drinks do not contain real juice and may contain sugar and artificial flavorings.

Be prepared for two year olds who don't like vegetables, three year olds who aren't hungry at lunchtime but want snacks all afternoon, four year olds who eat nothing but peanut butter and jelly, and finicky five year olds. Although there are no easy solutions for dealing with fussy eaters, I have found that children do eat when they are hungry. Overeating or filling up on junk food is more likely to be the problem. Since it is your house, you can set limits. If you feel that a child is eating too much junk food and it takes you half a day to calm him down due to the energy level sparked by sugar, you should not hesitate to ask parents to refrain from bringing cookies, candy, cakes, and soda.

In order to cut down on the amount of time spent planning meals, try planning daily menus for one month. You can reuse the same monthly meal plan, varying the fruits and vegetables to take advantage of what is in season. Parents appreciate seeing your meal plan posted so that they can plan their own family's daily meals.

Remember that most of us do not like to have food forced on us. You may want to encourage children to take a taste rather than forcing them to eat everything on their plates.

Nap Time

From the start, I would make a nap or rest period part of your daily routine. Everybody needs a break, and this is your chance to unwind, rest, or do things that are important to you.

The best time for such a nap or quiet time is usually after lunch. At that time children are usually very tired. After the children eat lunch, they can expect to put away toys, have a story read to them, and pull down the shades or close the curtains for their nap time. They can lie on beach towels, a soft rug, couch, mat, cot, or a bed. Tell them to close their eyes for a little rest while you turn on a music box, tuck them in with a favorite toy or blanket, give them a kiss, and quietly leave the room. Make sure that you stay in the same room or in the same general area of the house while the children sleep. (You will probably be ready for a nap by now!)

Children vary in the amount of sleep that they require. Although preschoolers need this rest, they are usually reluctant to admit it. A friendly bribe of a sticker on a chart may help motivate a child to nap or rest; those who don't get up or disturb the others can be given something special when they get up.

Older children who have outgrown the nap routine still need a quiet time. During this period, you may find that it works out best to give the older children coloring books, puzzles, or other quiet activities. Check on them often.

It is important that you explain to parents how crucial it is for their children to have a schedule at home too. Children need ten to fifteen hours of sleep each night. If a child goes to bed very late at home, he will be tired and out of sorts at your house. Be aware that not all families are like the ideal families portrayed on television. Routines may be utterly foreign to some homes. Always allow a tired child to curl up on the couch whenever he needs a little more sleep. You know how difficult it is to function when you haven't had adequate rest. There's nothing like a morning nap to put you back on schedule.

Closing Time

Parents do become annoyed when they are kept waiting while a child looks for a missing sock or misplaced toy. Do your best to make sure that the children are clean and neat and to gather all of their belongings in one spot so that time is not wasted looking for a lost article when parents arrive.

BUILDING
A GOOD
RELATIONSHIP
WITH PAREN TS

You will learn a great deal about getting along with people when you are in the child care business. I have found that it is best not to make hasty judgments about people. Billy's mother was someone who I thought just didn't care too much about her child. Billy always seemed in need of a bath. Mary often forgot to bring his lunch and just seemed so apathetic when it came to the well-being of her child. As I got to know her better, I found her to be a very good mother who had a lot on her mind. She was a single parent who had a severely handicapped older child. With three other children in elementary school, I understood why she might not be able to attend to being the "perfect mother." I knew that I could do no better if I had to cope with so many demands on my time and energy.

Parents really need to know that their child is special to you. It is music to a parent's ears, to receive a compliment about their child—even if it is "Oh, what a darling little outfit." I learned this when Robin was born. The day after she was born, the staff pediatrician came into the room and with a broad smile said, "Mr. and Mrs. Gallagher, your baby is in perfect health. She is the most beautiful baby that I have ever seen. You really struck gold!" My husband beamed with a new father's pride because he knew that this doctor had six daughters of his own and had been in practice for many years. John reasoned that of all the thousands of babies the doctor had cared for, we had the future Miss America right in our arms. John said to be sure to include this "most beautiful baby" quote in Robin's baby book. About eighteen months later, Katelyn was born at the same hospital and guess what? The same doctor came by to discuss the postbirth checkup. Once again, he had good news. Katelyn was in excellent health and . . . she was the most beautiful baby that he had ever seen. I leaned over to John and said, "We struck gold . . . again!" By the time Kristen was born, we knew exactly what to expect from this charming doctor. He knew what parents wanted to hear and we wanted to believe every word. The parents want to know that you see the beauty in their child—the inner beauty—so never miss an opportunity to praise their child.

Many working parents wish that the caregiver understood things from their point of view. Most people are not able to express their innermost fears and concerns. If you had a heart-to-heart talk with them, they would probably let you in on a few well-kept secrets.

- "I'm afraid that my child loves you more than me. It is very difficult to see you holding my child each day."
- "I sometimes wonder if I am missing important events in my child's life. I want to be the first one to discover a new tooth, or see a first step. If you see a first accomplishment, please keep it a secret. I want to discover it first."
- "I want the name 'Mommy' reserved for me."
- "I do not want anyone to give medicine to my child without my written permission (signed and dated)."
- "My child must always wear a seat belt or be in a car seat (no exceptions)."

- "It is hard for me to leave my child with you when he is screaming. Does he really stop as soon as I walk out the door?"
- "I feel guilty because I must work for emotional and/or financial reasons."
- "I hope you are not judging me."

I think that it is interesting to mention here that although I returned to my corporate job when Robin was 3½ months old, I did not put a photograph of her on my desk. I would have felt too bad and missed her too much if I had seen her big blue eyes staring at me. When I lead workshops, this short example always strikes a responsive chord. Mothers often nod in agreement and raise their hands to tell of their particular situation. It may seem easy to leave a child with someone else but appearances can be deceiving.

Understanding the
Working Parent's Feelings

Some providers may worry that if they give too much love and affection to the baby, the new mother will feel jealous. There is plenty of love to go around, and a baby can never get too much security. All of the attention that is focused on a baby builds a sense of self-esteem.

There were times when I worked and Robin was with a baby-sitter and I felt jealous. Robin seemed to be so content in Estelle's arms and also when she was with her grandparents. I hoped that she wasn't getting too much love from them and not enough from me. I remember when we were planning Robin's first birthday party. I invited all of our relatives to the gala event. Of course since Estelle "mothered" Robin during the week, I felt that she and her husband would enjoy coming too. I was surprised when Estelle hesitated and said that since grandparents and parents were going to be there maybe she shouldn't come. I read between the lines of what she was saying and realized she had thought of something that I had not. On this special day, commemorating the one-year anniversary of the most exciting event in my life, Robin's birth, my darling baby *might not want me exclusively*. She was most comfortable sitting on Estelle's lap like the little princess that she was in her home. Robin also cuddled up with her grandparents, which was more acceptable because after all they were part of our family. There is a part of the parent that wants you to adore their baby but there is also a very possessive instinct to be the mother. I guess what underlies this emotion for the working mother is the fear, "What if there is not enough love left for me?" Just being aware of a parent's fear will help you and the parents to trust each other. They will know that although you are attached to the baby because you feed, change, and play with him, you also know they are the parents. Can a child receive too much love? I don't think that there is a little child who was ever overloved. Parents, grandparents, baby-sitters and loving friends all offer something special. Parents should not fear an "alienation of affection." Victor Hugo, the famous nineteenth-century French author once said, "The supreme happiness in life is the conviction that we are loved." Psychoanalyst Anna Freud stated, "Unlike adults, who are generally capable of maintaining positive emotional ties with a number of different individuals, unrelated or even hostile to each other, children lack the capacity to do so. They will freely love more than one adult only if the individuals in question feel positively to one another. Failing this, children become prey to severe and crippling loyalty conflicts." As you think about the best interests of a child, both you and the parent must allow the child to love everyone freely and in his own special way.

Christopher was a perfect example of my feelings for the children I took care of. He was the sweetest little boy that you could ever imagine. I loved him in a special way and felt especially sad when his mother had to make other arrangements. A few months after he left, I met his mother in a grocery store and I was just so excited to see them both. It just came out naturally to say how much I missed him. I know that I offered to care for him on any weekend if she wanted to go away. I saw the look on her face as if she didn't understand why I would be inviting him to come over. Maybe in a way she felt that I was getting too close. When I stopped working, and Robin and I had long days together while we were waiting for Katelyn to be born, Estelle asked, "Why don't you come over for a visit? Bill and I miss our little bird." In my heart, I remember feeling that I was afraid she might want to stay there.

The parents will probably leave their child with you and just drive away. Let me assure you that they are probably wondering and worrying, "How do I know what is going on when I am not there?" "Is my baby lonely, hungry, or thirsty?" "What are the long-term psychological effects on my child of my working?" and most importantly, "Does my child miss me?"

Although working parents may seem to leave their child with you willingly, there is probably a tugging in their hearts as they walk away. As a mother who has done just that, I can assure you that it is not easy. The transfer of your child from one set of comfortable arms to another is difficult. Of course, the parents want the child to be well taken care of but there is still a great need to be the special one in the child's life. Even though you are with the child for the greater part of the day, let the parent know frequently that the child knows that the parent is really number one!

You Are a Working Parent Too!

Caregivers often think that the working parent is not aware that they work all day too. Even though the parent may say, "I don't know how you do it," there is probably another parent who is thinking, "She has it easy." They reason that because you are home during the day you can do the wash, run errands, make phone calls, watch television, and have friends over for coffee. I was surprised on four occasions when the parents told me that their child would no longer need day care. They had decided to start a day care program in their home because it really looked like it would be a breeze.

Somehow, in a nice way, you will want to weave the following important points into your daily conversations.

- "I am a full-time working mother like you."
- "Our family life is important, and I need to know that my day begins at a certain time and ends at a certain time. When people arrive early or late, it causes confusion in my schedule and builds resentment in me that I am being used."
- "I count on the money as my paycheck. We have bills to pay."
- "I am entitled to occasional vacation days, sick days, and paid holidays."
- It is not an easy job. As a matter of fact, I rarely sit down."
- "Please treat me with respect. I do a very important job."
- "Please don't make demands on me or give me orders about the care of your child."
- "Your child really does stop screaming soon after you leave."
- "Please be patient when your child who is supposed to be potty trained wets his pants. Accidents do happen at this stage of development."
- "I would like to hear some words of appreciation. Even though you are paying me, I yearn to hear a few words of praise or recognition. It will make my job even more satisfying."
- "When your child moves on to another school or day care center, please keep in touch. We get attached to the children and miss them when they leave."

Showing Parents
That You Care

I remember a bulletin board in my fifth grade classroom that said, "No act of kindness—no matter how small—is ever forgotten." I don't know how true that maxim actually is, but I do know that it is the friendly and considerate things that you do that enhance the relationship between parent and caregiver.

Even if it is hectic in the morning, be sure to ask the parent when the child ate last, when he woke up, and how he's feeling. Any event that occurred the night before or that morning will no doubt affect the child in your care. Ask how the parent is feeling too. The parent's emotional health is very important to the child. Be sure to wish the mother a good day and assure her that everything will be fine at your house too.

When Estelle began watching Robin, she gave me little notes each day about what Robin's schedule had been. She told me when and how much Robin ate, how she slept, and she always told me what a wonderful child she was and how much she enjoyed caring for her. This really made me feel good! Once when she mentioned how much work caring for a baby was, I was shocked. She had done such a convincing job of telling me what a great baby Robin was, I had begun to believe that her day was a cinch. Since I began caring for children in my home, I know that although you love the children, it is a very tiring job and you as a provider look forward to the time when the children leave so you can relax with your own family. On the last day our caregiver watched Robin she gave us a handprint which she and Robin had made with red paint. Attached to it was this poem which I treasure:

> Sometimes I get discouraged
> Because I am so small
> and always leave my fingerprints
> On furniture and walls.
> But everyday I'm growing
> I'll be grown up some day
> And all these tiny fingerprints
> Will surely fade away.
> So here's a final handprint
> Just so you can recall
> Exactly how my fingers looked
> When I was very small . . .

These very special and unexpected bonuses will be treasured by the parents and give them a happy surprise.

- Ask parents for a photograph of their family that you can hang on the refrigerator.

- Let parents know regularly that their child talks about them lovingly.
- Don't give "helpful advice" unless asked.
- Invite the families over for a picnic on a weekend.
- Have coffee or tea for parents after work occasionally.
- Call parents occasionally in the evening to let them know how special their child is to you.
- Ask them if they would like their child to call them at work every once in a while to say "I love you." What parent would not enjoy hearing those words any time of the day?
- Be honest and kind. Show respect for the parent's point of view.
- Facilitate good two-way communication. Face issues squarely.
- Do not talk about the families of the children you care for. Respect their right to privacy and hopefully they will respect yours. It's not good business to gossip.
- The young single mother may still be a kid herself. You may be able to assist her in a special way if she is interested in your ideas about helping her baby develop. If she is still in school she is probably under a lot of pressure at home and at school.
- Separated or divorced parents often have personal stresses and pressures. Support money may be late or not available, the job may be stressful, and they may be quite lonely. You may be able to extend yourself to this family and include them at your home for holidays or special occasions.
- Parents appreciate an occasional note in their child's lunch box saying how the child is doing generally.
- Parents often have weeks when money is in short supply. Occasionally, they may ask you to allow them to pay you a day or two late. You would not want to make this a regular practice but an occasional exception to policy may be in order to reduce the stress about money for a particular family.
- Place a bulletin board in the kitchen for the day care families. Parents can post little announcements for each other to see (clothing exchange, bike for sale, new baby an-

nouncement). You can use the bulletin board as a way to remind parents of the little things that are important to you, for example, "Please take your child's wet boots off before they walk on the rugs."

- Invite parents to help out with field trips, holiday parties, special activities, or make something for the group.
- Share information on nonchild-related topics that you know the parent has expressed interest. Perhaps you have seen an article in a magazine or know of a support group that would assist the family.
- Tell parents what you have done during the day so they can ask their children about the activities.
- Discuss your meal plans with the parent if you are serving lunch to the child.
- Surprise the parent with a scrapbook entitled "All About Me" which includes drawings, cute expressions, and a photograph or two of the child.
- Be friendly and warm but be sure that parents understand that your work with children is a business, and for that reason you have policies that must be adhered to and you need everybody's cooperation.
- Remember that parents work hard all day and that they do not want to hear minor problems that come up during your day.
- Take a personal interest in the family but don't get too involved with discussions of divorce, custody battles, and the family's troubles.

Despite your best intentions, you will have situations when the parents will have a gripe. Try to remain calm and discuss it with them without involving the children as an audience. If they call you on the phone during the day, you could call them back when the children are napping or return their call at night. There are times that you must address the problem immediately. Just like the retail policy of "The customer is always right," in day care homes you want to be as agreeable as possible without making concessions that will alter the harmony of your program. Use words that will enhance your understanding of the situation such as, "I agree," "I understand your concern," or "You have a right to feel upset." When you are about to lose your temper, you may want to express your sentiments in a less emotional way. Explain the problem from your perspective by saying, "I feel that . . . ," "I hope that . . . ," or "It would help all of us if we could . . ."

DAILY
ACTIVITY
PLANS

This chapter contains twenty-five sample daily activity plans. Don't hesitate to rearrange the activities to suit your own schedule and the ages of the children in your care.

As discussed in Chapter 6, most children need a morning nap or rest period. You may be able to use that time to prepare for lunchtime.

If you choose to experiment with the plans in this chapter, I would suggest that you take the time to gather the following boxes of items in advance. These items are used in many of the activities suggested.

Odds and Ends Box—This box should contain junk mail, lace doilies, magazines, foil, used greeting cards, coupons, postcards, ribbons, lace, yarn, paper bags, paper plates, pipe cleaners, straws, crayons, paste, scissors, cardboard, and scrap paper.

Box of Boxes and Safe Cans—This box should contain boxes of all sizes—from aspirin boxes to cereal boxes. It should also contain coffee cans, soup cans, baby formula cans, and any other type of can that strikes your fancy—provided it does not have sharp edges.

"Let's Pretend" Box—Create an opportunity for make-believe activities with a box full of hats, ties, shoes, dresses, old jewelry, and old pocketbooks. These items will allow children to act out characters from a story you've told them or dress up for a "night on the town." Friends and relatives are usually pleased to donate their treasures to the collection. (Keep a camera handy!)

Whether or not you follow the plans in this chapter, the key to success is being flexible enough to respond to the children's moods and confident enough to heed your own instincts. If you don't know the tune to a fingerplay or song that appears here, just make one up as you go along.

Day 1

9:30　S T O R Y T I M E

9:45　S O N G S	ABC's
	Count 1–20
	"Good Morning to You"
	(sung to the tune of
	"Happy Birthday," naming
	each child)

"Bullfrog"	
Here's Mr. Bullfrog	(Left hand closed, thumb upright)
Sitting on a rock.	
Along comes a little boy,	(Walking motion with index and third fingers)
Mr. Bullfrog jumps, *KERPLOP!*	(Thumb makes diving motion)

"Five Little Ducks"	
Five little ducks	(Hold up five fingers)
Swimming in the lake.	(Make swimming motion)
The first one said:	
"Watch the waves I make."	(Make motions of waves)

The second duck said:
"Swimming is such fun."
The third duck said:
"I'd rather sit in the sun."
The fourth duck said:
"Let's swim away."
The fifth duck said:
"Oh, let's stay."
Then along came a
motorboat
With a POP, POP, POP!   (Clap hands three times)
And five little ducks
Swam away from the
spot.

"Ten Little Fingers"
I have 10 little fingers
they all belong to me.
I can make them do
things.
Would you like to see?
I can shut them up tight.
I can open them wide.
I can put them together
And make them all hide.
I can put them up high.
I can put them down low.
I can fold them together
And keep them just so.

10:15 S N A C K S

10:30 T A B L E   A C T I V I T Y

Charm Bracelets
Seal an envelope (or take a used envelope and reseal by pasting down flap). Have the child color or paint the

envelope. Draw horizontal lines at one-inch intervals. Have child cut along the lines. Open the strip. See the bracelet!

11:00 F R E E P L A Y

Boxes
Provide boxes of all sizes. Shoe boxes and smaller boxes can hold things. Children can use them to make a miniature city. Egg cartons can be used for sorting. Preschoolers love to pretend larger boxes are cars, boats, planes, swimming pools, castles, and so on. Children can be given crayons or magic markers to decorate giant boxes.

11:30 R E C O R D P L A Y E R O R G A M E T I M E

11:45 L U N C H

12:15 N A P O R Q U I E T T I M E

2:30 K I D R O B I C S (physical exercise)
Bend, stretch, jump, crawl, run in place, shrink small, hop on one leg, tiptoe, and so on.

2:45 A F T E R N O O N S N A C K

3:00 C R E A T I V E A C T I V I T Y

What Is It?
Put a number of objects without sharp edges in a big bag—toys, cups, diaper, clothes pin, glove, and so on. Hold the bag in front of the child. He covers eyes with one hand and reaches into bag. He guesses what he has picked without uncovering his eyes.

Scouring
Scouring a blackened pan uses many muscles, big and small. It's surprising to see the black disappear as the pot gets shiny.

3:30   C I R C L E   T I M E
Name things that are yellow.
Name things that are round.

3:45   O U T D O O R   F R E E   P L A Y   O R   I N D O O R
F R E E   P L A Y

4:45   Clean up toys, gather belongings, wash faces and hands.

5:00   Selected educational television program or read books.

5:30   Children are picked up by parent.

Day 2

9:30 S T O R Y T I M E

9:45 S O N G S

ABC's
Count 1–20
"Good Morning to You"
(sung to the tune of
"Happy Birthday," naming
each child)

"Five Little Fishes"
Five little fishes were   (Hold up five fingers.
swimming near the shore.   Starting with thumb, bend
One took a dive, then   down one at a time as
there were four.   verse progresses)
Four little fishes were
swimming out to sea.
One went for food, then
there were three.
Three little fishes said:
"Now what shall we do?"
One swam away, and
then there were two.
Two little fishes were
having great fun.
But one took the plunge
Then there was one.
One little fish said:
"I like the warm sun."
Away he went and then
there were none.   (Put hand behind back)

"Fred and His Fishes"
Fred had a fish bowl.   (Form shape of bowl with
                                               hands)

In it was a fish,   (Hold up one finger)

Swimming around
With a SWISH, SWISH,   (Make swimming motion)
SWISH!
Fred said, "I know what I
will do,
I'll buy another
and that will make——.   (Children supply number
                              and hold up two fingers)

"Pancake"
Mix a pancake—stir a   (Suit actions to words)
pancake
Pop it in a pan.
Fry a pancake—toss a
pancake
Catch it if you can!

10:15   S N A C K S

10:30   T A B L E   A C T I V I T Y

Macaroni Necklace and Bracelet
String painted macaroni on long or short pieces of string
or elastic to make necklace or bracelet.

11:00   F R E E   P L A Y

Dress-Up Time
Provide clean used clothing for use as costumes (pocketbooks, shirts, scarves, safe jewelry, and so on). You'll
enjoy watching the children "act out" the costume they
put on!

11:30   R E C O R D   P L A Y E R   O R   G A M E   T I M E

11:45   L U N C H

12:15   N A P   O R   Q U I E T   T I M E

2:30 K I D R O B I C S (physical exercise)
Bend, stretch, jump, crawl, run in place, shrink small, hop on one leg, tiptoe, and so on.

2:45 A F T E R N O O N S N A C K

3:00 C R E A T I V E A C T I V I T Y

Homemade Puzzles
Paste a colorful picture on a shirt cardboard or any light-weight piece of cardboard. Cut it into pieces to be assembled as a puzzle. Make each piece large. Cut on straight lines.

Walkie-Talkie
One open-ended smooth frozen juice container with a hole punched in closed end, together with medium thickness cord makes an adequate walkie-talkie for two children to use. String would be knotted inside cans. It works well with a distance of 12 to 15 feet on the string.

3:30 C I R C L E T I M E
Name things that are red.
Name things that are square.

3:45 O U T D O O R F R E E P L A Y O R I N D O O R
F R E E P L A Y

4:45 Clean up toys, gather belongings, wash faces and hands.

5:00 Watch selected educational television program or read books.

5:30 Children are picked up by parent.

Day 3

9:30   S T O R Y T I M E

9:45   S O N G S

ABC's
Count 1–20
"Good Morning to You"
(sung to the tune of
"Happy Birthday," naming
each child)

"Washing Clothes"
Here's a little washtub   (Cup hands to make tub)
And here's a cake of soap.   (Clench one fist)
Here's a washboard   (Use back of hand turned
                                               sideways and rub across
                                               fingers)

And this is how we rub
Here's a clothesline way   (Form high imaginary line
up high,   with hands)
Now the clothes are
drying
W-o-o-o-o the wind comes   (Sweeping motion with
by   hands)
Now the clothes are dry.

"Teapot"
I'm a little teapot   (Place right hand on hip,
Short and stout.   extend left hand, palm
Here's my handle,   out)
And here's my spout.
When I get all steamed up,
I just shout,
"Tip me over and pour   (Bend to the left)
me out."
I can change my handle   (Place left hand on hip
And my spout.   and extend right hand
                                               out)

"Tip me over and pour	(Bend to the right)
me out."	

"Balloons"

This is the way we blow	(Pretend to blow,
up our balloons,	rounding hands as if
Blow, blow, blow	holding a balloon,
	spreading farther and
	farther apart)
This is the way we break	(Clap hands together on
our balloons,	each "Oh!")
Oh! Oh! Oh!	

10:15 S N A C K S

10:30 T A B L E A C T I V I T Y

String Painting
Have two or three shades of paint, cardboard or paper, and a heavy piece of string. Let the child dip the string into the paint and swirl it across the paper.

11:00 F R E E P L A Y

Milk Carton Blocks
Sturdy blocks can be made for free. Simply cut the tops from two milk cartons and insert one into the other. Be sure to press hard so that one is firmly inside the other.

11:30 R E C O R D P L A Y E R O R G A M E T I M E

11:45 L U N C H

12:15 N A P O R Q U I E T T I M E

 2:30 K I D R O B I C S (physical exercise)
Bend, stretch, jump, crawl, run in place, shrink small, hop on one leg, tiptoe, and so on.

2:45 A F T E R N O O N S N A C K

3:00 C R E A T I V E A C T I V I T Y

Footsteps
Trace the outline of the child's foot (barefoot or with shoes) and use these to make a path or run a relay race—it's fun!

Portraits
Put one child on a chair (side profile) between a lamp and the wall where a piece of drawing paper has been mounted. The profile can be traced around the shadow and this can be colored, cut out, and mounted.

3:30 C I R C L E T I M E
Name things that are green.
Name things that are triangular.

3:45 O U T D O O R F R E E P L A Y O R I N D O O R F R E E P L A Y

4:45 Clean up toys, gather belongings, wash faces and hands.

5:00 Watch selected educational television program or read books.

5:30 Children are picked up by parent.

Day 4

9:30 STORYTIME

9:45 SONGS

ABC'S
Count 1–20
"Good Morning to You"
(sung to the tune of
"Happy Birthday," naming
each child)

"I'm Bouncing"
*I'm bouncing, bouncing
everywhere
I bounce and bounce into
the air
I'm bouncing, bouncing
like a ball
I bounce and bounce, then
down I fall.*

(Bounce with knees
relaxed, drop to floor on
last line)

"Jack in the Box Sits
So Still"
*Jack in the box.
Sits so still.
Won't you come out?
Yes, I will.*

(Hands closed—thumb
inside)

(Thumb jumps out)

"Five Soldiers"
*Five little soldiers,
Standing in a row.
Three stood straight,
And two stood so.
Along came the captain,
And what do you think?
Those soldiers jumped up,
Quick as a wink!*

(Hold up five fingers—
right hand)
(Right thumb holds
forefinger down, other
three fingers stand up)

(Thumb and forefinger
raise up)

10:15 S N A C K S

10:30 T A B L E   A C T I V I T Y

Dangling Necklace
Cut out a piece of cardboard in the shape of a circle or
square. Color this or cover with colored paper. Place a
picture or design on it, punch a hole in the top, string it,
and use as a necklace.

11:00 F R E E   P L A Y

Grocery Store
Collect empty containers, boxes, plastic dishes, margarine tubs, and so on. Save grocery bags and boxes. Children arrange items to play store. Use cut-up paper as
money.

11:30 R E C O R D   P L A Y E R   O R   G A M E   T I M E

11:45 L U N C H

12:15 N A P   O R   Q U I E T   T I M E

 2:30 K I D R O B I C S (physical exercise)
Bend, stretch, jump, crawl, run in place, shrink small, hop
on one leg, tiptoe, and so on.

 2:45 A F T E R N O O N   S N A C K

 3:00 C R E A T I V E   A C T I V I T Y

Treasure Hunt
Hide three spoons in the play area while the children
cover their eyes. When they go to find them, tell them
they are "hot" when they come close to a spoon, and
"cold" when they move away from a spoon.

3:30 C I R C L E T I M E
Name things that are orange.
Name things that are square.

3:45 O U T D O O R F R E E P L A Y O R I N D O O R
F R E E P L A Y

4:45 Clean up toys, gather belongings, wash faces and hands.

5:00 Watch selected educational television program or read books.

5:30 Children are picked up by parent.

Day 5

9:30   S T O R Y T I M E

9:45   S O N G S   ABC'S
                                    Count 1–20
                                    "Good Morning to You"
                                    (sung to the tune of
                                    "Happy Birthday," naming
                                    each child)

"Going to Bed"
This little boy is just   (Use forefinger for boy.
going to bed   Lay finger crosswise on
Down on the pillow he   hand using thumb for
lays his head.   pillow. Use fingers for
He wraps himself in the   cover)
covers tight,
And this is the way he
sleeps all night.
Morning comes, he opens
his eyes
Off with a toss the covers
fly.
Soon he is up and dressed
and away,
Ready for fun and play
all day.

"Me"
My hands upon my head I   (Do actions as described,
place,   then bring hands down
On my shoulders, on my   slowly and place them in
face,   lap)
On my knees, and at my
side,
Then behind me they will
hide.

Then I raise them up
s-o-o high
'Til they almost reach the
sky.
Swiftly count them—
1, 2, 3,
And see how quiet they
can be.

"Use Your Eyes"
Use your eyes, use your
eyes,
You can look and see;   (Leader calls for various
If you have on brown   colors of clothing)
shoes
Come and stand by me.

10:15 S N A C K S

10:30 T A B L E A C T I V I T Y

<u>Stringing Beads</u>
A piece of string and circle-shaped dry cereal make
stringing beads.

11:00 F R E E P L A Y

<u>Playing House</u>
Cardboard boxes should be saved to be used as refrig-
erators, sinks, and stoves. Toy mops, dust pans, dolls,
and carts are good props.

11:30 R E C O R D P L A Y E R O R G A M E T I M E

11:45 L U N C H

12:15 N A P O R Q U I E T T I M E

2:30   K I D R O B I C S (physical exercise)
Bend, stretch, jump, crawl, run in place, shrink small, hop on one leg, tiptoe, and so on.

2:45   A F T E R N O O N   S N A C K

3:00   C R E A T I V E   A C T I V I T Y

Fingerpaints
Whip Ivory Flakes with an egg beater, add coloring. Let children paint on paper or brown paper bags. They also enjoy cleaning up from this activity.

3:30   C I R C L E   T I M E
Name things that are pink.
Name things that are round.

3:45   O U T D O O R   F R E E   P L A Y   O R   I N D O O R
F R E E   P L A Y

4:45   Clean up toys, gather belongings, wash faces and hands.

5:00   Watch selected educational television program or read books.

5:30   Children are picked up by parent.

Day 6

9:30 S T O R Y T I M E

9:45 S O N G S   ABC's
                                      Count 1–20
                                      "Good Morning to You"
                                      (sung to the tune of
                                      "Happy Birthday," naming
                                      each child)

"Brave Little Indian"
The brave little Indian   (Hold index finger at side
went hunting   of head like a feather in
for a bear.   the hair)
He looked in the woods   (Hands over eyes in
and everywhere.   "seeing" gesture. Hands
                                      make sweeping gesture)

The brave little Indian   (Repeat first and second
found a big bear.   instructions)
He ran like a rabbit   (Clap hands)
Oh, what a scare!   (Hand on ear to indicate
                                      scare)

"The Little Elf"
This little elf likes to   (Hold up thumb. Pretend
hammer   to hammer)
This little elf likes to saw.   (Hold up index finger.
                                      Pretend to saw)
This little elf likes to   (Hold up tall finger.
splash or paint.   Motion of painting)
This one has pictures to   (Hold up ring finger.
draw.   Motion of drawing)
And this little elf likes   (Hold up little finger.
best of all   Bend and cry, "Mama,
To put the cry in the baby   Mama")
doll.

"Five Little Indians"

Five little Indians stood in a row.	(Left hand fingers up straight)
Three stood up straight, but two stood just so.	(Touch thumb and index finger together)
Along came the big chief, and what do you think?	(Thumb of right hand)
Those two lazy Indians stood up quick as a wink!	(Thumb and index fingers up quickly)

10:15 S N A C K S

10:30 T A B L E   A C T I V I T Y

Sewing Cards
Make design on stiff cardboard. Punch holes along outline. Let children sew or string thread or yarn through the cards. The designs can also be colored.

11:00 F R E E   P L A Y

Fort
Build a fort or pretend house using four chairs and a blanket; drape the blanket over a table. Children love to construct their own hideout, cave, or fort.

11:30 R E C O R D   P L A Y E R   O R   G A M E   T I M E

11:45 L U N C H

12:15 N A P   O R   Q U I E T   T I M E

 2:30 K I D R O B I C S (physical exercise)
Bend, stretch, jump, crawl, run in place, shrink small, hop on one leg, tiptoe, and so on.

 2:45 A F T E R N O O N   S N A C K

3:00 C R E A T I V E A C T I V I T Y

Number Bingo
Take old calendar, cut a month's page in half, cut numbers from another page. Give half a sheet to each of two children or more as needed. Hold up numbers. Child takes number and covers corresponding number on his sheet. The one who covers his sheet first or gets a full line wins.

Comb Painting
Cut a piece of medium-weight cardboard not longer than the pan or dish holding the paint. Cut notches along one edge of the cardboard making sure the "teeth" are flat. Let the child dip the "comb" into the paint and make designs on old newspaper or colored construction paper.

3:30 C I R C L E T I M E
Name things that are purple.
Name things that are soft.

3:45 O U T D O O R F R E E P L A Y O R I N D O O R
F R E E P L A Y

4:45 Clean up toys, gather belongings, wash faces and hands.

5:00 Watch selected educational television program or read books.

5:30 Children are picked up by parent.

Day 7

9:30 S T O R Y T I M E

9:45 S O N G S

ABC's
Count 1–20
"Good Morning to You"
(sung to the tune of
"Happy Birthday," naming
each child)

"Our Carpenter"
Can you be a carpenter,   (Suit actions to words)
At work the whole day
long?
You will need so many
tools
Your arms must be quite
strong.
First, you saw and saw
and saw,
Until the boards are cut;
Long ones, short ones,
every size
You need to build a hut.

10:15 S N A C K S

10:30 T A B L E A C T I V I T Y

Scrapbooks
Children enjoy cutting out pictures from old magazines.
Suggest that they cut out pictures of animals, toys, com-
munity helpers, or any other subject or related grouping.
These can be pasted on construction paper or cardboard.
Pages can then be clipped or tied together with yarn or
ribbon. Children can label these pictures. Booklets are
also fun to use over and over as the illustrations for "make

up as you go" stories. Old greeting cards and junk mail are also usable for this and many other things.

11:00 FREE PLAY

Musical Instruments
(Take a while to construct these and the children will learn how to take care of them. They should be kept in a special box and only brought out for music time.)

Tambourine:
Staple paper plate to another plate so that it is hollow inside. Before stapling, put in some objects that will shake or make a rhythm noise. An aluminum pie tin with holes punched and buttons dangling from it is great too. How about putting holes in bottle caps, stringing wire through the caps and bending the wire into a circle? You can even add bells.

Drums:
Use coffee cans, formula cans with plastic snap-on lids or oatmeal box. Use wooden spoons for drumsticks.

Mexican Maraca:
Empty salt, milk, or detergent containers and fill them with rice, beans, or macaroni.

Flute:
Take a cardboard tube left over from toilet paper or foil and punch three small holes along the top of the tube. Cover one end with piece of waxed paper. The child can hum into the open end and move his fingers along the top to create musical sounds.

Marching Sticks:
Use solid wooden spoons, rulers, pencils, or sticks (without pointed ends).

Guitar:
Use a shoebox with six rubber bands stretched around the box—it's great for plunking out a song.

Bell Jar:
Fill glass jars with various levels of water and add food coloring. By tapping the jars with spoons, you can create different musical sounds.

11:30 R E C O R D P L A Y E R O R G A M E T I M E

11:45 L U N C H

12:15 N A P O R Q U I E T T I M E

2:30 K I D R O B I C S (physical exercise)
Bend, stretch, jump, crawl, run in place, shrink small, hop on one leg, tiptoe, and so on.

2:45 A F T E R N O O N S N A C K

3:00 C R E A T I V E A C T I V I T Y

Toothbrush Painting
Old toothbrushes can make an interesting painting tool. Objects from nature, such as leaves of different shapes and sizes, twigs, or pine cones, can be placed on paper with cellophane tape underneath so they won't slide around. Toothbrush is dipped into paint and brushed on the objects. Remove the objects and clear outlines will remain.

3:30 C I R C L E T I M E
Name things that are tan.
Name things that are sharp.

3:45 O U T D O O R F R E E P L A Y O R I N D O O R F R E E P L A Y

4:45   Clean up toys, gather belongings, wash faces and hands.

5:00   Watch selected educational television program or read books.

5:30   Children are picked up by parent.

Day 8

9:30 STORYTIME

9:45 SONGS   ABC's
Count 1–20
"Good Morning to You"
(sung to the tune of
"Happy Birthday," naming
each child)

"I Have Two Eyes"
I have two eyes to see   (Suit actions to words)
with
I have two feet to run.
I have two hands to wave
with,
And nose I have but one.
I have two ears to hear
with,
And tongue to say "Good-
day."
And two red cheeks for
you to kiss,
And now I'll run away.

"If"
If your fingers wiggle.   (Wiggle fingers)
Cross them one by one   (Clasp hands together)
Until they hug each other.   (Fold fingers down)
It really is quite fun.

"I'm Hiding"
I'm hiding, I'm hiding,   (Suit actions to words)
And no one knows where,
For all they can see
Is my toes and my hair.

10:15 S N A C K S

10:30 T A B L E A C T I V I T Y

11:00 F R E E P L A Y

Bubbles
You can buy bubbles at the store or make your own from the recipe in Chapter 9. Dip a kitchen funnel in solution and blow through the narrow end. Empty wooden spools can also be used to blow bubbles. Straws can be used if you cut four short slits at the end of one straw and bend the cut sections apart just a little.

11:30 R E C O R D P L A Y E R O R G A M E T I M E

11:45 L U N C H

12:15 N A P O R Q U I E T T I M E

2:30 K I D R O B I C S (physical exercise)
Bend, stretch, jump, crawl, run in place, shrink small, hop on one leg, tiptoe, and so on.

2:45 A F T E R N O O N S N A C K

3:00 C R E A T I V E A C T I V I T Y

Necklaces
Pine cones make attractive necklaces when strung on heavy string.

3:30 C I R C L E T I M E
Name things that are white.
Name things that are square.

3:45 O U T D O O R F R E E P L A Y O R I N D O O R F R E E P L A Y

4:45 Clean up toys, gather belongings, wash faces and hands.

5:00 Watch selected educational television program or read books.

5:30 Children are picked up by parent.

Day 9

9:30 S T O R Y T I M E

9:45 S O N G S

ABC's
Count 1–20
"Good Morning to You"
(sung to the tune of
"Happy Birthday," naming
each child)

"The Church"

Here is the church	(Lace fingers)
And here is the steeple	(Index fingers together at tips)
Open the door,	(Spread thumbs open like door)
And see all the people	(Open hands)
Here is the parson	(Index finger makes
Going upstairs	walking motion)
And here he is	
Saying his prayers.	(Fold hands in prayer)

"Thumbkins"

Where is Thumbkin?	(Hands behind back)
Where is Thumbkin?	
Here he comes, here he comes.	(Bring hands to front, thumbs up)
Mighty glad to see you, Mighty glad to see you.	(Wiggle thumbs at each other)
There he goes, there he goes.	

"Tommy Thumb"

This is little Tommy Thumb,	(Point to each finger in turn)
Round and smooth as a plum.	

There is busy Peter
Pointer
Surely he's a double-
jointer.
This is mighty Toddy
Tall.
He's the biggest one of all.
This is dainty Reuben
Ring,
He's too fine for anything.
And this little wee one,
maybe,
Is the pretty Finger Baby.

10:15 S N A C K S

10:30 T A B L E A C T I V I T Y

<u>String Picture</u>
Coat string or yarn with glue and make a design by laying
the yarn or string on a piece of colored paper.

11:00 F R E E P L A Y

Make a Train
Put little chairs, pillows, and boxes in a row. Cut out
small pieces of paper for tickets. Let the children pretend
they are on a train.

11:30 R E C O R D P L A Y E R O R G A M E T I M E

11:45 L U N C H

12:15 N A P O R Q U I E T T I M E

 2:30 K I D R O B I C S (physical exercise)
Bend, stretch, jump, crawl, run in place, shrink small, hop
on one leg, tiptoe, and so on.

2:45 AFTERNOON SNACK

3:00 CREATIVE ACTIVITY

What Am I Wearing?
Drape a tablecloth or large towel over your body (except your head) and ask the children to tell you what you were wearing. This teaches good observation skills. Take turns by going from one child to the next asking, "What am I wearing?"

3:30 CIRCLE TIME
Name things that are brown.
Name things that are hard.

3:45 OUTDOOR FREE PLAY OR INDOOR FREE PLAY

4:45 Clean up toys, gather belongings, wash faces and hands.

5:00 Watch selected educational television program or read books.

5:30 Children are picked up by parent.

Day 10

9:30 STORYTIME

9:45 SONGS

ABC's
Count 1–20
"Good Morning to You"
(sung to the tune of
"Happy Birthday," naming
each child)

"Fire! Fire!"
Fire! Fire! Fire! Fire!
Hear the siren blowing.
Fire! Fire! Fire! Fire!
Everybody's going.
Climb the ladder, squirt
the hose.
With a Sh! Sh! Sh! Sh!
Out the fire goes.

(Suit actions to words)

"Fire Engine"
This is the fire engine.
This is the hose.
The firemen work fast
When the siren blows.
Up goes the ladder
Up goes the hose
The fire is out
When the last siren blows.

(Suit actions to words)

"Where is Thumbkin?"
Where is Thumbkin?
Where is Thumbkin?
Here I am.
Here I am.
How are you today, sir?
Very well, I thank you.

Run and play,
Run and play.
(Substitute other finger
names: Pointer, Tallman,
Ringman, Pinky, and
family)

10:15   S N A C K S

10:30   T A B L E   A C T I V I T Y

<u>Finger Paint</u>
Refer to the craft recipes in Chapter 9 to find the mixture
for finger paint. Let the children use paper, newspaper,
box tops, or junk mail to paint on.

11:00   F R E E   P L A Y

<u>Hide the Music Box</u>
Hide a musical toy, alarm clock with ringing bell, or music
box. The children must try to find it before the sound
stops. Keep all of the children in one room for this activity.

11:30   R E C O R D   P L A Y E R   O R   G A M E   T I M E

11:45   L U N C H

12:15   N A P   O R   Q U I E T   T I M E

2:30   K I D R O B I C S (physical exercise)
Bend, stretch, jump, crawl, run in place, shrink small, hop
on one leg, tiptoe, and so on.

2:45   A F T E R N O O N   S N A C K

3:00   C R E A T I V E   A C T I V I T Y

Collage

Have the children tear pieces of paper, foil, and advertisements. Give each a little bit of glue (about the size of a half dollar). They can glue these small pieces on an 8½-inch by 11-inch piece of paper to make a decoration. (My recommendation is to not allow the children to use scissors unless very closely supervised.)

3:30 C I R C L E   T I M E
Name things that are blue.
Name things that are small.

3:45 O U T D O O R   F R E E   P L A Y   O R   I N D O O R   F R E E   P L A Y

4:45 Clean up toys, gather belongings, wash faces and hands.

5:00 Watch selected educational television program or read books.

5:30 Children are picked up by parent.

Day 11

9:30 STORYTIME

9:45 SONGS

ABC's
Count 1–20
"Good Morning to You"
(sung to the tune of
"Happy Birthday," naming
each child)

"My Hands"
Open them, shut them.   (Suit actions to words)
Open them, shut them.
Give a little clap.
Open them, shut them.
Open them, shut them.
Put them in your lap.

"My Friend"
Hello, hello, how are you?
You are my friend and I
love you.
(Child's name, child's
name), how are you?
You are my friend, and I
love you.

"Everybody Says"
Everybody says, I look
just like my mother.
Everybody says, I'm the
image of Aunt Bea.
Everybody says, I've a
nose just like my father's.
But I want to look like
ME!

10:15   S N A C K S

10:30   T A B L E   A C T I V I T Y

Make a Mask
Make a mask for each child using a large grocery bag. Cut out holes for eyes and mouth. The children can decorate the bags with yarn for hair, and foil for a nose.

11:00   F R E E   P L A Y

Hatbox
Collect baseball caps, nurse's caps, policeman's hat, and fancy hats. Keep them in a large hatbox for fun time.

11:30   R E C O R D   P L A Y E R   O R   G A M E   T I M E

11:45   L U N C H

12:15   N A P   O R   Q U I E T   T I M E

 2:30   K I D R O B I C S (physical exercise)
Bend, stretch, jump, crawl, run in place, shrink small, hop on one leg, tiptoe, and so on.

 2:45   A F T E R N O O N   S N A C K

 3:00   C R E A T I V E   A C T I V I T Y

Paper Plate Hat
Decorate paper plate with magic markers or crayons. The rim of the plate is the brim. Add ribbon to tie under the chin. Decorate with odds and ends.

 3:30   C I R C L E   T I M E
Name things that are black.
Name things that are fuzzy.

3:45 OUTDOOR FREE PLAY OR INDOOR FREE PLAY

4:45 Clean up toys, gather belongings, wash faces and hands.

5:00 Watch selected educational television program or read books.

5:30 Children are picked up by parent.

Day 12

9:30 STORYTIME

9:45 SONGS   ABC's
                               Count 1–20
                               "Good Morning to You"
                               (sung to the tune of
                               "Happy Birthday," naming
                               each child)

"The Eensy Weensy Spider"
The eensy, weensy spider   (Suit actions to words)
went up the water spout.
Down came the rain and
washed the spider out.
Out came the sun and
dried up all the rain.
So the eensy, weensy
spider went up the spout
again.

"B-I-N-G-O"
There was a farmer had a   (Suit actions to words)
dog,
And Bingo was his
name-O
B-I-N-G-O, B-I-N-G-O,
B-I-N-G-O,
And Bingo was his
name-O.
There was a farmer had a
dog,
And Bingo was his
name-O
B-I-N-G-X, B-I-N-G-X,   (X indicates claps instead
B-I-N-G-X,   of saying letters)

*And Bingo was his
name-O.
There was a farmer had a
dog,
And Bingo was his
name-O.
B-I-N-X-X, B-I-N-X-X,
B-I-N-X-X,
And Bingo was his
name-O.
There was a farmer had a
dog,
And Bingo was his
name-O.
B-I-X-X-X, B-I-X-X-X,
B-I-X-X-X,
And Bingo was his
name-O.
There was a farmer had a
dog,
And Bingo was his
name-O.
B-X-X-X-X, B-X-X-X-X,
B-X-X-X-X,
And Bingo was his
name-O.
There was a farmer had a
dog,
And Bingo was his
name-O.
X-X-X-X-X, X-X-X-X-X,
X-X-X-X-X,
And Bingo was his
name-O.*

"Ten Little Indians"
One little, two little, three   (Suit actions to words)
little Indians,
Four little, five little, six
little Indians,
Seven little, eight little,
nine little Indians,
Ten little Indian boys.
"And do you know what
they did? They got in
their boats very carefully.
Be very careful you don't
tip over."
They rowed, and they
rowed, and they rowed to
the shore.
The rowed, and they
rowed, and they rowed to
the shore.
They rowed, and they
rowed, and they rowed to
the shore.
Ten little Indians boys (or
girls).

10:15 S N A C K S

10:30 T A B L E A C T I V I T Y

<u>*Water Painting*</u>
(Outside activity for warm, sunny day)
Each child will have a milk container of water and a large
paintbrush. Pretend that the water is paint and "paint"
the sidewalk, house, and mailbox.

11:00 F R E E P L A Y

Tractor Tire Sandbox
Buy 50 pounds of sand at a garden center, hardware store, or lumber yard. You can find a tire by calling a tractor supply shop or a tractor repair shop. Have a special box of outdoor toys which you use only for sandbox time.

11:30   R E C O R D   P L A Y E R   O R   G A M E   T I M E

11:45   L U N C H

12:15   N A P   O R   Q U I E T   T I M E

 2:30   K I D R O B I C S (physical exercise)
Bend, stretch, jump, crawl, run in place, shrink small, hop on one leg, tiptoe, and so on.

 2:45   A F T E R N O O N   S N A C K

 3:00   C R E A T I V E   A C T I V I T Y

Jump the River
Lay two parallel pieces of string on the floor (about 1½ feet apart). Children try to jump across "the river" without getting wet.

 3:30   C I R C L E   T I M E
Name things that are red.
Name things that are sharp.

 3:45   O U T D O O R   F R E E   P L A Y   O R   I N D O O R
F R E E   P L A Y

 4:45   Clean up toys, gather belongings, wash faces and hands.

 5:00   Watch selected educational television program or read books.

 5:30   Children are picked up by parent.

Day 13

9:30 STORYTIME

9:45 SONGS

ABC's
Count 1–20
"Good Morning to You"
(sung to the tune of
"Happy Birthday," naming
each child)

"Teddy Bear"
Teddy Bear, teddy bear
Turn around.
Teddy bear, teddy bear,
Touch the ground.
Teddy bear, teddy bear,
Show your shoe.
Teddy bear, teddy bear,
That will do.
Teddy bear, teddy bear,
Go upstairs.
Teddy bear, teddy bear,
Say your prayers.
Teddy bear, teddy bear,
Turn out the light.
Teddy bear, teddy bear
Say "Goodnight!"

(Standing in place, suit
actions to words)

"I Stuck My Head in a
Little Skunk's Hole"
I stuck my head in a
little skunk's hole,
And the little skunk said
before my soul,
"Take it out, take it out,
take it out,
Remove it."

I didn't take it out, and
the little skunk said,
"You better take it out or
you'll wish you had.
Take it out, take it out,
take it out."
So-o-o I removed it.

"Head, Shoulders, Knees, and Toes"
(To the tune of "There is a
Tavern in the Town")

Head, shoulders, knees,
and toes,
Knees and toes,
Head, shoulders, knees,
and toes,
Knees and toes.
Eyes and ears and mouth
and nose.
Head and shoulders,
Knees and toes, knees and
toes!

(Point to various parts of the body while singing the song; then begin pointing only, eliminating words)

10:30 TABLE ACTIVITY

Dribble Glue

Each child will need a piece of shirt cardboard and white glue. By dribbling glue on the cardboard, you can make an interesting design. Allow the papers to dry overnight. The next time the children come, they will paint the whole cardboard with one color of paint. The paint will not stick to the glued design so it will stand out raised and shiny against the colored background.

11:00 F R E E P L A Y

Bowling
Clean ten half-gallon milk cartons. Decorate the sides
with large numbers made from colored paper. Use a nerf
ball and your kitchen or hallway for a bowling alley.

11:30 R E C O R D P L A Y E R O R G A M E T I M E

11:45 L U N C H

12:15 N A P O R Q U I E T T I M E

2:30 K I D R O B I C S (physical exercise)
Bend, stretch, jump, crawl, run in place, shrink small, hop
on one leg, tiptoe, and so on.

2:45 A F T E R N O O N S N A C K

3:00 C R E A T I V E A C T I V I T Y

Guess What It Is
Put an item in a sock. Pass it around. Let each child try
to guess what is in the sock.

3:30 C I R C L E T I M E
Name things that are yellow.
Name things that are dangerous.

3:45 O U T D O O R F R E E P L A Y O R I N D O O R
F R E E P L A Y

4:45 Clean up toys, gather belongings, wash faces and hands.

5:00 Watch selected educational television program or read
books.

5:30 Children are picked up by parent.

Day 14

9:30   S T O R Y T I M E

9:45   S O N G S   ABC's
                                                    Count 1–20
                                                    "Good Morning to You"
                                                    (sung to the tune of
                                                    "Happy Birthday," naming
                                                    each child)

"Ready to Listen"
Let your hands go clap,   (Suit actions to words)
clap, clap.
Let your fingers go snap,
snap, snap.
Let your lips go up and
down.
But do not make a sound.
Fold your hands and close
each eye.
Take a breath and softly
sigh, AH!

"1, 2, 3"
1, 2, 3, there's a bug on   (Pretend to brush it off)
me!
Where did he go?   (Look around)
I don't know.

"Monkey Song"
A little monkey likes to   (Suit actions to words)
do,
Just the same as you and
you.
When you sit up very tall,
Monkey sits up very tall.

When you pretend to
throw a ball,
Monkey pretends to throw
a ball.

10:15 S N A C K S

10:30 T A B L E A C T I V I T Y

Paper Chains
Children will need paste and a number of narrow strips
of paper. Take one strip of paper and bend it to make a
circle and paste the ends together. Your chain could be
a necklace, a Christmas tree decoration, or a party decoration.

11:00 F R E E P L A Y

Trash Can Basketball
Crumple a sheet of newspaper in the shape of a ball.
Secure it with masking tape so it is firm. Make about
twelve balls. Use a clean, empty wastebasket. Let each
child take turns aiming to score points by tossing the ball
into the wastebasket.

11:30 R E C O R D P L A Y E R O R G A M E T I M E

11:45 L U N C H

12:15 N A P O R Q U I E T T I M E

2:30 K I D R O B I C S (physical exercise)
Bend, stretch, jump, crawl, run in place, shrink small, hop
on one leg, tiptoe, and so on.

2:45 A F T E R N O O N S N A C K

3:00 CREATIVE ACTIVITY

Jack Be Nimble
Each child stands behind any small object (a book, toy, or plastic cup). Pretend that the item is a candlestick. "Jack be nimble, Jack be quick, Jack jump over the candlestick!" (All jump over their candlestick.)

3:30 CIRCLE TIME
Name things that are brown.
Name things that are dry.

3:45 OUTDOOR FREE PLAY OR INDOOR FREE PLAY

4:45 Clean up toys, gather belongings, wash faces and hands.

5:00 Watch selected educational television program or read books.

5:30 Children are picked up by parent.

Day 15

9:30 STORYTIME

9:30 SONGS

ABC's
Count 1–20
"Good Morning to You"
(sung to the tune of
"Happy Birthday," naming
each child)

"Five Little Elephants"
Five little elephants.
Rowing toward the shore.
One fell in.
Then there were four.
Four little elephants
Climbing up a tree.
One slid down.
Then there were three.
Three little elephants
Living in the zoo.
One walked off.
Then there were two.
Two little elephants
Playing in the sun
One fell asleep.
Then there was one.
One little elephant
Isn't any fun.
Abra-ca-da-bra!
Then there were none!

(Hold up five fingers and
suit actions to words)

"Nap Time"
"Come little children,"
Calls mother hen.
"It is time to take
Your nap again."

(Beckoning motion)

And under her feathers	(Fingers of right hand
The small chicks creep	creep into folded left
And she clucks a song	hand)
Till they fall asleep.	

"I Had a little Poodle"

I had a little poodle	(Hold up clenched fist for
His coat was silver gray	poodle)
One day I thought I'd	
bathe him	
To wash the dirt away.	
I washed my little poodle.	(Scrub fist with other
	hand)
Then dried him with a	(Pat fist with other hand
towel	as if drying)
My poodle seemed to like	
his bath	
He didn't even growl.	

10:15 S N A C K S

10:30 T A B L E A C T I V I T Y

Caterpillars
Save cardboard egg cartons. Turn them upside down. They will resemble the back of a caterpillar. Use pipe cleaners to make two antennae on the first cup which will be the head. Fill in the eyes and the mouth. Color or paint the body.

11:00 F R E E P L A Y

Building with a Deck of Cards
Delicately balance the cards on a carpeted area. Try to build with them by leaning them against each other.

11:30 R E C O R D P L A Y E R O R G A M E T I M E

11:45 L U N C H

12:15 N A P O R Q U I E T T I M E

2:30 K I D R O B I C S (physical exercise)
Bend, stretch, jump, crawl, run in place, shrink small, hop on one leg, tiptoe, and so on.

2:45 A F T E R N O O N S N A C K

3:00 C R E A T I V E A C T I V I T Y

Hand Shadow Show
Find a blank wall to create a hand shadow. Place a lamp without the shade across from a blank wall. The room should be dark otherwise. Show the children a few basic ways to create animals on the wall using your fingers and hands.

3:30 C I R C L E T I M E
Name things that are gold.
Name things that are good to eat.

3:45 O U T D O O R F R E E P L A Y O R I N D O O R F R E E P L A Y

4:45 Clean up toys, gather belongings, wash faces and hands.

5:00 Watch selected educational television program or read books.

5:30 Children are picked up by parent.

Day 16

9:30 STORYTIME

9:45 SONGS

ABC's
Count 1–20
"Good Morning to You"
(sung to the tune of
"Happy Birthday," naming
each child)
"Row, Row, Row Your
Boat."

"The Wind"
The wind came out to
play one day.
He swept the clouds out of   (Make sweeping motion
his way: with arms)
He blew the leaves and   (Make fluttering motions
away they flew.   with fingers)
The trees bent low, and   (Lift arms and lower
their branches did, too.   them)
The wind blew the great   (Repeat sweeping
big ships at sea,   motions)
The wind blew my kite
away from me.

"The Top"
Wind the top,   (Winding motion)
Wind the top,
Round and round and   (Spinning motion)
round.
Now it makes a little hop,   (Hopping motion)
And spins along the
ground.
Faster, faster, faster,
Whirling, whirling,
whirling,

Spinning round and
round again.
Twirling, twirling,
twirling.
Wobbly, wobbly, wobbly!   (Wobbling motion)
It's running down I fear.
Slower, slower, slower   (Spinning slowly)
Now it falls! Oh dear!

"Doctor Day"
My mother said, "It's
doctor day."
Then she and I were on
our way
To see our friend, the
doctor who
Would check on me as
doctors do.
He had more things than
I can tell
To help him keep the
people well.
He checked me up and all
the while
He wore a big and
friendly smile.
So now I hope that
someday you
May go to see the doctor
too.

10:15 S N A C K S

10:30 T A B L E A C T I V I T Y

Crazy Collage
Children love to tear up pieces of newspapers and magazines. Paste the scraps on to a larger sheet of paper. They

can also add fabric scraps, sparkles, and herbs to their design.

11:00 F R E E P L A Y

Spaghetti and Meatballs
The children cut white yarn into pieces so that it looks like spaghetti. Color Ping-Pong balls for meatballs. Add paper plates. Small red pieces of tissue paper can be the spaghetti sauce.

11:30 R E C O R D P L A Y E R O R G A M E T I M E

11:45 L U N C H

12:15 N A P O R Q U I E T T I M E

2:30 K I D R O B I C S (physical exercise)
Bend, stretch, jump, crawl, run in place, shrink small, hop on one leg, tiptoe, and so on.

2:45 A F T E R N O O N S N A C K

3:00 C R E A T I V E A C T I V I T Y

Physical Exercise
"Touch your head
Touch your toes
Stretch ..." (Name body parts)

3:30 C I R C L E T I M E
Name things that are purple.
Name things that are cold.

3:45 O U T D O O R F R E E P L A Y O R I N D O O R
F R E E P L A Y

4:45 Clean up toys, gather belongings, wash faces and hands.

5:00 Watch selected educational television program or read books.

5:30 Children are picked up by parent.

Day 17

9:30 STORYTIME

9:45 SONGS

ABC's
Count 1–20
"Good Morning to You"
(sung to the tune of
"Happy Birthday," naming
each child)

"Farmer in the Dell"
The farmer in the dell
The farmer in the dell
Hi, ho, the dairy-o
The farmer in the dell.
(The farmer takes a wife
. . . takes a child . . . takes
a nurse, etc.)

"Baa, Baa, Black Sheep"
Baa, baa, black sheep
Have you any wool?
Yes sir, yes sir
Three bags full.
One for my Master,
One for the Dame,
One for the little lad [or
lass]
Who lives in the lane
Baa, baa black sheep
Have you any wool?
Yes sir, yes sir
Three bags full.

"Jack and Jill"

Jack and Jill went up the   (Suit actions to words)
hill
To fetch a pail of water.
Jack fell down and broke
his crown
And Jill came tumbling
after.

10:15   S N A C K S

10:30   T A B L E   A C T I V I T Y

<u>*Scissor Fun*</u>
Each child has several pieces of colored paper. They use
their scissors to make different shapes. (Younger children should just rip the paper.) The older children will
attempt to cut circles, triangles, and so on, while the
younger ones will just cut nondescript pieces. Save all of
these scraps for a day when you want to "wallpaper" a
large box by letting the children paste them on.

11:00   F R E E   P L A Y

<u>*Let's Go on a Picnic*</u>
Today is "Let's go on a picnic day." Each child can bring
a stuffed animal with him. Spread a cloth on the floor
and imagine a picnic in the forest. Use your plastic dishes,
picnic basket, cooler, and jug.

11:30   R E C O R D   P L A Y E R   O R   G A M E   T I M E

11:45   L U N C H

12:15   N A P   O R   Q U I E T   T I M E

2:30 K I D R O B I C S (physical exercise)
Bend, stretch, jump, crawl, run in place, shrink small, hop on one leg, tiptoe, and so on.

2:45 A F T E R N O O N   S N A C K

3:00 C R E A T I V E   A C T I V I T Y

Train
Children hold on to a rope or scarves tied together to make a train. The engine leads them around the house. The children can take turns being the engine, caboose, or coal car. While you are walking look for a particular thing. Make stops when you see things that are mostly orange, green, yellow, and assorted color combinations.

3:30 C I R C L E   T I M E
Name things that are orange.
Name things that are hot.

3:45 O U T D O O R   F R E E   P L A Y   O R   I N D O O R   F R E E   P L A Y

4:45 Clean up toys, gather belongings, wash faces and hands.

5:00 Watch selected educational television program or read books.

5:30 Children are picked up by parent.

Day 18

9:30 STORYTIME

9:45 SONGS

ABC's
Count 1–20
"Good Morning to You"
(sung to the tune of
"Happy Birthday," naming
each child)

"Little Miss Muffet"
Little Miss Muffet sat on
a tuffet
Eating her curds and
whey.
Along came a spider and
sat down beside her
And frightened Miss
Muffet away!

"Rain, Rain, Go Away"
Rain, rain, go away
Come again some other
day.
Rain, rain, go away
Little [child's name]
wants to play!

"Mary had a Little Lamb"
Mary had a little lamb
Little lamb, little lamb.
Mary had a little lamb,
Its fleece was white as
snow.
Everywhere that Mary
went,
Mary went, Mary went

Everywhere that Mary
went
The lamb was sure to go.

10:15 S N A C K S

10:30 T A B L E A C T I V I T Y

Make a Sandwich
Give each child a slice of bologna, cheese, and day-old bread. Let each child select a cookie cutter in animal or other shape. Each child can experiment by cutting out his treat on different textures of food to make a silly sandwich!

11:00 F R E E P L A Y

Mailbox
Use a large carton, taped at the ends. A pillowcase can be the mailbag. Save junk mail and used envelopes. Use magic markers and construction paper to decorate the box. Cut along the top to make a slot for deposit of mail. Make a door flap in front to retrieve mail. Put the words MAILMAN or MAILWOMAN on a circular piece of paper. Attach it to a hat which the mail carrier can wear.

11:30 R E C O R D P L A Y E R O R G A M E T I M E

11:45 L U N C H

12:15 N A P O R Q U I E T T I M E

2:30 K I D R O B I C S (physical exercise)
Bend, stretch, jump, crawl, run in place, shrink small, hop on one leg, tiptoe, and so on.

2:45 A F T E R N O O N S N A C K

3:00   C R E A T I V E   A C T I V I T Y

Tin Can Bank
Save coffee cans, formula cans, and nut cans with plastic lids. Cut a slit in the top through which money can be deposited. Cover the tin part of the can with decorated paper or paper which the children have decorated themselves. Yarn, string or ribbons can also be glued to the can.

3:30   C I R C L E   T I M E
Name things that are green.
Name things that are old.

3:45   O U T D O O R   F R E E   P L A Y   O R   I N D O O R
F R E E   P L A Y

4:45   Clean up toys, gather belongings, wash faces and hands.

5:00   Watch selected educational television program or read books.

5:30   Children are picked up by parent.

Day 19

9:30 STORYTIME

9:45 SONGS   ABC's
                                         Count 1–20
                                         "Good Morning to You"
                                         (sung to the tune of
                                         "Happy Birthday," naming
                                         each child)

10:15 SNACKS

10:30 TABLE ACTIVITY

Bottle Decorations
Save empty clear bottles or jars. Remove labels, rinse, and clean. Children fill with different textures such as hard white beans, dry cereal, and corn kernels. One at a time the children spoon the ingredients into their bottles to create a pattern with different layers of food. Fasten lid and tie a bow at the top.

11:00 FREE PLAY

Paper Cup Building
Save used paper cups (all the same size) and spring-type clothespins. Stand the cups upright and attach one to the other. Children can make an interesting construction project by attaching fifty to one hundred cups together with clothespins.

11:30 RECORD PLAYER OR GAME TIME

11:45 LUNCH

12:15 NAP OR QUIET TIME

2:30   K I D R O B I C S (physical exercise)
Bend, stretch, jump, crawl, run in place, shrink small, hop
on one leg, tiptoe, and so on.

2:45   A F T E R N O O N   S N A C K

3:00   C R E A T I V E   A C T I V I T Y

Straw Necklaces and Bracelets
Cut thick straws into small pieces. Connect the straws
with string or pipe cleaners to make some exciting jewelry.

3:30   C I R C L E   T I M E
Name things that are white.
Name things that are new.

3:45   O U T D O O R   F R E E   P L A Y   O R   I N D O O R
F R E E   P L A Y

4:45   Clean up toys, gather belongings, wash faces and hands.

5:00   Watch selected educational television program or read
books.

5:30   Children are picked up by parent.

Day 20

9:30 S T O R Y T I M E

9:45 S O N G S
                             ABC's
                             Count 1–20
                             "Good Morning to You"
                             (sung to the tune of
                             "Happy Birthday," naming
                             each child)
                             "Here We Go Round the
                             Mulberry Bush"
                             "London Bridge"
                             "Hickory Dickory Dock"

10:15 S N A C K S

10:30 T A B L E   A C T I V I T Y

Noodle Jewelry
Color pasta noodles with crayons or magic markers. These simple dress-up accessories are fun to make by just stringing the noodles together. Use a decorated shoe box for a "jewelry box."

11:00 F R E E   P L A Y

No-Bake Cereal Cookies
½ cup chunky peanut butter
⅓ cup honey
½ cup flaked coconut
2 cups of a favorite cereal

Mix peanut butter, honey, and coconut in a large bowl. Stir in only ½ cup of cereal. Scoop out peanut butter mixture and form into large balls. Then roll the balls in the remainder of the cereal so they are covered by the cereal mixture. Save for your afternoon treat!

11:30 RECORD PLAYER OR GAME TIME

11:45 LUNCH

12:15 NAP OR QUIET TIME

2:30 KIDROBICS (physical exercise)
Bend, stretch, jump, crawl, run in place, shrink small, hop on one leg, tiptoe, and so on.

2:45 AFTERNOON SNACK

3:00 CREATIVE ACTIVITY

Matchbox Car Track or Animal Farm
Use the reverse side of a plastic tablecloth to draw a series of roads, houses, farms, trees, and so on. Give the children small cars or plastic animals. They will amuse themselves for quite a while with this activity. (You can ask them to bring their own cars or small animals.)

3:30 CIRCLE TIME
Name things that are black.
Name things that are fuzzy.

3:45 OUTDOOR FREE PLAY OR INDOOR FREE PLAY

4:45 Clean up toys, gather belongings, wash faces and hands.

5:00 Watch selected educational television program or read books.

5:30 Children are picked up by parent.

Day 21

9:30   S T O R Y T I M E

9:45   S O N G S

	ABC's
	Count 1–20
	"Good Morning to You"
	(sung to the tune of
	"Happy Birthday," naming
	each child)
	"Rock-a-Bye Baby"
	"Twinkle, Twinkle, Little
	Star"
	"Humpty Dumpty"

10:15   S N A C K S

10:30   T A B L E   A C T I V I T Y

Indian Headdress
Cut out band of construction paper to fit around head
of each child. Cut out feathers from construction paper.
Children can decorate band and feathers prior to pasting
them together.

11:00   F R E E   P L A Y

Let's Pretend Birthday Party
Set up small tables and chairs. Give children cake pans,
cupcake papers, napkins, and plastic dishes. Ribbons and
empty gift boxes can be used to enhance their fun.

11:30   R E C O R D   P L A Y E R   O R   G A M E   T I M E

11:45   L U N C H

12:15   N A P   O R   Q U I E T   T I M E

2:30 K I D R O B I C S (physical exercise)
Bend, stretch, jump, crawl, run in place, shrink small, hop on one leg, tiptoe, and so on.

2:45 A F T E R N O O N S N A C K

3:00 C R E A T I V E A C T I V I T Y

Vegetable People
Use colored toothpicks to make vegetable people from cucumbers, potatoes, eggplant, green tomatoes, and so on. Wash, store in refrigerator, and use later for a snack or salad.

3:30 C I R C L E T I M E
Name things that are yellow.
Name things that are funny.

3:45 O U T D O O R F R E E P L A Y O R I N D O O R
F R E E P L A Y

4:45 Clean up toys, gather belongings, wash faces and hands.

5:00 Watch selected educational television program or read books.

5:30 Children are picked up by parent.

Day 22

9:30 S T O R Y T I M E

9:45 S O N G S   ABC's
                                  Count 1–20
                                  "Good Morning to You"
                                  (sung to the tune of
                                  "Happy Birthday," naming
                                  each child)
                                  "Ring-Around-A-Rosy"
                                  "Are You Sleeping?"
                                  ("Frère Jacques")
                                  "Oh, Susanna"

10:15 S N A C K S

10:30 T A B L E A C T I V I T Y

Rock Art
Children can look for flat, smooth rocks during their afternoon outdoor free play period. Paint some designs on
them or funny faces. Paint them all one color or teach
them how to draw circles, triangles, rectangles, and other
shapes.

11:00 F R E E P L A Y

Making Your Own Butter
You will need a container with a clear plastic lid and ¼
cup heavy cream. Also buy some salty crackers. Pour the
cream into the container and secure the lid tightly. Give
each child a turn to shake the container. Shake for approximately four minutes. At the end of that time, remove
the liquid. You will see a ball of butter sitting in some
liquid. Pour off the liquid so only the butter remains.
Spread the butter on the salty cracker since the butter
may taste bland. (You could also do this in a blender

letting the children take turns pressing the buttons.) This treat can be saved for afternoon snack.

11:30   R E C O R D   P L A Y E R   O R   G A M E   T I M E

11:45   L U N C H

12:15   N A P   O R   Q U I E T   T I M E

2:30   K I D R O B I C S (physical exercise)
Bend, stretch, jump, crawl, run in place, shrink small, hop on one leg, tiptoe, and so on.

2:45   A F T E R N O O N   S N A C K

3:00   C R E A T I V E   A C T I V I T Y

Paper Plate Clock
Turn a paper plate to the back side. Show the children how to fill in numbers with crayons or magic markers. Use a round-headed paper fastener to fasten the hands of the clock. Then decorate the face of the clock.

3:30   C I R C L E   T I M E
Name things that are brown.
Name things that are big.

3:45   O U T D O O R   F R E E   P L A Y   O R   I N D O O R
F R E E   P L A Y

4:45   Clean up toys, gather belongings, wash faces and hands.

5:00   Watch selected educational television program or read books.

5:30   Children are picked up by parent.

Day 23

9:30   S T O R Y T I M E

9:45   S O N G S   ABC's
                                    Count 1–20
                                    "Good Morning to You"
                                    (sung to the tune of
                                    "Happy Birthday," naming
                                    each child)

10:15   S N A C K S

10:30   T A B L E A C T I V I T Y

Egg Carton Finger Puppets
Cut out each individual egg holder of an egg carton and
use them as little caps covering your fingers. Use magic
markers to draw faces on the little heads. You can glue
cotton or yarn to the egg-cup heads for hair.

11:00   F R E E P L A Y

Spaceship
Build a spaceship with large boxes and magic markers.
Don't forget the controls!

11:30   R E C O R D P L A Y E R O R G A M E T I M E

11:45   L U N C H

12:15   N A P O R Q U I E T T I M E

2:30   K I D R O B I C S (physical exercise)
Bend, stretch, jump, crawl, run in place, shrink small, hop
on one leg, tiptoe, and so on.

2:45   A F T E R N O O N S N A C K

3:00   C R E A T I V E   A C T I V I T Y

Vegetable Friend
Cut raw vegetables (cucumbers shaped like circles, carrots in sticks, etc.) Children can make faces with mushrooms, radishes, parsley, and so on. Use for afternoon snack.

3:30   C I R C L E   T I M E
Name things that are blue.
Name things that are scary.

3:45   O U T D O O R   F R E E   P L A Y   O R   I N D O O R   F R E E   P L A Y

4:45   Clean up toys, gather belongings, wash faces and hands.

5:00   Watch selected educational television program or read books.

5:30   Children are picked up by parent.

Day 24

9:30 S T O R Y T I M E

9:45 S O N G S   ABC's
                                   Count 1–20
                                   "Good Morning to You"
                                   (sung to the tune of
                                   "Happy Birthday," naming
                                   each child)
                                   "Little Miss Muffet"
                                   "Hot Cross Buns"
                                   "Rain, Rain Go Away"

10:15 S N A C K S

10:30 T A B L E A C T I V I T Y

Print It!
Trace around a child's footprint and handprint on a piece
of paper. The child can color it in and then paste it to a
piece of cardboard with the date written on the back.

11:00 F R E E P L A Y

11:30 R E C O R D P L A Y E R O R G A M E T I M E

11:45 L U N C H

12:15 N A P O R Q U I E T T I M E

 2:30 K I D R O B I C S (physical exercise)
Bend, stretch, jump, crawl, run in place, shrink small, hop
on one leg, tiptoe, and so on.

 2:45 A F T E R N O O N S N A C K

3:00 C R E A T I V E   A C T I V I T Y

Edible Snowman
In preparation for this activity, place three round scoops of ice cream on a plate. Put back in freezer to harden. Arrange raisins, maraschino cherries, coconut, and so on, on another plate. When the children are seated around a table, they take turns adding to decorating the snowman. When finished, divide the ice cream and serve for snacks.

3:30 C I R C L E   T I M E
Name things that are green.
Name things that smell pretty.

3:45 O U T D O O R   F R E E   P L A Y   O R   I N D O O R
F R E E   P L A Y

4:45 Clean up toys, gather belongings, wash faces and hands.

5:00 Watch selected educational television program or read books.

5:30 Children are picked up by parent.

Day 25

9:30   STORYTIME

9:45   SONGS

ABC's
Count 1–20
"Good Morning to You"
(sung to the tune of
"Happy Birthday," naming
each child)
"Bumblebee"
"I've Been Working on the
Railroad"
"She'll Be Coming Around
the Mountain"

10:15   SNACKS

10:30   TABLE ACTIVITY

Pencil Holder
Save a small frozen juice can or a soup can. Make sure
there are no rough edges. Cover the can with construction
paper, wrapping paper, wallpaper, contact paper, and so
on. Use ribbon, trim, or bric-a-brac for decorating.

11:00   FREE PLAY

Cave
Make a cave for play using boxes.

11:30   RECORD PLAYER OR GAME TIME

11:45   LUNCH

12:15   NAP OR QUIET TIME

2:30   K I D R O B I C S (physical exercise)
Bend, stretch, jump, crawl, run in place, shrink small, hop
on one leg, tiptoe, and so on.

2:45   A F T E R N O O N   S N A C K

3:00   C R E A T I V E   A C T I V I T Y

Milk Carton Porcupine
Lay carton on its side. Draw a mouth and one eye (profile)
at the printed part of the carton. Punch holes in the container and insert drinking straws which the children can
cut in half.

3:30   C I R C L E   T I M E
Name things that are pink.
Name things that are sad.

3:45   O U T D O O R   F R E E   P L A Y   O R   I N D O O R
F R E E   P L A Y

4:45   Clean up toys, gather belongings, wash faces and hands.

5:00   Watch selected educational television program or read
books.

5:30   Children are picked up by parent.

CRAFT
RECIPES

Most children love arts and crafts, not only because it gives them the chance to be creative, but because they enjoy messy activities. Since many parents do not welcome projects that drip, smear, and spill in their own homes, I like to have "Messy Day" once a week in my home. The parents know that their children should wear old clothes or bring a smock that day because they will be making clay, paint, and papier-mâché.

Although the substances described in this chapter can be purchased, I believe that youngsters can learn a great deal when an adult spends time showing them how to measure, pour, and mix different ingredients. This can be a fun and effective way to teach numbers, measurements, and other concepts to children.

Here are a few rules of thumb to keep in mind:

- Decide how many children can participate at one time without causing chaos, and divide the children into two groups if necessary. You may want to supervise the project yourself while another adult keeps the rest of the children occupied.

- Have all supplies on hand so you don't have to leave the children unattended for even a minute.
- When using glue, put only a small amount on a jar lid or a small piece of cardboard. Teach the children that a small dab will do the job.
- Use newspaper, linoleum, brown paper, or old tablecloths to protect your work area.

Parents will appreciate it when their children do not come home with their good clothes stained with paint and food coloring. When I first began working with children, I didn't know that food coloring permanently stains clothes. I knew I had made a serious mistake when a little boy greeted his mother with green food coloring spattered all over his new outfit, and she turned to me with a look of horror.

To guard against stains, use old aprons or make your own apron by draping two towels over a child's shoulders so that one towel covers his front and one hangs over his back. (Use diaper pins to join the towels). Or how about one of dad's old work shirts? Simply cut the sleeves to the proper length.

Warning: Although some of the recipes which follow may look "tasty" to children, none of them are meant to be eaten. Stress this before you begin any activity. One time while my group of children was painting, we used a blue drinking cup filled with water to wash out our paintbrushes. One boy saw the blue cup and took a big gulp of water mixed with paint. Luckily, he was fine but that taught me a lesson. Designate a special container for rinsing paint brushes that is clearly separate from your drinking cups.

M O D E L I N G   C L A Y

Ingredients:

2¼ cups non-self-rising
   wheat flour
1 tablespoon powdered alum
   (available at a pharmacy)

1 cup salt
4 tablespoons vegetable oil
1½ cups boiling water
food coloring

What to do:

1. Mix flour, alum and salt.
2. Add vegetable oil.
3. Add boiling water. Stir vigorously with a big spoon until mixture sticks together.
4. Children can knead the dough until smooth.
5. Divide the dough into several piles.
6. Add a few drops of food coloring to each pile.
7. Store in airtight containers.

FINGERPAINT #1

Ingredients:

½ cup cornstarch
¾ cup of water
1 envelope unflavored gelatin
¼ cup cold water

2 cups boiling water
small jars with screw tops
food coloring

What to do:

1. Combine cornstarch with ¾ cup of water to form a smooth paste in a saucepan.
2. Put gelatin in a separate pan in ¼ cup of cold water. Put aside until ready to use.
3. Pour boiling water slowly into the cornstarch mixture, stirring as you pour.
4. Cook over medium heat, stirring constantly until mixture boils and is clear.
5. Remove from heat. Mix in the gelatin mixture.
6. Cool and put into different jars for different colors. Stir food coloring into each jar until well blended.
7. Use medicine droppers, sponges, cotton swabs, toothbrushes, string, orange halves, evergreen branches, straws, potato halves, or apple halves as "brushes."
8. Use old newspaper, paper bags or shelf paper to paint on! To make cleanup easier, you could put a plastic bag in the

jar and secure with a rubber band. After use, bags can simply be thrown away.

FINGERPAINT #2

Ingredients:

½ cup flour
2 cups water

1 tablespoon glycerine
food coloring

What to do:

1. Mix flour with a *little* water to form a thick paste.
2. Add remaining water.
3. Cook over low heat and stir constantly until mixture is thick and clear.
4. When cool, add glycerine.
5. Put in separate muffin tins and add food coloring.

CRYSTALS

Ingredients:

1 cup epsom salts
1 cup boiling water

What to do:

1. Mix an equal amount of epsom salts and boiling water.
2. Let cool.
3. Paint a picture with this solution.
4. When water dries, crystals will sparkle on your artwork.

PAPIER-MÂCHÉ

Ingredients:

newspaper
hot water

*wheat paste (can be
    purchased at wallpaper or
    paint store)*

What to do:

1. Rip newspaper into tiny pieces.
2. Add hot water so paper is completely wet.
3. Squeeze out excess water.
4. Add wheat paste to the mixture until it has the consistency of clay.
5. Form into desired shape.
6. Poke a hole in the bottom to speed up drying process.
7. Put aside to harden.

FUN DOUGH

Ingredients:

3 cups flour
1 cup salt
water to mix in dough

1 teaspoon cooking oil
food coloring

Combine all ingredients. Knead to smooth consistency. Add food coloring. Store in refrigerator.

You can also leave the food coloring out and just let the children play with the dough. They can make an animal out of it and let it harden. When it is hard, they can color it with markers or they can paint it. Fun dough can be hardened by putting it on a windowsill overnight or by placing the object in the oven at 225 degrees F. (Bake until hard: 15–60 minutes). After the paint is dry, you can protect the object by coating it with two or three layers of clear nail polish.

DOUGH SCULPTURE

Ingredients:

4 cups flour   *shellac*
1 cup salt

What to do:

1. Preheat oven to 350 degrees F.
2. Mix flour with salt.
3. Add water until it forms a ball that holds its shape and doesn't crumble.
3. Create a shape out of the dough.
4. Bake for approximately two hours.
5. Let it cool.
6. Coat it with shellac so it will last a long time.

SILKY FUN DOUGH

Ingredients:

1 cup salt   *2 cups soap flakes (not*
2 cups flour   *powder)*
1 cup water

What to do:

1. Combine all ingredients.
2. Use rolling pin and cookie cutters to create shapes.
3. Store in airtight plastic bag for repeated use.

PAPER PASTE

Ingredients:

⅓ cup non-self-rising wheat
flour
2 tablespoons sugar

1 cup water
¼ teaspoon oil of peppermint

What to do:

1. Mix flour and sugar together.
2. Gradually add water, stirring rapidly to prevent lumps.
3. Cook over low heat until clear, stirring constantly.
4. Remove from stove.
5. Add oil of peppermint.
6. Stir until well blended.

CREPE PAPIER-MÂCHÉ

Ingredients:

tiny pieces of crepe paper
water
plastic tablecloth to use in
work area

1 cup flour
1 teaspoon salt

What to do:

1. Tear crepe paper into tiny pieces. Put the ripped pieces in a bowl.
2. Add just enough water to cover paper and soak until soft (about 15 minutes).
3. Drain off excess water.
4. Mix the flour and salt together.
5. Add the flour and salt mixture to crepe paper to make a stiff dough.
6. Knead it until it is all blended together.

7. Sculpt animals, ashtrays, candy dishes, birds, or whatever you can imagine. It will dry to a hard finish.

C O R N S T A R C H P A I N T

Ingredients:

3 tablespoons cornstarch
2 cups water

1 tablespoon glycerine
food coloring

What to do:

1. Mix cornstarch with small amount of water.
2. Stir to form smooth paste.
3. Add remaining water.
4. Cook over low heat and stir constantly until boiling point.
5. Let cool and add glycerine.
6. Add food coloring.

T E M P E R A P A I N T

Ingredients:

powdered tempera paint
  (from artist supply store)
water

large sheet of paper
cardboard tube from paper
  towel roll

What to do:

1. Buy powdered paint at the store.
2. Mix powder and water in a shallow baking pan.
3. Roll the towel roll in pan and then let it roll across a large piece of newspaper. You could also dip the open end of roll in paint and press to make circles all over the paper.
4. You could also mix the paints in empty small juice cans.

Put six cans in a soft drink carton. Then you can easily carry the paints to the project table.

SOAP BUBBLES

Ingredients:

¼ cup Ivory detergent
½ cup water

1 teaspoon sugar
a few drops of food coloring

What to do:

1. Mix all ingredients.
2. Bend a piece of thin wire or a piece of a hanger to form the wand to blow bubbles.

SOAP POWDER CLAY

Ingredients:

1½ cups soap powder
2 tablespoons warm water

What to do:

1. Mix soap powder and water in mixing bowl.
2. Beat with electric mixer until thick. It should look like clay.
3. Shape as desired and allow to dry.

COOKIE CUTTER CLAY

Ingredients:

1 cup salt
4 cups flour

1½ cups warm water

What to do:

1. Preheat oven to 275 degrees F.
2. Dissolve salt in warm water.
3. Add flour and mix.
4. Knead for five minutes.
5. Shape as desired or roll out like pastry.
6. Cut out with floured cookie cutters.
7. Bake for one hour on greased cookie sheet.
8. Paint or shellac when cool and hard.

HOW TO REMOVE STAINS

Even when you do your best to keep spills to a minimum, accidents do happen. These hints may help you remove some "not-so-smart art" and other stubborn stains.

Crayon on walls. Use Formby (blue liquid) furniture cleaner to remove crayon "art" from walls or scrub the crayon smears lightly with a *dry* soap-filled steel wool pad, or scrub gently with baking soda sprinkled on a damp cloth.

Magic Marker on rugs. Try "Scuttle," a spray and wash product manufactured by Kirby.

Chewing gum or candlewax. Try a dry cleaning solvent such as Energine or Carbona (available at hardware stores). If the candlewax has hardened, use a warm iron covered with wax paper. Place an absorbent towel over the wax which will soak up the melted wax.

Food coloring or soft drink stains. Use 1 tablespoon of ammonia diluted in ½ cup water.

Blood. Soak garment in cold water for thirty minutes, apply straight ammonia, and rinse.

Grass. Sponge with dry cleaning solvent. Soak in a solution of 1 quart warm water, 1 teaspoon laundry detergent, and 1 tablespoon white vinegar for fifteen minutes. Then rinse and launder.

Clay in hair. Wait until the clay has hardened at which point it can be removed easily because it will crumble in your hands.

PLAY AND
LEARN
ACTIVITIES

Everyday Opportunities
to Learn

It is important to your self-esteem as a day care provider to feel that you are helping the children to get off to a good start in life. As a caregiver and mother who cares for eleven children in my home, I know you must be resourceful when trying to keep everyone creatively entertained and safe. There are days when one activity just doesn't seem to keep the children's interest, so I have to be flexible and quickly shift to something else. My goal is to help children feel good about themselves and be happy.

At the same time, I want to teach children skills which will help them to excel in their later life. All children have a talent that is just waiting to be discovered. By praising a child's drawing, painting, singing, or ability to catch a ball, you are instilling confidence that will lead to a lifelong sense of self-esteem. In our family, my parents encouraged each of their five children to excel in one particular area. We did not feel competitive toward each other because we each had our own "claim to fame" in the family hierarchy. When you did not make the basketball team or secure a part in the school play, a little voice cushioned the disappointment and said, "But at least I know that I am really good in spelling or swimming." As you enjoy the time that you spend with each child, look for a special interest and try to develop it by saying, "Wow, Katelyn, you are really an artist," or "Gee, Robin, you are such a fast runner—swift like a deer."

Some people are under the impression that children need expensive toys and state-of-the-art technology to learn. My husband wanted to buy Robin and Katelyn some computer programs for Christmas. Although that may be an excellent way to learn, I lean toward gaining competency by engaging in normal play activities. Problem-solving skills are learned by simple activities such as building a bridge with blocks or trying to determine how to organize plastic animals according to length, width, or height.

Children learn responsibility when they are taught to put all of the toys back on the proper shelves. They understand that the pieces will not get lost and they will be accessible the next time. Children create little challenges for themselves as they throw a ball, chase each other around the yard, or draw a picture. You do not need to teach in a structured way. Allow the children to follow their natural inclinations.

I recently observed a four-year-old cousin playing a video game with his friend. Over and over again, David and Josh made the little man on the screen dive into the water. They were laughing and playing and developing their problem-solving skills. A neighbor asked, "Why do you keep doing the same thing over and over?" Obviously this person did not understand that preschoolers benefit from repetition and that a child's future learning is based on this sort of competency.

My ideas are not meant to be academic in the true sense of the word, but I believe that skills, lessons, and concepts are learned as children identify common household objects, learn by touching and discern complicated concepts by playing with plastic clay, matching shapes, measuring long and short objects, and in general playing full time.

Children can learn all the math and reading readiness skills by sharing time with you as they play with shapes, make a calendar, talk about the weather, construct easy arts and crafts projects and enjoy your attention and affection.

Explain to the parents that children are learning in a very natural way. You can help children learn by incorporating descriptive words into your daily conversation.

Colors

Noah, would you like a *green* cup?

I am pouring juice from a *red* and *yellow* pitcher.

Let's look for *green* and *brown* leaves.

Shapes

Who would like a *round* cookie?

The brownies are cut into *squares*.

Would you like me to cut your sandwich into two *triangles?*

Counting

Let's count the steps as we walk up and down.

How many flowers are growing in this row?

Let's count the panes of glass on the window.

Recognizing Letters

When you write a child's name on his worksheet or artwork, pronounce each letter as you write it. The other children will listen as you say, "I am going to write Eric's name on his paper: E-R-I-C."

Combining Concepts

Mandy, would you like *two white* marshmallows?

The primary purpose of play and learn activities is to have fun. You must be patient and relaxed when working with children. Do not allow yourself to be distracted by the phone ringing or friends dropping by to chat when you are working on an art activity or organizing games. The children's attention span is very short and when they have to wait for glue or paint, they may lose interest altogether.

Keep one golden rule in mind when enjoying these activities. There should be lots of flexibility with the rules, and plenty of room for creative expression when making the crafts. Every child's artwork should be considered a masterpiece. Praise each work of art. When playing games, it is very hard to be eliminated from a game and be told that you are "out." Find ways to make each child feel like a winner by commenting on how fast they run, how well they can catch, or how clever they are. Also be careful about choosing teams when playing a competitive game. You probably can remember a time when you were young and were not selected when choosing sides and how hurt you felt.

On the pages that follow, you will find lots of ways to instill a love of learning through indoor and outdoor activities, no-cook baking ideas, and grab bag delights that show you how to further enjoy your time together.

Mix and match the activities, and you can be assured that your little ones will be ready to start any school experience with confidence and competence.

Supplies from Your Community

When I first began caring for children in my home, I spent a fortune purchasing supplies. I have since learned that most of the companies in my neighborhood have great "junk" (surplus materials) and they are happy to share it with you. Simply walk down a busy commercial street in your area and visit your local merchants. Tell them you care for children in your home and are looking for supplies that they might be planning to discard. These surplus materials are perfectly suited for making arts and crafts and outdoor play equipment.

One recent evening, I went to my local office supply store to buy easel paper. I was shocked at how expensive it was. As I left without purchasing the paper, I noticed a computer shop. I

walked in and explained to the man that I needed blank paper
to teach an alphabet lesson to some youngsters. He was more
than happy to give me a hundred sheets of computer printout
paper that had been used on only one side. This was a great
"freebie." Then I noticed a wallpaper store, and I explained the
same problem to the salesperson. She had ten discontinued wallpaper books in the back storeroom which they had planned to
throw away. I assured her that the children of Miss Trisha's play
group would enjoy cutting and pasting the colorful pages.

My favorite sources of free supplies are the retail stores, video
shops, supermarkets, and shopping centers. As I walk around,
my eyes are always peeled for the holiday decorations that most
merchants discard after each season. For example, I approach
the managers of greeting card stores and ask them what they
plan to do with the Valentine displays after February 14. Most
people say that they toss them because the franchiser supplies
them with new decorations annually. If any store owners are
planning to discard them, I ask if they would save them for me
and I will pick them up after the holiday. Their holiday decorations are great for bulletin boards. Video stores have given me
Walt Disney-type posters to decorate the walls of our playroom.
Our supermarket recently had a frozen food promotion. I noted
that they had three-foot-high displays of black and white pen-
guins cut out of Styrofoam. The manager did not plan to save
them so we put them to good use. (Did you ever play Pin the
Nose on the Penguin?)

There are also many good books which introduce numerical
and reading concepts. In an educational supply store you can
buy the reproducible pages and copy them for all the children.

The following is a list of some locations where I have obtained
free arts and crafts supplies.

Paint Store—sample paint charts

Cut up the sample charts into individual squares. Make a sort of
matching game. "Who has a green square like me?" "Try to put
your square in the same order as mine: a green square, pink
square, two yellow squares . . ."

Lumberyard—scraps of wood (pine is preferable), pieces of lumber

Building blocks can be made from all the different shapes and sizes of wood found at a lumberyard or construction site. Sand the edges so the children don't get splinters. Be sure that the wood has not been chemically treated in case a small child puts it in his mouth.

Carpet Store—floor samples

Carpet squares are great for a game of Musical Rug derived from the traditional game of Musical Chairs. When the music stops, remove one carpet sample. Use the squares for story time. Each child has his favorite rug.

Fabric Store—spools, scraps, eyelets, ribbons, buttons

All of these items are used for collages or to enhance an art project.

Tobacco Shop—cigar boxes

Use boxes to store small toys or as art boxes for individual children which contain scissors, glue, and crayons. The boxes can also be used to make jewelry boxes.

Printer—all sizes, shapes, and textures of paper

Printers have lots of scrap paper which remain after they have cut larger pieces of paper and cardboard. Sometimes they make an error and have to throw away large quantities of colored paper, carbon paper, labels, and envelopes. All of this paper can be used to make great art projects.

Garment Factory—pieces of fabric

Fabric is used for collages. Cut the materials into small pieces. Large sections are used in our dress-up corner as a king's cloak or a bride's veil.

Label Factory—stickers

Adhesive label manufacturers often have stickers and mailing labels that are slightly flawed and thus unacceptable to their customers. Their error in production is definitely our gain because kids love the stickers that manufacturers are pleased to give away.

Furniture, Appliance Store, Moving Companies—large boxes

Large boxes are used for caves, forts, tunnels, garages for riding toys, and pretend tables for an afternoon tea party. Be sure to remove any copper staples that may be in the boxes. Paint them, color them, wallpaper them!

Farm Store—ice cream cartons

Ice cream stores have large containers which are used for storing small toys and baby supplies such as ointments, powders, and pins.

Computer Centers—printout paper

Computer paper is great for art projects. It can also be used to provide a clean pad for diapering a baby.

Cabinetmakers—wooden color samples

All of those wonderful wood samples can be used for counting and matching games. The varied grains teach children about differences in colors and textures.

Medical Suppliers, Clinics, Drugstores—tongue depressors and Styrofoam

These items are great for details on 3-D pictures. Cut out a cat from a heavy piece of cardboard and tape a tongue depressor to the back of it. It becomes a puppet.

Post office—end sheets of stamps.

Color the zip code man. Design a stamp on the blank squares.

Newspaper—end rolls

Newspapers have paper that remains after a production run. Since it is not an adequate quantity to use the next day, many publishers are glad to give excess paper away. End rolls can be used as a table cover, a wall mural project, or placed on the floor for body tracings.

Bar or Restaurant—wine corks

Wine corks are fun for general art projects or for demonstrating items that float in a pail of water.

Airlines—plastic eating supplies

Plastic cups, sugars, salt, silverware, and plates have all been donated by airline carriers. The little ones love to pretend to buckle up their seat belts and fly away as they are served by their friends.

Architectural Firm—drafting paper

Drafting paper has small squares. Children enjoy coloring in the squares with colored pencils or pens.

Billboard Companies, Bottling Companies, Container Companies—sheets of colored paper, bottle caps, large sheets of cardboard

All of these items are used for art projects.

Contractors—building scraps, linoleum pieces

By laying linoleum on the floor with a plastic tool kit, children can remodel an existing fort or construct something new.

Power Companies—telephone poles, spools

Telephone and electrical wire are supplied on large wooden spools. We used these spools for tables and also as a backyard climbing activity. Telephone poles placed on a slight angle and securely anchored can be used as a tightrope for future gymnasts.

Candy Manufacturers—cans and boxes

Cans and boxes can be decorated for pencil holders.

Gift Shop—Styrofoam packing pieces

With a dark-colored marker, the child first prints his name on a piece of cardboard. Styrofoam packing pieces are glued to the surface to spell the child's name.

Fast-Food Outlets—plates, napkins, empty sour cream containers, margarine containers, egg cartons

Since fast-food restaurants serve large numbers each day, they buy in bulk. I have asked them for egg cartons which are constructed to contain thirty-six eggs rather than twelve, and we use them for sorting games such as separating colored dry cereal or multicolored pasta noodles. The sour cream container and margarine tubs are huge and great for mixing paint and for storage of craft recipes. Since the plastic lids fit securely, the plastic clay and modeling clay retain their freshness.

Tire Store—truck or tractor tires

At a truck tire outlet, the owner was thrilled to give me an unlimited number of tractor tires because usually they have to pay someone to haul them away. When placed on the ground in your backyard, the possibilities for uses is limited only by the children's imagination. One day the tires are a boat and the next day a train. If you decide to use a tire as a sandbox, be sure to poke holes in the interior rim of the tire so that water drains after a heavy rain.

Parents Can Help Save Too

"One man's junk is another man's treasure." No truer words were ever spoken, especially with children. The odd items we throw away without thought can provide pleasurable hours of activities for children. Ask parents to keep a box or bag in a cabinet. Their children will be thrilled to issue reminders to save paper towel rolls and margarine containers. One important aspect of day care is to have the children and parents share an experience and this is a perfect way to do it. But I want to warn you that it won't be long before you'll have more than ample supplies. Parents mention to grandparents and friends that Lauren needs margarine containers or brown paper bags and before you know it, you'll have more than enough.

Here's a list of items parents can save and bring to your home. You are sure to think of other items you can use.

Margarine containers
Plastic lids of all sizes
Empty oatmeal
   containers
Old magazines and
   catalogs
Baby food jars
Egg cartons
Shirt cardboards
Lightweight cardboard
   of any kind
Paper rolls from paper
   towels, foil, plastic
   wrap
Toilet paper rolls
Junk mail
Pipe cleaners
Brown paper bags
Tin cans with plastic lids
Frozen juice cans
Clean old clothes

Shoe boxes
Long shoelaces
Heavy string
Half-gallon milk
   containers
Paper plates
Old calendars
Construction paper
Old greeting cards and
   wrapping paper scraps
Ribbon, yarn
Old toothbrushes
Pine cones
Foil
Large paintbrushes
Old tractor tire
Masking tape
Corn kernels
Hard white beans
Deck of cards (full or
   partial)

Used paper cups	Ping-Pong balls
Clothespins	Fabric scraps
Straws	Cotton balls
Large boxes	

Indoor Activities

You can never have too many good ideas. Use these suggestions to keep the children creatively entertained while educating them too.

Pasting, Pouring, Punching, and Painting

Indoor Sandbox

Partially fill a baking pan or a gift box with salt. Children can bring their own little cars or plastic animals to play with in the "indoor sand."

Hole Puncher Activities

Let the children punch holes in junk mail, scrap paper, or wallpaper. Punch the holes while working over a newspaper so that your cleanup task is easy.

Indoor Wading Pool

Place a child's pool on a plastic tablecloth on your kitchen floor. The pool is used to blow bubbles, float objects, and to experience water play using strainers, dippers, plastic containers, and other kitchen toys. (This is an activity that must be supervised at all times.)

Picture Puzzles

Paste brightly colored magazine pictures to a piece of shirt cardboard. Draw puzzle lines on the back of the cardboard and cut out. The number of puzzle pieces should be determined by the ability and age of the child.

Toothpick Designs

Children who can handle sharp objects safely can glue the fancy hors d'oeuvres toothpicks to colored paper and make a design.

Soldier Doll Miniatures

Paint clothespins to look like soldier dolls or whatever else strikes your imagination. After making the face with magic marker, glue or paste bits of yarn on the head for hair.

Instrument Panel

Use a sturdy piece of corrugated cardboard and a variety of objects like spools, buttons, and pieces of foil to make an instrument panel in a plane, ship, or submarine. An old mirror could be pasted on too!

Potato Puppet

Draw a face on a piece of paper and glue it to the potato. Insert a popsicle stick in the potato to hold it up.

Sewing Cards

After the children have mastered the use of a hole puncher, you can make sewing cards. Punch many holes in very heavy paper or cardboard. The holes can form a simple design. Cut several long pieces of yarn or string. Wrap a piece of masking tape around the end of the yarn to form a point. The tape makes it easier for the child to thread the yarn through the holes.

Indoor Gardens

Milk Carton Garden

Let the child plant some flower, vegetable, or grass seeds in small pots or milk cartons (cut out the side of the cartons and partially fill with dirt). Dampen the soil. After planting, place in a well-lighted room. Talk about how seeds germinate and plants grow.

Growing Experiment

Each child needs a carrot and a container. Cut off the leaves. Cut about one inch from bottom of carrot (thick end). Put the little piece in the container with the thickest part down. Put small stones around it so that it doesn't fall. Add water halfway up the carrot and keep in the sunny part of the house. Children will enjoy watching the progress of its new growth.

Sponge Grass

Show the child how to grow grass indoors. Gather the following materials: a sponge, bowl, or deep dish; some grass seed; and a fork or little stick (popsicle stick). Follow the directions carefully: put the sponge in the bowl and fill about halfway up with water. Sprinkle with the grass seed, not too heavily. Put the seeds gently down into the sponge with the fork or stick so they are soaked with water but not under the water. Keep adding water to the dish (not pouring over the sponge) every day or two so that the sponge stays wet. Soon little sprouts will grow. After a few weeks, you'll have a tiny lawn you can trim with scissors.

Indoor Gardening

Cut a sweet potato in half lengthwise. Place in a bowl of water, open face down, and use toothpicks stuck around the potato to let it hang on the lip of the bowl. Keep it in a dark place until you start to see sprouts. Then take it out and put it on a windowsill where you can watch it grow. Water it so the bottom half of the sweet potato is covered all the time.

Paper Bags, Paper Plates, Paper Rolls

Binoculars

Tape two empty toilet paper rolls together—side by side. Use magic markers or crayons to decorate. Cover the open ends with colored cellophane.

Paper Plates

Give a child six paper plates with identical designs except for one plate. The child shows you the plate that is different. Ask about the colors on the plate. Count the plates. Ask the child to duplicate a pattern with his set of plates. This activity develops perception skills in young children.

Paper Bag Puppets

Stuff a brown lunch bag with crumpled newspaper. Glue yarn for hair, and paint the features on the face of the bag. Place a toilet paper roll into the open part of the bag as the neck. Tape it securely. Insert your fingers in the toilet paper roll so you can manipulate your puppet. You can kneel behind a chair so that the top of the chair is a stage for your puppet.

Paper Towel Tube Puppets

Glue a plain paper cup upside down on the tube. Provide yarn for hair and cut out eyes, nose, and mouth. Decorate the body of the tube with markers or crayons.

Paper Bag Butterflies

Place two child-size shoes on a paper bag spread out on the floor. Trace the shape with a magic marker or crayons. It will look like the wings of a butterfly. Add antennae and cut out. Color it in with brightly colored crayons.

Gift Ideas

Potholder Holder

Take two paper plates. Cut one in half. Staple one to the other so that there is a hollow space to put a potholder on the inside. Decorate the plates with cutouts or crayons. Poke a hole at the top and tie a piece of yarn on it so you can hang the holder up. You can also make paper plate pictures by coloring or painting a picture in the center. You could cut a picture from a magazine and glue it on. Hang with a piece of ribbon at the top of the plate.

Jewelry Boxes

Glue all sorts of odds and ends to the top of a cigar box. People will be glad to donate their Styrofoam packing pieces which look very nice. Adorn the box with pebbles, popcorn kernels, and pieces of fabric. On the inside, glue a piece of plain paper. Drop a marble in some paint, put it in the box and tape the lid tight. Shake the box and the marble will make an interesting design!

Wallpaper Books

Most wallpaper stores will save their outdated books and give them to you at no charge. Cut the pages of these books up and use for decorating many projects. Use these cutouts to decorate plain paper plates and white gift boxes.

Paper Clip Jewelry

Attach large paper clips end-to-end to make necklaces. I have done this activity with children over the age of four providing close supervision so they do not put the paper clips into their mouths.

Macaroni Jewelry

Mix 1 teaspoon of food coloring with ½ cup of water. Dip macaroni pieces in for about 30 seconds and lay them out to dry on paper towels. They will take a while to dry so you might want to do the coloring a day ahead of time and string them the next day. Put a piece of tape around one end of the string to make the point of the needle.

Blackboards

Take four popsicle sticks and a square of black construction paper. Glue the four sticks together like a picture frame and glue a piece of black paper to the back so that it fits perfectly. Tie a piece of yarn to the top of the frame so you can hang it up. Use a piece of white chalk to write a message on the pretend blackboard. The child can give it to his parents with the message "Be My Valentine."

Awareness of Shapes and Numbers

Colored Shapes Activity

Make cutouts of different shapes. Make several of the exact same shape and color by cutting through four pieces of paper at the same time. The adult can ask the children to sort by shape, color, and size. "What color is the circle?" "Put all green squares in the tray." "What else is shaped like a square?" This activity aids the children in making comparisons, in color recognition, and in classification.

Guess the Shape

Start with a box of different-shaped blocks. One child closes his eyes and picks a shape. He must guess which shape he is holding.

Changing Your Shape

Ask the children to try to change their own body shape so that they're shorter, taller, wider, thinner, bigger, or longer. They will usually listen intently and then follow your instructions.

Stickers

Buy some plastic ribbons like the type you see at Christmastime. Cut the ribbon into different shapes—circles, triangles, squares, or rectangles. Moisten the pieces. They will adhere to things like the door of your dryer, the front of the stove or windows, and sliding glass doors.

Hike Through the House

Emphasize a color and shape each day. Then take a walk through the house and look for things that are red or blue or shaped like a circle or square.

Milk Cartons

Use milk cartons for building blocks. Open the peak of the milk carton. Wash thoroughly. Close back up when dry. These can make great castles or igloos. What shape can you make from rectangular boxes?

Counting Objects

Place a number of crayons in several cups. Ask the children which cup holds the most crayons and which the least, and which cup is the heaviest and which is the lightest. Count the crayons in each cup. Ask about the colors of the cup and crayons. This activity helps in associating numerals with a number of objects.

Counting Exercise

Place ten plastic cups upside down on the floor (in a row). Use a spoon to tap on the bottom of each cup. As you tap each cup, count. This is the way that children learn one-to-one correspondence. It is good counting practice to say each number as you march ten steps or clap your hands ten times. Don't forget to count your fingers and toes at least once a day. Count the chairs at the table before you sit down for snacks and lunch. Count the numbers on the kitchen clock.

Talk About a Calendar

Show the children you are placing a star on the dates that mark their birthday, Christmas, Easter, and other special days. Each day count aloud the number of days that are left in the month. Each day make a game of counting the days of the week.

Learning About Coins

Learn about textures (rough edges, colors, sizes). The exercise also introduces the names of unusual colors like copper and silver and different sizes.

Deck of Cards

Give children a deck of playing cards and ask them to sort the cards by numbers, colors, and suits.

All About Animals

Walk Like an Animal

This game is another version of Simon Says. One child is the leader. He gives commands such as "the rabbit hops" or "the cow moos." The children follow the commands, unless the leader says something silly like "the duck meows." Then they do not imitate him or his animal sound. Any child who does, sits out for one round.

Noah's Ark

Take a shoe box or a wax milk carton. Use a straw for the mast and cut out portholes on the side. Cut a triangular sail. Use plastic animals or animal crackers to decorate. Another idea is to cut out pictures of animals from magazines or catalogues.

Poor Little Puppy

Children are seated in a circle. One child is designated to be the puppy. He goes over to another child and the other child has to pet the puppy's head four times. If he laughs, then he becomes the new puppy. The object is to try not to laugh.

Mystery Pets

What animal likes carrots, celery, lettuce, likes to chew through wood, and runs on a wheel? This animal also bites when frightened and is small (hamster). What animal likes to drink milk or cream, sometimes sleeps in a basket, likes to chase a string, and may hook its claws in the sofa? (cat). Each child gets a turn to think of a mystery pet and give a few clues so the other children can guess.

Picnic with the Bears

Place a blanket on the floor. Pretend you are having a picnic. Place picnic-type items on the blanket (picnic basket, dishes, and napkins). The children close their eyes while you remove one item. You tell them a bear came into the forest and took something. The children have to figure out which item is missing.

Cotton Drawings

Paste cotton or yarn onto coloring book pages to trace the outline of an animal. If the picture is of a lamb, use cotton balls to create white woolly fur. If it is a picture of a dog, cut out bits of yarn to glue on as fur.

Barnyard Friends

Place toy animals in a box. The children take turns lining them up on the floor in order of their size. This activity reinforces the skills of selection, classification, and series of objects.

Fun with Water

Bathtub Finger Painting

Use washable finger paints and let the children paint in an empty bathtub. You can also buy special bathtub crayons.

Floating Sailboat

Cut a triangular sail from construction paper. Tape the sail to a toothpick and insert into a bar of soap that will float.

Water Play

Put water in a tub, bucket, sink, or bathtub. Give the children plastic toys, soap bubbles, and funnels to play with. Never leave the children unattended.

Practice in Pouring

Fill a measuring cup with rice or water. Demonstrate how to pour from one measuring cup to another. Let each child try to pour without spilling.

Washing a Table, Kitchen Chair, or Cabinet

Fill a bucket with water and a rag or sponge. Show the children how to squeeze really hard before beginning to wipe a surface. After one child cleans, teach another child how to dry the surface with a towel.

Bubbles

Bubbles are easy to make and it's much more fun than buying them. Let each child use a shallow baking pan, and add some liquid dish detergent to a pan and some water. Each child has his own individual pan and straw. If he blows gently into the pan, he will create a bubble sculpture. The ratio is ½ cup of detergent to 1 quart of water.

All About Me

Maps of the Neighborhood

You will need a large piece of paper and crayons. Start by drawing your house and street. Then add the other important places like a friend's house, park, school, and store.

Body Portraits

The child lies down on a large piece of wrapping paper or paper bags taped together. Trace the outline of his body. The child can either draw his features or can tape some old clothes on the picture. Hang up the picture so everybody can admire it.

Show and Tell

Ask the children to bring something special from home. They'll enjoy telling the others about it and passing it around.

Name Cards for Each Child

Print the child's name on heavy paper. Each day, make a game out of holding up the name and as a group pronouncing each letter. You will be surprised at how quickly the children will learn to recognize their own names as well as the others.

Learning About Child's Favorites

Encourage the children to verbalize their feelings and communicate to them that what they have to say is important. "If you could have any toy in the world, what would it be?" "What pet or animal would you like to take care of and why?" "Do you like the garden?" "Who is your favorite cartoon character?" "What is your favorite color?"

Surprise Letter

A child dictates a letter so you can print it. The child then decorates the letter, puts it in an envelope, and mails it to his home address. It is a great surprise for his parents.

Family Trees

Use old photographs and a large sheet of paper. The child is the focus of the tree. Talk about how each child is related to the other people in the tree and point out how the children look similar or different from their relatives.

Dressing Skills

On a rainy day, teach the children about their clothing and how things work, like a zipper, shoelaces, or buckles. Show them how to put on boots and put on gloves.

No-Cook Baking Ideas

Children enjoy learning to cook. Since I want to keep things as simple as possible when caring for children in a group setting, I have included some easy to make no-cook baking ideas. The recipes require adult supervision but are intended for the children to make. You can use this opportunity to discuss nutritious foods and begin to teach concepts about numbers and measuring. As you prepare these snacks, talk about what you are doing. This is a good chance to reinforce sequence skills, such as what comes first, next . . . , watching the clock to tell time, and stressing the importance of following directions exactly.

An important part of this activity is allowing the children to help you clean up. No-bake cooking time is also a way to involve parents. In advance, ask parents if they would like to help make special recipes. You could sign one mother or father up each month if you decide to do a special activity on the first Friday of each month.

As a preparatory activity, you could show the different sizes of measuring spoons, several size measuring cups, and bowls. Let the children pretend that they are mixing pancakes in a mixing bowl. Be sure to give each child his own job, such as mixing, spreading, shaking, serving, or pouring.

Peanut Butter "Play Dough"

Mix:
   1 cup peanut butter
   1 tablespoon honey
   1 cup dry powdered milk
Knead "dough."
Cut into shapes with cookie cutters.
Decorate with raisins.

Healthy Snack

In a container, mix dry cereal with the following ingredients:
  1 cup coconut
  1 cup raisins
  1 cup peanuts
  Sprinkle of wheat germ
  1 cup of miniature marshmallows
Shake it up and enjoy as a healthy snack.

Crunchy Balls

Mash 1 cup peanut butter and 1 stick soft butter.
Mix in:
  2 cups oatmeal
  1 cup chocolate chips
  1 cup raisins
  ½ teaspoon vanilla extract
Roll the mixture with clean fingers into balls.
Roll balls in shredded coconut.

Banana Treats

Mash 4 bananas until mushy.
Add:
  6 ounces cream cheese
  1 stick butter
Mix well.
Add:
  5 tablespoons cocoa
  2 cups finely chopped nuts
  1 cup coconut
  2 tablespoons maple syrup
  3 cups of your favorite rice cereal
Spread the mixture flat on two dinner-sized paper plates.
Place in the refrigerator for 1 hour.

Special Cookies

Buy a box of plain cookies, a can of vanilla frosting, and sprinkles
or chocolate drops. Give each child a small dish of icing, some

decorations, and a knife. Children love to decorate their own cookies.

Ginger Snap Cookies

Buy tube frosting and let the children decorate the cookies with their names, happy faces, or holiday designs.

Peanut Butter Treats

Mix:
    1 cup peanut butter
    1 cup powdered milk
Add:
    ½ cup honey
    ¼ cup toasted wheat germ
    Jelly
Flatten a spoonful of mixture on a cookie sheet for individual cookies.

Put a dollop of jelly in the center of each pancake-shaped cookie and roll up in a ball.

Chill for 1 hour.

Refrigerated Date-Nut Bars

Mix:
    1½ cups graham cracker crumbs
    ¼ teaspoon salt
    1 cup chopped dates
    1 cup chopped nuts
    1 cup very, very small marshmallow pieces
Pour slowly 1 cup of heavy cream into crumb mixture until moistened.

Refrigerate and after 1 hour cut into squares.

Banana Sandwich

Remove the crust from bread and cut into shapes with cookie cutters.

Have the children mix 3 ounces of very soft cream cheese with

1 tablespoon of jelly and 2 large tablespoons of very finely chopped nuts.

Spread this mixture on bread.

Slice a banana into thin slices and place on the mixture.

Coconut Balls

Beat a very soft 8-ounce package of cream cheese with 2½ cups of confectioner's sugar (powdered sugar).

Beat in:

¼ teaspoon vanilla

A dash of salt

A dab of food coloring

(Children take turns stirring and beating.)

Shape into balls.

Refrigerate for one hour, then roll balls in grated coconut.

Place coconut balls on waxed paper or cookie sheet.

Refrigerate for three hours, and enjoy!

Coconut Toast

Toast bread and butter it. While it is hot, sprinkle it with shredded coconut.

Cinnamon Toast

Toast bread and let the children spread softened butter on it. Then sprinkle with sugar and cinnamon.

Cocoa Toast

Mix cocoa powder, a pinch of cinnamon, and a drip of honey on a piece of warm toast.

Applesauce

Peel, seed, and core 6 large apples.

Cut the apples into very small pieces.

Put 3 of the apples into the blender with 1 tablespoon lemon juice, ¾ cup apple juice, and 1 teaspoon cinnamon.

Blend at highest speed until very smooth.

Add remaining apples and blend again.

Fruit Cubes

Have the children pour any kind of fruit juice into ice cube trays. Cut maraschino cherries, pineapples, and peaches and place in the trays. Freeze thoroughly and then add the fancy ice cubes to glasses of fruit juice.

Tropical Tantalizer

Mix:
   ½ gallon orange juice
   8 apples (chopped very small)
   4 thin lemon slices (no seeds)
   Chopped strawberries
   Pinch of sugar
Mix in blender with a few ice cubes.

Peanut Butter Milkshake

Mix in a blender:
   4 cups milk
   ⅔ cup peanut butter
   2 tablespoons molasses or honey
   ½ teaspoon cinnamon

Super Shake

Mix:
   Three jars of strained peach baby food
   3¾ cups cold water
   4½ tablespoons honey
Mix with a blender or shake in a container.
Add 1 cup of dry powdered milk and blend again.

Eggnog

Mix:
   3 eggs
   6 tablespoons honey
   ½ teaspoon vanilla extract
   A pinch of salt
   2 cups milk
Freeze for 15 minutes.

Blender Bliss

Mix:
   2 cups yogurt
   4 cups milk
   1 tablespoon molasses
   4 bananas broken into small pieces
Blend in blender.
Add 1 egg for a richer, more delicious flavor.

Yogurt Art

Empty a container of yogurt on a dinner plate. Give each child a spoon, sliced peaches, bits of pineapple, raisins, banana slices, or other pieces of fruit. Use a spoon to draw a face and then trim with the treats.

Listening Skills

Monkey See, Monkey Do

Make a circle with string. The children stand on the string. One child is in the middle. He is the monkey. He instructs the children to do something specific such as, "Jump two times." As they jump, they chant, "Monkey see, monkey do, monkey does the same as you!"

Following Directions

Have the children sit in a circle. Give directions to one child at a time while the others watch, for example "Knock on the door two times" or "Open the closet door." Depending on the age of the children involved, the directions may vary in complexity.

Nursery Rhymes

Read a nursery rhyme and let the children act out the story. Also read the rhyme leaving out a word. Let them guess what was left out.

  Little Miss Muffet
  Sat on a _____
  Eating her curds and _____.
  Along came a _____
  And sat down beside her,
  And frightened Miss Muffet away.

Reading Aloud

Even though I graduated with a teaching degree, I learned a very important lesson from my assistant who had more experience than I in reading to children. Maria's four children were grown and she helped me out as a substitute on an occasional basis. I noticed that when she read a story, she really seemed to have the children's rapt attention. They were engrossed in what she had to say because she read the story slowly, used expression, allowed plenty of time to see the pictures, and encouraged the children to participate by asking them questions about the characters.

Reading aloud to children on a daily basis is an important way to develop a healthy interest in books. Reading stories, poems, and fingerplays develops listening and speaking skills. These skills form the basis for beginning reading (see Appendix C for recommended books).

Here are some tips for reading to children. Read to a small group so you can seat the children comfortably around you. Be realistic about the expectations for the age group when you are reading a story. Select a time when you can read a story without being interrupted by the telephone ringing or babies babbling. Plan the story for a particular time each day such as right after lunch or mid-morning. Purchase or borrow durable books that are designed to withstand the handling and mishandling by small children.

I remember a valuable lesson on the subject of books that I learned when I began my program. I visited the library and was delighted when the librarian told me that I was permitted to check out twenty books. I chose books that had simple stories and bright colorful pictures. During the story time at my house, the children were allowed to read the special library books. The children were quiet and I felt that this daily activity was a great success. I returned the books within the two-week period and was shocked to receive a call from the children's librarian. She chastised me for the horrible condition of some of the returned books. I did not realize that the children had ripped pages and colored on the inside of each book. Remember, I did say they were unusually quiet during book time. Now I know why! They were completely engrossed in their own art projects. Needless to say, that led to a lesson in taking care of books and less independence when it came to reading stories.

An alternative to borrowing from the library is to trade with friends, relatives, and other day care providers. A lending library of this sort is of benefit to everyone because of the great variety of toys and games that each family is able to share.

Guests of Honor

There are so many important lessons and skills that the children will learn from the preceding indoor activities. To encourage interaction with day care children and other interesting people, you can invite parents, grandparents, and friends to share their unique knowledge and various hobbies with the children. Even the people in your local community we see every day could answer some of the children's questions, like the mailman who might show the children his mail pouch and show off his uniform. And how about the man who is trimming your trees with a big chain saw, or the lady who does alterations on your spring coat?

At a birthday party my neighbor was giving for her son, I saw a wonderful clown entertain the children. After the show, when I was talking with "Daisy The Dancing Clown," she mentioned that she had difficulty finding someone to watch her child while she was performing in people's homes. Instantly an idea popped into my mind. What about a trade? I offered to watch her child and she came in to surprise my day care children with wonderful tricks and games.

My father always fascinated our relatives with his magic tricks. He was called upon to perform his famous disappearing tricks. My mother is an artist and really enjoys those messy art projects. She visited on many occasions and painted the older children's faces with hearts and rainbow designs. My brother owns a farm. He brought a variety of eggs to show the children. When baby ducks or chicks were born, he stopped by to surprise us with a visit. One of the mothers of the children was a school bus driver. She stopped by on her way to pick up schoolchildren and let the kids examine a real school bus. Here are some other people you might meet in your area who could share their experiences with your children.

Gardener

If you know someone who has a vegetable garden, invite him or her to tell the children when to plant, and how gardens grow.

Florist

Invite a florist to come and demonstrate how to make a floral arrangement. Encourage discussion on when and why people send flowers and where to buy supplies.

Nurse/Doctor

Children are fascinated by instruments, charts, and machines in a doctor's office. A nurse or doctor can explain the tools of the trade and discuss the reasons he or she selected the profession.

Fire Fighter

A community fire fighter can relate incidents about real life situations in which a fire could have been prevented. This is a good opportunity to practice a fire drill, test smoke alarms, demonstrate the use of fire extinguishers, and explain the purpose of fire hydrants and the fire alarm bell. A discussion of safety practices is also appropriate.

Seamstress

The children can find out how clothing is made by hand or learn how a sewing machine works. They can learn how to sew a large button with only two eyes in it on a piece of material.

Farmer

Ask the farmer to explain how he or she plants, harvests, and sells goods. What about milking machines? How much does a cow eat? A discussion of daily chores would be of interest to school-age children.

Ambulance Paramedic

The paramedic is often a volunteer who would welcome the chance to talk to children about safety in the home and on the playground. The children could even be taught basic first aid and what to do in an emergency.

Crossing Guard or Traffic Policeman

The policeman can explain the movements of his or her hands and arms to protect children crossing or directing traffic at a busy intersection. He or she can also talk about the uniform and training.

Computer Operator

The computer enthusiast could be a high school student, perhaps the older brother or sister of one of the children in your care, or anyone who enjoys working with computers. No doubt he or she could learn something from one of the prodigies in your care.

Gas Station Attendant

The visitor could answer questions like the following: How do you pump air in a bicycle tire, car tire, or truck tire? Is it fun to pump gas? What about self-service? What other services does your station perform?

Greenhouse Owner

Children could pose questions like these: How can you grow beautiful flowers even when it's cold outside? When do you do it? What do you do with all of the plants?

Mail Carrier

With the mail carrier, children can hear about stamps, packages, and mailing letters across town and around the world. What happens to undeliverable mail and packages?

Carpenter

A few screws, hammer, and simple tools can provide a learning experience for school-age children who visit a carpenter. Talk about what carpenters fix and construct.

Camper (Eagle Scout, Girl Scout Leader)

Children can ask questions like these: How do you cook? Where do you sleep? What animals did you see? Where did you go? How do you build a campfire?

Acrobats/Cheerleaders/Musicians

Invite high school or college students who would like to show a few of the basics in tumbling, dancing, singing, or playing a musical instrument. How do you learn these tricks? How long do you practice each day?

Special Needs Teacher

Children must learn to accept all types of people. A teacher from a school for visually handicapped or hearing impaired could show the children how other students learn despite certain limitations.

Holiday Surprise

Around Christmas, Mary's father made a surprise visit as Santa Claus. The children had prepared a special treat because we told them we were going to have a surprise guest. The Halloween witch or the Easter bunny could pay a visit to your house too.

Tapping Community Resources

As you explore community resources, you will undoubtedly learn of exciting programs available to you and the children. I joined the local Chamber of Commerce because I felt their members needed to know that child care providers are more than just neighborhood baby-sitters. I hope that message was conveyed, but in the process I also learned of merchants in the area who were willing to allow children to visit their businesses.

I also found out about civic projects that appeal to children, such as a Halloween Safety Coloring Kit. Another social group's project provided materials that warned children about accidental poisoning. A call to a local hospital uncovered a free puppet show on the subject of nutrition. A very kind dentist invited us to her office, demonstrated the equipment, and gave each of the children a book of stickers about dental hygiene.

If there is a Head Start Program or any type of funded early childhood program nearby, it doesn't hurt to call them. Ask if it would be possible for the children you are caring for to participate in any of their activities. The old faithfuls are the local police and fire departments, who always seem to be willing to talk to children about a variety of safety issues. Perhaps a Girl Scout or Boy Scout troop in your area would be interested in helping you in some way. They are often trying to earn merit badges that require volunteer work. Senior citizens have a great deal to offer to children, and little children respond well to extra hugs and kisses. Perhaps a healthy, energetic senior citizen would like to work with you occasionally.

Outdoor Activities

Weather permitting, children need fresh air each day, even if it is for a very short period of time. Keep in mind that they should not play outside without supervision. If you take them for a neighborhood walk, you could tie scarves together to make a train. Children must hold on at all times—no matter how trustworthy you think they are. Fear of an approaching dog, a bumblebee, or seeing their parent's car may cause them to dart from the group.

Outdoor Fun

Plant a Garden

Everyone can help you plant some seeds for flowers or vegetables. Talk about the size and shapes of seeds or bulbs.

Sky Gazing

Bring a blanket outside. Children can look up at the fluffy clouds. What shapes and pictures do they see when they look at them?

Collecting on a Nature Walk

Bring a paper bag so that the group can collect feathers, interesting rocks, leaves, pine cones, and pebbles. When you return inside, these items can be used as part of a show and tell exhibit and displayed in muffin tins or egg cartons. Children can write or draw by putting tiny pebbles next to each other to make a numeral or a house.

Walk Around the Neighborhood

As you walk outside, tell the children to listen carefully and try to hear the sounds of construction workers hammering, birds singing, people talking, and cars, trucks, motorcycles, and airplanes.

Jump in the Leaves or Roll Down a Grassy Hill

Follow the Leader

The leader jumps, hops, takes giant steps, or skips while the others follow. Let the children take turns being the leader.

Rock Collection

Collect stones of various sizes. Rock animals can be made from rocks, glue, cotton, and construction paper. Make a bunny rock with a cotton tail, or a cat rock with a nose and whiskers.

Hide and Seek

One person covers his eyes and counts to twenty. The others hide in one place *as a group*. This allows you to supervise everyone. The person who is "it" tries to find the group.

Obstacle Course

The children will enjoy going under a picnic table, through some open boxes, around the bike, and tiptoeing around the garden.

There are probably so many places right in your community that would be a learning experience for your children. Going on a walk through the park or to your neighbor's backyard to look at her garden will give you plenty of opportunities to ask the children questions about animals, gardens, or the weather. Teach the children to notice the small details of a bush, or the sounds of the birds, or a worm crawling in the ground. Besides being enjoyable, these activities are ways to sharpen the children's senses and for them to learn about seeing the minutest detail that makes up their environment.

Even though the outdoor activities are exciting for preschoolers, occasionally you may want to really give the children a treat by taking them on a fun-filled adventure away from your home. Here are some answers to questions that will help you organize a more extensive learning experience with the children.

Field Trips

My recommendation is to ensure that the children in your care are as safe as possible. It is not wise to risk any type of accident. Check with your insurance agent to see if you and your assistant are covered for field trips and transporting children. If you are adequately insured, you may wish to plan outings that are appropriate for the age of children in your care (zoo, bakery, veterinarian, playground, movie, dairy farm, local parks, and wildlife sanctuary). Do not tell the children too far in advance that you are going on a trip. Small children do not comprehend the concept of days and weeks and may become anxious and overly excited when anticipating a special event.

When taking a walk, the children should hold hands or, as I mentioned earlier, hold on to a piece of rope or scarves tied together with you in the lead. Do not walk near the street. By walking on the grass, you can keep the children safe!

They are your responsibility at all times. Don't take chances. When you are going to a special place, it is a good idea to bring an extra adult to help you. Children can become overexcited and may need extra attention. You could ask the parents of the children if they would like to join the group. You or the parents can take a few instant pictures so that you can follow up the activity with discussions, retelling of the event, and posting the pictures on your kitchen bulletin board.

Bring the following items for your well-planned trip:

Tissues
Snacks
First Aid kit to manage minor cuts

Emergency list which includes all parents' telephone numbers

Consent forms for all children (be sure all parents are informed of all trips)

Identification tag for all children attached to their wrists (name, phone number, name of group, provider's name)

Car Safety (Be sure you have adequate gas and your tires are in good condition)

Check the cars for bees before departing.

Provide seat belts or car seats for all (make sure that they are not twisted and are properly adjusted).

Lock all doors before starting the car.

No eating or drinking is allowed while the car is in motion.

No sharp objects such as pencils or pens are allowed.

Never leave children alone in the car.

Adults should get out of the car before children.

Field Trip Safety

Prepare children in advance. Tell them where you are going and what you will see there. Practice staying together as a group.

Reinforce rules about staying together and not running ahead of the group.

Establish a "what if you get lost" plan.

Keep an "emergency snack pack" in case you are delayed or have to wait for an event to begin (raisins, cookies, crackers).

Never allow children to visit rest rooms by themselves.

If you do have an emergency, try to remain calm. Sing with the children, play a simple game, or read a book that you have in your emergency pack. Pads of paper and crayons may also be useful to add to your pack for unexpected situations.

Places of Interest in Your Community

The following list describes some places that might be near your house where you can take the children.

SPCA or Pet Store

Inquire about the possibility of bringing a few animals to your house. A discussion about how to care for pets would be appropriate.

Supermarket

Arrange for a tour of the produce or meat department of your local supermarket. Talk about the weighing scale, how the products are displayed, the utensils and tools needed to process the meat for sale, and the prevention of spoilage.

Pumpkin Farm

Children might ask questions like these: How do pumpkins grow? What purpose do they serve? What can you make with them?

Apple Orchard

A local grower could answer questions like these: How do you take care of an orchard? What do you do with the apples? Why are there different kinds?

Paint Store

Children can learn how paint is mixed, how colors are coordinated in a decorating scheme with wallpaper. The clerk might also talk about how paint and wallpaper are removed when the home owner decides it is time for a change.

Library

Libraries offer more than just books. The librarian may explain language cassettes, record collections, the microfilm machine, and books in Braille.

Bakery or Pizza Shop

The baker could answer questions like these: What does it mean to bake from scratch? How do you measure? How do your machines operate? Where do you learn the skills to be a baker?

Hardware Store

Children could ask questions like these: Who buys all these gadgets? Where does the store owner purchase the tools, machines, and materials?

Don't forget your local park and recreation center, museums, and the YMCA or YWCA. Additional places of interest include a stable, post office, small airport, printer, church, clock store, barbershop, or botanical garden.

Thank you notes are always appreciated by your host, so why not make that a follow-up activity? Children could write a letter or draw a picture that illustrates their perceptions of the visit and expresses gratitude.

Grab Bag Ideas

Here are some more games and ideas to keep the children amused and occupied inside and outside.

Nesting Games

Look in your cabinets for a variety of cans, bowls, boxes, pots, pans, and cups. Try to fit the different sizes into one another or turn them all upside down and try to stack them high without falling.

The Chalk Trail

Follow a trail that you have made with chalk, leaves, sticks, or stones to find the prize at the end of the trail. Use a small stuffed animal as the prize.

Tunnels

Open both ends of several large refrigerator boxes. Children can drive bikes or riding toys through the tunnel. It makes a great hiding place for hide-and-seek!

Organizing Cabinets

If you have a low cabinet with pots and pans, empty the pots and pans and let the children reorganize the shelves for you. Make sure there is nothing in the cabinet that is sharp or harmful for children to play with.

Learning to Care for Books

Teach the children to respect both their own books and those that are borrowed from a library. Make sure their hands are clean before handling the books and show them the correct way to turn the pages without ripping them. Discuss why you should never write in or rip the book. You can also help each child to make a personal bookmark that can be decorated with the picture of a favorite animal, toy, or their name.

Clothespin Basketball

The children try to drop clothespins into a clean juice or milk bottle standing just above the bottle placed on the floor.

Who Is the Clapper?

One child leaves the room. The other children sit in a circle. One person claps their hands four times. When the other child rejoins the group, he has to guess who the clapper was.

Hiding

Pretend that you are a tiny monster and you are hiding in the car. The children have to ask questions such as, "Are you in the glove compartment?" Whoever guesses correctly is the next one to hide.

Matching Pairs

Place six pairs of shoes in a large box. Mix them up on the floor. One at a time, let each child try to match the pairs.

Candy Hunt

Hide wrapped pieces of candy. Each child carries a bag to find the treasures. You can also use dried fruit for a healthier hunt.

Masking Tape Roads

Toy cars and trucks can speed up and down the roads created on your kitchen floor with masking tape. Some children enjoy trying to make letters with the tape on their blackboard on the floor. Don't put tape on a floor near direct sunlight or it will be difficult to remove.

Taste Test

One child closes his eyes and puts out his tongue or his hand. You give him a small taste of something and he has to guess what it is. This activity develops an awareness of the senses. A discussion can follow as to what it tasted like—sweet, sour, or salty.

Potpourri Pictures

Gather together corn kernels, macaroni, and crayons. Keep these things in a shoe box and bring them out occasionally. As the children are seated at a table, let them draw a picture by arranging these odds and ends in a design on the tabletop.

Find the Right Store

Write the words BAKERY, HARDWARE STORE, GROCERY, PRODUCE MARKET on index cards and glue each one to a box. Gather items from around the house such as cellophane tape, apples, soup cans, or cookies and ask the children, "In which store would you find the cookies?" Show them the properly labeled box to put it in. Spell the word GROCERY for them as they place the cookies into the correct box. This activity develops the ability to classify, make judgments, and learn the names of foods and other household items.

Chalk Drawings

Cut a brown paper bag and dampen it with a sponge. Tell the children to turn pieces of colored chalk on their sides as they draw a picture or design.

A Crepe Paper Wall

Hang a piece of string from one wall to the other. Cut strips of crepe paper and dangle them over the hanging string between the two walls. Children can pretend this is a stage and can wait behind the stage until it is their turn.

Dry Chalk Pictures

Make a picture with colored chalk and then write over it with another color and yet again another color. With your fingers, blend together to give a new look to the picture.

Movement Skills

There will be days when you will need an outlet for your frustrations or you feel that the kids are a little too spirited. Perhaps the weather is inclement or they are just overly excited about the thought of Santa Claus coming to town. For whatever reason, you will find that exercise is a great way to release tension. Instead of just jumping up and down or hopping on one foot, try asking the children to follow your instructions as you lead them in some of the following movements. Some people may wonder how such simple things could be interesting to kids. They probably are not aware that all of these activities are new to children. We have done these things over and over again in our lives, but activities like this encourage children to be creative, to follow directions, to pretend, to develop rhythm, and are also a great outlet for their amazing energy.

In early childhood education, college students are taught the importance of helping children develop locomotor and nonlocomotor skills. For our purposes, we want to have fun while at the same time teach the children how to follow directions and perform locomotor skills such as running, jumping, and hopping.

Have the children take turns being the leader as they tell the children to do the following movements.

Wriggling	Sliding	Swaying
Hopping on one foot	Skipping	Shaking
	Pointing	Tying
Hopping on two feet	Dancing	Rolling
	Walking fast	Rubbing
Stretching	Tapping	Kicking
Bouncing up and down	Clapping	Squirming
	Patting	Waving
Spinning	Swimming	Snapping

Let's Pretend

Pretending lets the imagination of the children run wild. Encourage the children to be free with their movements. This is a great outlet for their energy as well as an experience in developing rhythmic movement. Ask children to imagine the following and act out what they see:

a snake hissing	a boat rocking
a caterpillar crawling	a wind blowing
a bear growling	a cloud floating
a scarecrow shaking	a kitten purring
a clock ticking	a clown balancing
a bird chirping	a baby stretching

Involving Children in Your Activities

Children love to help out around the house and are often happy to assist you in preparing food, cleaning up after lunch, or folding clothes. It may be tempting to dismiss their offers if you are in a hurry to get the job done. However, you may want to be guided by the Montessori philosophy of learning and view everyday activities as important stepping-stones in a child's learning development. Such everyday activities include sweeping, mopping, dusting, polishing glass, setting the table, cutting flowers, cleaning shoes, raking leaves, and weeding a garden.

Although these are basic tasks that may seem unexciting to you, accomplishing them will help children gain self-confidence and motivation. Experts in the field of early childhood development recommend that caregivers allow children as much independence as possible so long as they do not endanger themselves or others. By allowing children the freedom to participate, you will be helping them build a healthy and happy future.

TROUBLE-
SHOOTING

Dealing with
Behavior Problems

Experts tell us that discipline is not meant to punish but to teach. If you yell at children, you will be teaching them to yell as a means of resolving a problem.

As a caregiver you must be fair, firm, and warm. Your patience will be tried many times during the day as you hear the children exclaim, "No!", "That's mine," or "I had it first."

Sometimes when children whine, fight, or have temper tantrums, it is related to feelings of frustration, helplessness, hunger, sickness, or anger. By recognizing the reasons why they feel upset, you may be able to avoid potential outbursts. Try to prevent misunderstandings before they erupt into conflict. Children need praise and attention when they are well behaved. By positively reinforcing good behavior with hugs, kisses, smiles, and praise, you are encouraging them to repeat what is rewarded.

Think about what you consider to be the rules of the house. There are several tried and true techniques that are effective

with children. Practice using these methods in your daily interactions with children.

Children may be fighting over toys because you do not have
an adequate supply. One riding toy for seven children is not
sufficient. Part of your responsibility as a caregiver is to teach
the children to cooperate and share things with other children.
If two children want the same toy, you could use an egg timer
and allow each child to have the toy for a specified number of
minutes. Another idea is to give the problem to them. Ask them
for their ideas about how to resolve the conflict. This works well
with older children when they feel that you might be doling out
too harsh a disciplinary measure. Turn the tables around and
let them choose an appropriate method, like spending the day
without television, or one hour of extra reading for school.

When two children are fussing with each other, try touching
one of them lightly on the shoulder and removing him from the
conflict. Give him time to explain to you what happened. Children
who are away from home for long periods of time have lots of
emotions tucked inside. Be a good listener. Let them share their
hidden feelings with you. Assure them that you understand. Let
the children know frequently that you love them, but you cannot
allow them to hurt each other physically or emotionally. Follow
up a reprimand with kind words. Explain that when you correct
them it is because they are doing something that is not acceptable
at your house.

The time-out chair is popular. When a child is not conforming
to your codes of behavior, you ask him to sit in the chair for a
few minutes. The rule of thumb might be that a three year old
should sit for three minutes, a four year old for four minutes,
and a five year old for five minutes. Any period of time longer
than that is an eternity for a child and would be an extreme
measure of discipline. I visited a day care center and observed
a two year old in the corner for at least thirty minutes. Every
time the poor little child would try to join the group, he was
reprimanded and sent back to the bad boy corner. It broke my
heart to see this because obviously the teacher knew very little
about caring for children. It also saddened me because I knew
that his parents were completely unaware of the treatment that

their little boy was receiving at day care. The final insult to the child's dignity was when a thoughtless aide lashed out in frustration and said, "Now I know why your mommy leaves you here." Remember that children are human beings too. You don't want to humiliate them or disgrace them in front of their peers. I hope the days are gone when the dunce cap was placed on a child's head as he sat in the corner of the room facing the wall. A friend of mine had a brother who years ago was punished this way because he was left-handed and the teacher felt that this was just inappropriate behavior and had to be broken.

You could use the same time-out chair for yourself where you can go and relax. The children should know that when you are sitting in that certain chair, you need quiet time too! And it shows the children that it isn't so bad to be sent to the time-out chair because you use it too.

Give a child a warning when it is time to stop an activity and go on to the next. When a child is playing with blocks and you tell him it is nap time, his reaction will probably be negative. After all, you are interrupting his play environment. Try this approach. Tell the child that it is almost time to stop playing and that you will be back in a few minutes. Encourage him to end his play because it is getting close to nap time.

Some children do things just to get your goat. If it is not hurting you or the other children, you may wish to ignore the small annoyances. If you do not give attention to every act of misbehavior, it may diminish because you are not responding to it.

Develop a certain tone of voice or a look in your eyes that says very clearly you are not pleased about something. This method is better than losing your temper, and most children are very attuned to someone's change in expression or sound of their voice.

Try to use more do's than don'ts in your conversations with children. Listen to yourself. Are you constantly saying "No" when children ask you if they can do something? Give them independence if it is not going to hurt anyone. Some people have the bad habit of always trying to control children. Perhaps they feel it is the way they were raised, but there are alternatives to just saying "No" all of the time. The more freedom you give a child on a limited basis, the less he will want to step over the boundaries. Children know you have given them your trust. In other words, if they feel they already have the freedom, they will not need to test it quite so much.

Taking Care of Your Own Family

If you have a family of your own, you may find that running a child care business requires a period of adjustment for all of the family members. Each person will have to be prepared to make some changes in his or her expectations of you as a mother and as a wife. The reason that I began child care was so I could have more time with my own children rather than going out to work and leaving them in someone else's care. Because Robin and Katelyn were very young, I could not explain to them that they were going to have to share their mother with a houseful of kids. To assure them their status as my special children was not threatened, I was sure to save them a seat on my lap at story time and gave them lots of hugs and kisses throughout the day. In the evening, I took them with me on my errands and told them how much I loved being with them. It would not be truthful if I said that things run smoothly all of the time. There are times when children are possessive of their mother's affection, which is a very natural feeling. Jealousy is a strong emotion even for adults so it is certainly understandable that a child would want his mother to be his "one and only."

If your children are able to understand they will have to make some adaptations in their home life, you should have a family discussion in which you explain why you have chosen to work as a caregiver and how they can help you. In addition to having chores around the house, you could offer an increase in their allowance if they help you with the day care children. One mother has designated Friday night as a special night and takes her own children ice skating or to a fast-food restaurant if everyone cooperates during the week. It is important that everyone understands they will experience some loss of privacy because so many different people will be passing through each day.

If you have an elderly relative living with you, you may find that his or her philosophy is that "Children should be seen and not heard." This is definitely not possible in the home day care business.

Keep the lines of communications open with each family member. In the beginning it may be a little tough as everyone adjusts to a new situation, but with a little time you will find that new routines will be established and you will be able to balance adeptly both family and business needs.

Common Problems Caregivers Face

No matter how painstakingly you follow the suggestions in this book and the advice of other caregivers, everything will not be perfect. Remember I mentioned earlier that you are going to have good days and bad days just like with any other job.

In this section I discuss some of the common problems that caregivers experience. After each quote, I offer solutions that have helped other people.

1. "The parents don't seem to respect me. They arrive late to pick up their child. They bring sick kids. They have even given me bad checks. They do not bring the supplies we have discussed such as formula, diapers, baby food, a second set of clean clothes, and ointment."

You may want to review your professional attitude. In order to be successful and have people respect you, you must be firm about the rules of your business. Be clear about your hours, fees, vacation and holiday schedules, and sick policy. You are a very successful businesswoman, so you must show proudly by your words and actions that in order for you to offer this arrangement, the parents must play by *your* rules.

Communicate with the parents regularly and honestly. The best way to resolve a problem with a parent is to discuss the issue when you have cooled off and can speak without flying off the handle. Relate the problem in such a way that it is not threatening or insulting to the parent.

Sometimes you may consider yourself as only a baby-sitter. You need to reconsider your status. You have a tremendous responsibility. You are performing a very valuable service. You must treat yourself with respect and expect others to treat you that way. Take pride in your appearance and in the condition of your home.

Remember there are other careers that you could have selected, but you chose child care because you love children. If the parents do not appreciate the value of your commitment, then they will have to look elsewhere for child care.

2. "A friend recently asked me to care for her handicapped child. I felt torn between my loyalty to her as a friend and the limits of my own abilities to handle special needs in a group setting."

Not everyone is able to offer special needs child care. It is important to consider each case individually. Talk to the specialists in your community who offer programs for disabled children and ask what resources are available to give you guidance and ongoing support if you decide to accept such a child. One provider told me of the enormous satisfaction she felt when she was able to care for two sisters with cerebral palsy. Their mother needed a break from the demands of caring for handicapped children, and Andrea enjoyed having them for three hours a day. Read all that you can about children who have physical and emotional challenges before you make your decision. A very good friend of ours has a blind child. He is a sweet little boy who would greatly benefit by joining a few children in a home setting. If you are energetic and not intimidated by special needs children, you might offer to take them (just for a few hours initially).

3. "The children are driving me crazy. Everything is starting to get on my nerves. Nobody is helping me with family chores. My husband thinks because I am home all day that I can schedule appointments, take care of the lawn, do the housework, and iron his shirts. I just can't do everything by myself."

There are lots of jobs that have to be done to keep your household functioning. If you attempt to houseclean, prepare meals, do laundry, take care of the pets, and manage the lawn care duties, you will not have a minute for yourself and will feel very resentful. Plan a family meeting. You should write a list describing all of the jobs that will have to be shared by the family members. Discuss who will be responsible for specific chores by the week or the month. To make the selection more agreeable, you could let family members pull the job assignments out of a hat or have a sign-up sheet. You could also design a workwheel which is turned weekly to assign everyone a new share of chores. You might also consider hiring a few helpers. Two neighborhood girls come over each day to help me vacuum the playroom, sweep the kitchen floor, and put some of the toys away. They are not involved with the children because that is my responsibility, but they are a great help in taking some of the pressure of house cleaning away from me.

4. "Other providers make me feel inadequate because they tell me they never have to advertise and they have a long waiting list of people who need their service. I can't seem to attract enough customers."

This common problem can be due to a variety of circumstances. If you live off the beaten track or out in the country, your service may not be as needed as someone who lives in the middle of a busy town.

Look at your home and yourself with a critical eye. Are you projecting a professional image to the prospective parents? Ask a friend or other caregiver to give you some constructive criticism. You may be unconsciously sending signals to the prospective parents by your telephone manner or by some action that you are not aware of. Your house may look lived in to you but unkempt and unsafe to a parent of small children.

Be sure you are advertising enough. Signs have to be posted where parents can see them. You could send a flyer or letter to the local elementary school secretary. Better yet, you could visit in person so that the school personnel can see you are a professional day care provider. Let the PTA, church groups, and large companies in your area know that a quality home day care service is operating in their area. Be sure that your local resource and referral group knows that you exist so they can recommend their clients to you.

5. "It is really hard for me when a new child begins. The other children become out of sorts and I feel very frustrated."

Beginnings can be difficult for both you and the children. You may want to have a friend help you when a new child starts. Tiny babies usually adjust more easily because they can be comforted with singing, a warm bottle of milk, and the distraction of watching other children. When babies are about eight months old, they may begin to feel strange. They know you are not their mother. It will be an adjustment for them to learn they can trust you when it seems to them that their beloved mother has deserted them.

In the beginning, some little toddlers and preschoolers will revert to babyish behavior. They may wet their pants, suck their thumb, or show off around the group. If you understand this is normal behavior, it will be easier for you.

Prior to a new child coming into the group, prepare the other children for the newcomer. Tell them a little bit about the child and emphasize how we all want to make him feel welcome. Ask the children for their suggestions: he can draw a picture with us, take a walk, and we'll show him what to play with outside, explain the safe areas in the house where we play, and learn everybody's name. You can involve the older children in the preparation by having them set up the playpen and select baby toys from the toy box. Within the group, everyone's position will change. The baby who is eighteen months old may not be considered the baby anymore and the six year old who was considered the leader might feel depressed when a third grader joins the group for after-school care. You can help all of the children to make a comfortable adjustment by helping each one to feel secure and loved within the day care family.

6. "I have a hard time keeping track of everything that I have to do. There seem to be so many personal and business commitments."

You could buy a large wall calendar with large squares for writing in information, or an appointment book and write everything down; doctor's appointments, the story hour at the library, the days you plan to take off, and all of the children's birthdays should be clearly indicated. Keep it next to the phone so you can mark the days you are interviewing parents or someone is coming to inspect your home.

7. "There seem to be conflicts about individual parent requests. Some mothers tell me that they don't want their babies to take a bottle when they go in for a nap, and I don't really believe in seat belts and car seats. Should I do things the way I raised my own children or follow the new mother's requests?"

There are many mothers who have successfully raised their own children and grandchildren but many practices that were recommended in the past have been revised. For example, pediatricians today recommend that babies do not take bottles to bed with them so they fall asleep with the bottle in their mouth. The sugar in juice and milk remaining on the teeth while the child is sleeping can begin to decay the teeth. This is commonly referred to as "nursing bottle syndrome." As much as possible, you should follow the parents' instructions for their child, although at times you will want to add your own opinions. If you see a real danger to the child, don't hesitate to speak up, because the parents may not realize the jeopardy in which they are placing their child. Remember, too, that in most states seat belts and car seats are mandatory.

8. "Why doesn't the parent notice all of the positive things that we do instead of being critical about a toilet-learning experience?"

Some of the parents may be uptight about toilet training and may say to you, "I don't know why he wets here, he is always fine at home." Don't worry about that type of comment because sometimes new behavior such as toilet training seems to be forgotten when a new situation arises, like Mommy leaving the child at someone else's home. Toilet training can be a manageable experience if you do not make a big deal out of it. Wait until the child is ready. Take the child in the bathroom so he can watch the other children. This is the most effective way to learn. Give praise appropriately and don't scold about accidents.

9. "What can I do about the phone ringing? It seems that just when I am reading a story, fixing lunch, or changing a diaper, someone calls and it disturbs everything."

I remember many occasions when I had to run in from the outdoor play area to answer the phone. You never know if it is a parent calling about a child or one of those annoying telephone solicitors doing a survey or announcing that you have been selected to win a million-dollar prize. An answering machine will record messages and you can hear them. If you are changing a diaper, giving a bath, or reading a story, you do not want to leave the child or the group without supervision. When it is convenient, you can return the call. If it is a parent, you might decide to respond right away. If it is a friend, you can remind him or her that you can't talk while you are working. A friend should understand that it is your job and that it is impossible to sit down and talk when you are responsible for young children.

10. "Sometimes I feel so isolated and wonder if I am ill-suited for this type of job. Any suggestions?"

If you feel isolated, gather the children for a trip to the library or a fast-food restaurant that has a playground. You will all have a change of scenery and you will get a chance to talk to other adults—even if it is only the cashier. I personally knew that I wanted adult companionship during the day. I hired a helper while I cared for the children. Since I had a teaching background, I knew that I could handle a large group with the assistance of another competent adult. We enjoyed working together and became very good friends because we shared so much with each other about our family life and growing up experiences. This satisfied my need for adult contact.

A group of providers recently shared their favorite stress reducers with me. They suggested playing with clay as a way of pounding out your frustrations, reading a comic book so that things do not seem so serious, counting to ten, going out for fresh air and letting the kids run around, calling a neighbor to come in so you can take a break, or keeping a box of toys which are special. (Call it a trinket box.) You should definitely join a group of other day care providers one evening a month for fun and friendship. You will have so much in common, and these providers can be your source of support when you are having a bad day. Pick up the phone and call them when you need a little pep talk to get you through a tough day.

11. "I hear so much about child abuse. What if someone misinterprets something that I do and falsely accuses me of harming the child?"

There are ways to prevent the possibility of such an accusation. Have an open door policy for all of the parents whose children come to your home. Do not confuse this to mean that you should just allow parents to enter your home without knocking. To ensure the safety of the children so that they do not walk or crawl out of an unlocked door, you should have the doors locked. The environment should be friendly and open in the sense that the parents can just drop in for lunch or a visit at their convenience. You should not take photographs of the children in any stage of undress as this could be misconstrued by a parent (see photograph release form in Appendix D).

12. "I have a problem with parents who send gum, candy, and chocolate cupcakes with their child. Besides being messy, the other children become upset because they do not have the same treats."

You may want to suggest to parents that you would prefer they do not bring treats to your home except for special occasions such as a birthday party. Fruit juices, raw vegetables, and fruit are healthier snacks and the children do not become overexcited after eating such nourishing foods. If you really feel strongly about this issue, you should include it in your initial policy sheet which establishes the framework for your business.

13. "I notice mood changes with some children and I don't know why they are so good some days and so out of control on other days."

Anything that has happened at home or en route to your home can affect the child's mood. If the parents were arguing or if the child overheard a troubling telephone conversation or if a family pet is sick, a little child can become depressed. When you observe a significant change in behavior or temperament, ask the parent if there is anything that you should be aware of so you can give extra attention to the child.

14. "Sometimes the toy room looks like a bomb hit it and I feel like I am so disorganized. The kids seem to be disorganized too."

One way to begin is to structure your home so that everything has a place. Teach the children to play with one toy and put it back in the proper bin before pulling out another box of toys (age three years and older). Do not overdo it by having too many toys and games. The toy box should not be a place to dump and pile toys. It is very frustrating for the child to have to dig to the bottom in search of a favorite toy. Teach the children that cleanup time is part of their job. Put a favorite record on and make a game of trying to put everything away before the song is over.

Be sure to have a rocking chair to soothe a child and yourself. Arrange the contents of your day care area so that you have separate areas for little tables and chairs, a rest area for a tired child, storage space, and space for active play. I caution you against too much open space or you will invite raucous behavior and running around. Your should establish rules stating that nobody is allowed to hurt another child. Children need time for quiet activities and active play. Be sure to allow them time for both. When outside, they can use their outside voice but when in the house, they must always use inside tones of voice.

15. "Although my policy states that a child who is sick may not come, two parents repeatedly bring an ill child."

This is a problem that causes harm to everyone. Since the preliminary visit with the parent you have asked them to have a contingency plan in effect in case their child has a fever, diarrhea, or contagious disease, you are certainly within your rights to refuse to allow a child to stay who exhibits symptoms of illness. Strep throat, pinkeye, and lice are diseases that will quickly infect all of the children in your care. One inconsiderate parent can cause great inconvenience and expense for everyone. The other parents will have to spend money for doctor's visits, throat cultures, and prescriptions, in addition to the work of caring for sick youngsters and possibly missing work time. Since children are highly susceptible to disease, parents need to know that you will enforce the ground rules concerning illness.

16. "I have had several children who were 'biters.' Besides being very painful and dangerous to the child who has been harmed, the parents are irate that I could allow this to happen, and I feel responsible."

The most important thing to do is immediately take care of the injured child. Then take the child who bites aside and explain that this kind of behavior is not acceptable in your house. If you cannot get him to stop this habit, the parents should be consulted and a solution must be worked out before the child does harm to someone else. Frustration in a child can be manifested physically through temper tantrums or biting. Ask yourself how you can prevent biting before it happens. Is the child getting enough personal attention from you? Look for signs that say this child is getting out of control and stop him if you can before he attacks another child. The behavior does not reflect on your ability as a caregiver and should not be considered a failure on your part when you have taken all the necessary steps to prevent another incident from happening in the future.

STARTING A MOTHER'S DAY OUT PROGRAM

In the preceding chapters, I discussed the steps involved in planning and organizing a full-time child care business. Now I would like to offer a suggestion for the person who is interested in providing a part-time child care service. A Mother's Day Out program is a great way to earn supplemental income while providing a very valuable service for nonworking mothers or those who work only a few days a week.

A Mother's Day Out program is a play group for profit. Children who are two years old and older come one day a week on a regular basis from 9:30 A.M. until 3 P.M. During that time, activities are planned and the children enjoy playing and learning while their mothers are free to pursue their own personal interests.

To set up a program that caters to the needs of the mother at home, you can follow the guidelines and procedures in the earlier chapters and simply modify the fees and hours to fit your specific program.

I have included a sample introductory letter, flyer, and classified ads to help you get off to a good start.

Sample Letter and Advertisements

Dear Parents:

In talking to neighbors and friends, I have found that many mothers in our area would appreciate an occasional break, and they would like their preschoolers to play and learn with others of the same age. Now that I am home with Robin and Katelyn, I have decided to offer a Mother's Day Out program in my home.

Beginning in September, you can plan to have a "Mom's Day Off." This is a great opportunity for you to shop, clean in peace, volunteer at the school, meet your friends for lunch, or just relax and read a book. You can be assured that your little ones will be safe and happy while you enjoy some time for yourself.

So that each child will receive lots of love and individual attention, my sister Jan will be here to help me if more than four children are in attendance at one time.

I have a teaching background and I love children. Both Jan and I have completed the Red Cross First Aid course and we are state-licensed. I would be happy to give you a tour of my home so that you can see some of the things we have planned. I have also attached a sample activity plan which we follow each week.

Please call me at any time so that I can share more information with you.

Sincerely,

Sample Flyer

CALLING ALL PRESCHOOLERS!

Would you like to come stay and play?

Does your mom need a few hours for herself?

Join our play group once a week!

- Arts and Crafts
- Educational Activities
- Songs
- Games
- State Approved
- Excellent Supervision
- Safe, Loving Atmosphere
- Small Group Setting
- Certified Teacher/Mother

Conveniently located near Brookside Mall
For information call 555-1234

555-1234	555-1234	555-1234	555-1234	555-1234	555-1234	555-1234	555-1234	555-1234	555-1234

Sample Ads

Calling All Moms!

Enjoy a day for yourself. Your child can join us
for games, arts and crafts, and lots of fun.
Certified teacher and loving mother offers
Mother's Day Out Program. For information,
please call 555-1234 (Plymouth area).

"Preschool Playtime"—Time Off for Moms
Arts, crafts, snacks, and play and learn
activities offered one day a week for
preschoolers. Safe, loving environment; state-
licensed. Please call 555-1234 for information.

Special Notes About a Part-time Program

- Give your program a catchy name such as Special Time For Mom, Give Mom A Break, Miss Carol's Play Group, Mother's Day Out, Mom's Day Off, or Preschool Playtime.
- Target your advertising to mothers who work part time, children who do not have siblings or neighborhoods kids to play with, people who are new to the area and do not have relatives to help them, mothers who have just had new babies and want to do something special for the older sibling, and mothers who just need time for themselves.
- Notify local day care centers and nursery schools that you offer a part-time program.
- Accept children ages two years and older.
- Enroll the children so that they come on a regular basis, thus ensuring that all of the children know each other and are familiar with your routine.

STATE LICENSING

BUREAUS

To find out the telephone number of the licensing bureau in your area, you can call the National Association for the Education of Young Children at 800-424-2460 (ask for Information Services) or the Children's Defense Fund at 202-628-8787 (ask for Child Care Division). Be sure to specify that you are inquiring about licensing for in-home day care rather than for a day care center. Or write to your state bureau (see the following list), addressing your letter to the Day Care Licensing Official. This list is current as of January 6, 1989. Source: Children's Defense Fund, 122 C. Street, N.W., Washington, DC 20001.

ALABAMA

Family and Children's
  Services
64 North Union Street
Montgomery, AL 36130-1801

ALASKA

Department of Day Care
  Licensing
Box H-05
Juneau, AK 99811-0630

ARIZONA

State Health Department of
  Child Day Care Licensing
701 East Jefferson
Phoenix, AZ 85034

ARKANSAS

Child Development Unit
Children and Family Services
P.O. Box 1437
Little Rock, AR 72203

CALIFORNIA

Community Care Licensing
  Division
744 P Street
Mail Station 17-17
Sacramento, CA 95814

COLORADO

Day Care and Home
  Licensing
Department of Social Services
1575 Sherman Street
Denver, CO 80203

CONNECTICUT

Day Care Licensing
Department of Health
  Services
150 Washington Street
Hartford, CT 06106

DELAWARE

Pauline Koch
330 East 50th Street
Wilmington, DE 19802

DISTRICT OF COLUMBIA

DCRA/SFRA
Supervisor of Licensing
614 H Street, N.W.
Room 1031
Washington, DC 20001

FLORIDA

Department of Health and
  Rehabilitative Services and
  Familes
Division of Children & Youth
1317 Winewood Boulevard,
  Bldg. 8
Tallahassee, FL 32301

GEORGIA

Child Care Licensing Section
  Director
Department of Human
  Resources
Office of Regulatory Services
P.O. Drawer 112
Madison, GA 30650

HAWAII

Department of Social Services
   and Housing
Public Welfare Division
P.O. Box 339
Honolulu, HI 96809

IDAHO

Department of Health and
   Welfare
450 West State Street
Boise, ID 83720

ILLINOIS

Licensing Specialist
Department of Children and
   Family Services
406 E. Monroe
Springfield, IL 62701-1381

INDIANA

Child Welfare Division
State Welfare Department
141 Meridian Street, 6th floor
Indianapolis, IN 46225

IOWA

Department of Human
   Services
Division of Adult, Children
   and Families
Hoover State Office Building,
   5th floor
Des Moines, IA 50319

KANSAS

State Department of Health
   and Environment
Child Licensing, 10th floor
900 Jackson
Topeka, KS 66620-0001

KENTUCKY

Division for Licensing and
   Regulation
275 East Main Street
CHR Building, 4th floor east
Frankfort, KY 40621

LOUISIANA

Division of Licensing and
   Certification
P.O. Box 3767
Baton Rouge, LA 70821

MAINE

Department of Human
   Services
Licensing Unit
State House Station 11
Augusta, ME 04333

MARYLAND

Department of Health and
   Mental Hygiene, Day Care
311 West Saratoga Street
Saratoga State Center
Baltimore, MD 21203

MASSACHUSETTS

State Office for Children
10 West Street
Boston, MA 02110

MICHIGAN

Department of Social Services
Office of Children and Youth
  Services
300 South Capital Avenue,
  9th floor
Lansing, MI 48926

MINNESOTA

Department of Human
  Services
Division of Licensing
Space Center, 6th floor
444 Lafayette Drive
St. Paul, MN 55155-3842

MISSISSIPPI

Division of Special Licensing
Department of Health
P.O. Box 1700
Jackson, MS 39205

MISSOURI

Division of Family Services
Licensing Unit
P.O. Box 88
Jefferson City, MO 65102

MONTANA

Bureau of Social Services
P.O. Box 8005
Helena, MT 59717

NEBRASKA

Nebraska Department of
  Social Services
Early Childhood Program
301 Centennial Mall South
P.O. Box 95026
Lincoln, NE 68509-5026

NEVADA

Child Care Services Bureau—
  Youth Division
505 East King Street
Carson City, NV 89710

NEW HAMPSHIRE

Division of Public Health
  Services
Bureau of Child Care
  Standards and Licensing
Health and Human Services
  Building
6 Hazen Drive
Concord, NH 03301-8584

NEW JERSEY

Division of Youth and Family
  Services
1 South Montgomery Street
CN 717
Trenton, NJ 08625

NEW MEXICO

Department of Health and
  Environment
Harold Reynolds Building
P.O. Box 968
Santa Fe, NM 87501

NEW YORK

State Department of Social
  Services
Office of Child Day Care
40 North Pearl Street
Section 11B
Albany, NY 12243

NORTH CAROLINA

Department of Human
  Resources
Division of Facility Services
Child Day Care Section
701 Barbaur Drive
Raleigh, NC 27603-2008

NORTH DAKOTA

North Dakota Department of
  Human Services
State Capitol
Bismarck, ND 58505

OHIO

Child Care Regulatory Unit
Department of Human
  Services
Columbus District Office
30 East Broad Street
Columbus, OH 43205

OKLAHOMA

Department of Human
  Services
Licensing Unit
P.O. Box 25352
Oklahoma City, OK 73125

OREGON

Department of Human
  Resources
Children's Services Division
198 Commercial Street, S.E.
Salem, OR 97310

PENNSYLVANIA

Department of Public Welfare
Office of Policy Planning and
  Evaluation
Day Care Division
P.O. Box 2675
Harrisburg, PA 17120

RHODE ISLAND

Department for Children and
  Their Families
610 Mt. Pleasant Avenue
Providence, RI 02908

SOUTH CAROLINA

Department of Social Services
Day Care Division Regulatory
  Unit
P.O. Box 1530
Columbia, SC 29204

SOUTH DAKOTA

Department of Social Services
700 Governors Drive
Pierre, SD 57501

TENNESSEE

Department of Human
  Services
Citizen's Plaza Building
400 Deadrick Street
Nashville, TN 37219

TEXAS

Department of Human
  Resources
P.O. Box 2960
Austin, TX 78769

UTAH

Department of Family
  Services
120 North 200 Street (west)
Salt Lake City, UT 84103

VERMONT

Department of Social and
  Rehabilitation Services
103 South Main Street
Waterbury, VT 05676

VIRGINIA

Department of Social Services
  Licensing
8007 Discovery Drive
Richmond, VA 23229-8699

WASHINGTON

Division of Children and
  Family Services
Mail Stop OB-41
Olympia, WA 98504

WEST VIRGINIA

Department of Human
  Services
1900 Washington Street East
Charleston, WV 25305

WISCONSIN

Division of Community
  Development
Office for Children, Youth
  and Families (Room 465)
P.O. Box 7851
Madison, WI 57307

WYOMING

Department of Health and
  Social Services
Division of Public Assistance
  and Social Services
Hathaway Building
Cheyenne, WY 82002-0710

SELECTED RESOURCES

Booklets for Day Care Providers

—"One Hundred and One Tips About Starting a Day Care" ($2.00)
—"One Hundred Ways to Keep Kids Happy" ($2.00)
—"How to Deal with Common Day Care Problems" ($2.00)

Home Child Care Updates
Box 442
Kind of Prussia, PA 19406
Invaluable reports for caregivers.

Equipment

Environments, Inc.
Early Childhood Division
P.O. Box 1348
Beaufort, SC 29902
1-800-EI-CHILD
This company's free catalog is an excellent source of toys, games, and equipment for day care needs.

Child Craft Education Corporation
20 Kilmer Road
Edison, NJ 08818
1-800-631-5652
Call for free catalog.

Educational Resources

Resources for Child Caring, Inc.
Toys 'N Things Press
906 N. Dale Street
St. Paul, MN 55103
1-800-423-8309
In Minnesota call: 1-612-488-7284
A national leader in publishing and distributing professional resources. Family Day Care Newsletter.

Pre K Today
Scholastic Inc.
730 Broadway
New York, NY 10003
Call 1-800-631-1586 (8 A.M. to 6 P.M. Eastern Standard Time). This magazine is filled with ideas for teaching and caring for infants to five year olds. Subscription available.

Totline Newsletter
Warren Publishing House, Inc.
P.O. Box 2255
Everett, WA 98203
Full of creative and challenging ideas for preschool children. Published six times annually. A year's subscription costs $12. (sample issue is $1.00).

Kimbo Educational
P.O. Box 477
10 North Third Avenue
Long Branch, NJ 07740

1-800-631-2187
In New Jersey call 1-201-229-4949

DLM Teaching Resources
P.O. Box 4000
Allen, TX 75002
1-800-527-4747
In Texas call 1-800-442-4711

C.A.P.E. Center, Inc.
5924 Royal Lane, Suite 216
Dallas, TX 75230
(214) 692-0263
Specializes in excellent training systems for family day care providers, preschool directors, nannies, and parents. Telephone for further information.

Family Day Care Curriculum Kits

Mrs. Greene's Kapers For Kids Curriculum & Craft Kits
2325 Endicott St.
St. Paul, MN 55114
1-800-882-7332
In Minnesota call: 1-612-646-8722
Offers excellent curriculum and craft kits, including a detailed schedule of activities. Materials for over a dozen craft projects are included for each child.

Little People's Workshop
Box 43900
Louisville, KY 40243
1-800-626-1554
In Kentucky or Canada call 1-502-245-4160
Step-by-step learning activities to stimulate children 2–5 years. Lessons for circle time, art, movement, and so on.

Home-Based Business Publications

Mothers at Home
Box 2208
Merrifield, VA 22116
Welcome Home Newsletter.

Homeworking Mothers Newsletter
P.O. Box 423
East Meadow, NY 11554

Sideline Business: The Newsletter for Part-time Entrepreneurs
JG Press
Emmanus, PA 18049

National Home-Based Business Report
Box 2137
Naperville, IL 60566

Child Care Organizations

National Association for Family Day Care (NAFDC)
815 Fifteenth Street NW, Suite 928
Washington, DC 20005
202-347-3356

National Association for the Education of Young Children (NAEYC)
1834 Connecticut Avenue NW
Washington, DC 20009-5786
1-800-424-2460
Centralized source on national child care issues.

Child Care Action Committee
99 Hudson Street #1233
New York, NY 10013
212-334-9595
Advocacy group for quality child care.

Day Care and Child Development Council
1012 14th Street NW
Washington, D.C. 20005
Family Day Care Provider newsletter

Children's Foundation
1420 New York Avenue NW
Washington, D.C. 20005
Information on Child Care Food Program. Also offers home-based providers a publication called "Family Day Care Bulletin."

School Age Child Care Project
Wellesley College
Wellesley, MA 02181
617-431-1453
New curriculum guide also available to train family day care providers to provide better care for infants and toddlers. For further information: 202-347-3300.

Insurance Information

BMF Marketing Insurance Services, Inc.
15250 Ventura Boulevard, Suite 1012
Sherman Oaks, CA 91403-3288
1-800-423-9733
In California call 1-800-624-0912
Call and ask for pamphlet "Recommended Minimum Insurance Requirements for Family Day Care."

Family Day Care Publications

Argus: The Journal of Family Day Care
P.O. Box 15146
Atlanta, GA 30333
A professional publication through which the family day care community shares information and ideas. Subscription available.

Zoning Guide for Family Day Care
Child Care Law Center
22 Second Street, 5th Floor
San Francisco, CA 94105
415-495-5498
Publication written for family day care providers, resource and referral agencies, day care advocates, and elected officials. Write to above address for current price.

Skippack Books
Box 792
Skippack, PA 19474
215-584-8244
Mail order book company for child caregivers. (Catalog free.)

RECORDS AND BOOKS

Records

Children love to listen to music and songs over and over again until they can sing along with the record. They also make up dances as they act out the song. Records are wonderful to play when you are trying to get your children to rest. They can close their eyes to sleep as they dream about the stories they are listening to.

Price/Stern/Sloan:
Wee Sing America 1983
Wee Sing Silly Songs 1982

Shoreline/A & M Records:
More Singable Songs by Raffi 1976
Baby Beluga by Raffi 1980

Golden, 1966:
The New Golden Song Book

Random House, 1979:
The Illustrated Disney Song Book

Simon and Schuster, 1966
The Fireside Book of Children's Songs

Educational Activities:
Getting to Know Myself by Hap Palmer 1972
Learning Basic Skills Through Music: Building Vocabulary by Hap Palmer 1975

Children's Books

This list contains both books for very young children and pre-schoolers.

Brown, Margaret Wise. *The Runaway Bunny*. Boulder, CO: Live Oak Media, 1985.

Burningham, John. *John Burningham's ABC*. New York: Crown, 1986.

Burton, Virginia L. *Katy and the Big Snow*. Grand Rapids, MI: Zondervan, 1974.

Campbell, Rod. *Dear Zoo*. New York: Macmillan, 1983.

Carle, Eric. *The Very Hungry Caterpillar*. New York: Putnam, 1981.

Carle, Eric. *Do You Want to Be My Friend?* New York: Harper & Row Junior Books, 1986.

DePaola, Tomie. *Tomie DePaola's Favorite Nursery Tales*. New York: Putnam, 1986.

Flack, Marjorie. *Angus y el gato*. New York: Scholastic, 1979.

Gag, Wanda. *Millions of Cats*. New York: Putnam, 1977.

Ginsburg, Mirra. *Good Morning, Chick*. New York: Greenwillow, 1980.

Keats, Ezra Jack. *The Snowy Day*. New York: Viking-Penguin, 1962.

Keats, Ezra Jack. *Kitten for a Day*. New York: Macmillan, 1974.

Kunhardt, Dorothy. *Pat the Bunny*. New York: Western, 1942.

Langstall, John. *Over in the Meadow*. San Diego, CA: Harcourt Brace Jovanovich, 1967.

Maxwell, Arthur S. *Uncle Arthur's Bedtime Stories, Volume One*. Washington, DC: Pacific Press Publishing Association and Review and Herald Publishing Association, 1976.

Miller, Jane. *Farm Counting Book*. Englewood Cliffs, NJ: Prentice-Hall, 1983.

Piper, Watty. *The Little Engine That Could*. Cuthchogue, NY: Buckaneer, 1981.

Potter, Beatrix. *The Tale of Peter Rabbit*. Mahwah, NJ: Troll, 1979.

Scarry, Richard. *Richard Scarry's Busiest People Ever*. New York: Random House, 1976.

Magazines

Since magazines are tax deductible for your business, you may want to subscribe. If not, why not check them out at your local library on a regular basis. You will find photographs, poems, activities, and articles of interest for everyone.

Sesame Street Magazine (preschoolers)
P.O. Box 2895
Boulder, CO 80321

Ranger Rick's Nature Magazine (older children)
Your Big Backyard
National Wildlife Federation
1412 16th Street NW
Washington, DC 20036

Highlights for Children (ages 2–12)
803 Church Street
Homesdale, PA 18431

Turtle Magazine for Preschool Kids
1100 Waterway Boulevard
Box 567
Indianapolis, IN 46206

Suggested Reading for the Caregiver

If you would like to learn more about of caring for your children, the books listed will give you good advice.

Brazelton, T. Berry. *Toddlers and Parents*. New York: Delacorte, 1974.

Dobson, James, M.D. *Hide or Seek*. Old Tappan, NJ: Fleming H. Revell, 1979.

Fraiberg, Selma. *The Magic Years: Understanding and Handling the Problems of Early Childhood*. New York: Scribner's, 1959.

Galinsky, Ellen, and Hooks, William. *The New Extended Family: Day Care That Works*. Boston: Houghton Mifflin, 1977.

Gallagher, Patricia C. *So You Want to Open a Profitable Day Care Center* . . . ($12.95) (A Guide for Teachers, Nurses, Corporate Personnel, College Students) *Robin's Play and Learn Book— How To Entertain Children At Home or in Preschool* ($12.95)
<u>Order Dept.</u>
    Child Care
    Box 555
    Worcester, PA 19490

Kelly, Marguerite, and Parsons, Elia. *The Mother's Almanac*. New York: Doubleday, 1975.

Spock, Benjamin, M.D. *Baby and Child Care*. New York: Pocket Books, 1974.

SAMPLE STATE

LICENSING FORMS

Forms required of home day care providers vary from state to state. The following forms are samples of those required for licensing in my home state of Pennsylvania. This is just to give you some idea of the type of information needed for state licensing.

APPLICATION FOR DAY CARE SERVICES
CHILD DAY CARE CENTERS · GROUP DAY CARE HOMES · FAMILY DAY CARE HOMES

	DATE OF APPLICATION
NAME OF CHILD	BIRTHDATE
ADDRESS	
MOTHER'S NAME · OR LEGAL GUARDIAN	FATHER'S NAME · OR LEGAL GUARDIAN
MOTHER'S HOME ADDRESS	TELEPHONE NO. · HOME
FATHER'S HOME ADDRESS	TELEPHONE NO. · HOME
MOTHER'S BUSINESS ADDRESS	TELEPHONE NO. · BUSINESS
FATHER'S BUSINESS ADDRESS	TELEPHONE NO. · BUSINESS
NAME AND ADDRESS OF PERSON TO BE CONTACTED IN EMERGENCY IF PARENTS ARE NOT AVAILABLE	TELEPHONE NO.
NAME AND ADDRESS OF CHILD'S PHYSICIAN OR SOURCE OF MEDICAL CARE	TELEPHONE NO.

SPECIAL DISABILITY · IF ANY

ANY SPECIAL MEDICAL OR DIETARY INFORMATION NECESSARY FOR MANAGEMENT IN AN EMERGENCY SITUATION · ALLERGIES, MEDICATIONS, SPECIAL CONDITIONS

ANY ADDITIONAL INFORMATION ON SPECIAL NEEDS OF THE CHILD

HEALTH INSURANCE COVERAGE FOR CHILD UNDER FAMILY INSURANCE POLICY OR MEDICAL ASSISTANCE BENEFITS, IF APPLICABLE

SIGNATURE OF PARENT OR GUARDIAN:

Commonwealth of Pennsylvania   Department of Public Welfare   CY 320 · 8-78

AGREEMENT

CHILD DAY CARE CENTERS · GROUP DAY CARE HOMES · FAMILY DAY CARE HOMES

A Fee of	Per-Day-Week, etc.	Will be paid · Daily, Weekly, etc.	By · Mother, Father, Other · Specify	
$				

This will include cost of · Care, Transportation, Meals, etc. · Specify Meals to be Served

Transportation will be supplied by		Medical Care · If required · will be paid by

Child will arrive at · Time	Depart · Time	Usually accompanied by · Mother, Father · Other	A Fee of	Per Min · Hr (Not applicable · Title XX)
			$	

Person(s) designated by parents to whom child may be released · specify all persons other than parents

Any additional conditions and/or services as agreed upon by both parties

Signature · Administrator, Director, Caregiver	Date	Signature, Parent or Guardian	Date

DATE OF CHILD'S ADMISSION · ENROLLMENT	DATE OF CHILD'S WITHDRAWAL

CY 321 · 3-78

PAYMENT OF FEE

DATE	AMOUNT	DATE	AMOUNT	DATE	AMOUNT	DATE	AMOUNT

EMERGENCY CONTACT INFORMATION
FAMILY DAY CARE HOMES

	Date of Application
Child's Name	Birthdate
Address	
Mother's Name - or Legal Guardian	Telephone No. *(Home)*
Address	
Business Address	Telephone No. *(Business)*
Father's Name - or Legal Guardian	Telephone No. *(Home)*
Address	
Business Address	Telephone No. *(Business)*
Name and Address of Person to be Contacted in Emergency *(If Parents Are Not Available)*	Telephone No.
Name and Address of Child's Physician or Source of Medical Care	Telephone No.

Special Disability *(If Any)*

Any Special Medical or Dietary Information Necessary for Management in an Emergency Situation *(Allergies, Medications, Special Conditions)*

Any Additional Information on Special Needs of the Child

Health Insurance Coverage for Child Under Family Insurance Policy or Medical Assistance Benefits *(If Applicable)*

Person(s) Designated by Parent(s) to Whom the Child May be Released

_____   _____
Signature of Parent or Guardian   Date

CY 73 - 4-81

PARENTAL CONSENT

☐ Child Day Care Centers	☐ Group Day Care Homes	☐ Family Day Care Center	CHILD'S NAME

KEEP THIS CONSENT FORM HANDY SO THAT IT CAN BE TAKEN WITH THE CHILD IN CASE EMERGENCY MEDICAL CARE IS NEEDED.

NAME AND ADDRESS OF FACILITY

WRITTEN CONSENT IS GIVEN FOR: (Please check those items for which you give your consent)

☐ EMERGENCY MEDICAL CARE ☐ ADMINISTRATION OF PRESCRIPTION MEDICATIONS (Physician's Current Written Instructions Must Be Provided)

☐ ADMINISTRATION OF NON-PRESCRIPTION MEDICATIONS; PLEASE LIST ALL THAT MAY BE ADMINISTERED, AND DOSAGE:

☐ ADMINISTRATION OF SPECIAL DENTAL OR DIETARY NEEDS; PLEASE LIST ALL THAT CAN BE ADMINISTERED, AND DOSAGE:

☐ TRIPS ☐ TRANSPORTATION BY THE FACILITY FOR TRIPS ☐ DAILY TRANSPORTATION PROVIDED BY THE FACILITY (Facility Has The Option to Offer)

IF YOUR CHILD IS TRANSPORTED BY THE FACILITY ARE THERE ANY INSTRUCTIONS FOR SPECIAL CARE FOR THE CHILD (E.G. MOTION SICKNESS, SEIZURES) DURING TRANSPORTATION? YES ☐ NO ☐ If yes, specify:

☐ SWIMMING ☐ HOMEWORK SUPERVISION

PARENT'S SIGNATURE	DATE	HOME TELEPHONE NO.	WORK TELEPHONE NO.

HOME ADDRESS

WORK ADDRESS

CY 38 - 7/84

CHILD HEALTH APPRAISAL

CHILD DAY CARE CENTERS ● GROUP DAY CARE HOMES ● FAMILY DAY CARE HOMES

DATE OF EXAM

CHILD'S NAME (Last, First, M.I.) BIRTHDATE

CHILD'S ADDRESS TELEPHONE NUMBER

1. REVIEW OF HEALTH HISTORY

2. MEDICAL INFO. PERTINENT TO DIAG. AND TREATMENT IN CASE OF EMERGENCY

3. SPECIAL INSTRUCTIONS TO PROVIDER REGARDING ANY MEDICATION REQUIRED DURING DAY CARE HOURS

4. RECOMMENDED MODIFICATIONS OR LIMITATIONS OF CHILD'S ACTIVITIES OR DIET (e.g. allergies, etc.)

5. VISION (Acuity)   Normal   Abnormal

6. HEARING (Audiometry or equiv.)

7. GROWTH MEASUREMENT
Ht. ___ ' ___ Percentile   Wt. ___ lbs. ___ Percentile   Circ. ___ " ___ Percentile

8. DENTAL SCREENING	YES	NO	9. MEDICAL				Normal	Abnormal	10. HGB		
				Normal	Abnormal				HGB	Normal	Abnormal
Caries			Ears, Nose			Abdomen			GM OR HCT	Normal	Abnormal
Missing Permanent Teeth			Eyes			Genitalia, Breasts			%		
Oral Infection			Mouth, Throat			Extremities/ Joints			11. BLOOD PRESSURE		/
Protrusion			Lungs			Spine					
			Cardio-Vascular			Skin, Lymph Nodes				Normal	Abnormal

12. DEVELOPMENTAL APPRAISAL

IS CHILD PROGRESSING NORMALLY WITH AGE OR GROUP?   YES   NO   DENVER DEVELOPMENTAL: Normal   Abnormal

13. IMMUNIZATIONS

DTP: Diptheria–Tetanus–Pertusis	DATE	TRIVALENT ORAL POLIO VACCINE	DATE	OTHER	DATE
1st (2 months)		1st (2 months)		Measles (15 months or older)	
2nd (4 months)		2nd (4 months)		Mumps (15 months or older)	
3rd (6 months)		3rd (18 months)		Rubella (15 months or older)	
Booster		4th (4 - 6 years)		HIB (Haemophilus b)	
Booster		Urinalysis		Tuberculin test	

14. RECOMMEND FURTHER MEDICAL TESTS OR EXAMINATION ON THE FOLLOWING:

VISION   GROWTH   HBG   HEAD CIRCUMFERENCE   HEARING   DENTAL   BLOOD PRESSURE

MEDICAL (Specify)

DEVELOPMENTAL PROGRESS (Specify)

IMMUNIZATION (Specify)

PRINTED NAME OF PHYSICIAN   TELEPHONE NO.

PHYSICIAN'S ADDRESS

PHYSICIAN'S SIGNATURE

DATE

00148A

CY 51 - 2/88

RECOMMENDATIONS FOR PREVENTIVE PEDIATRIC HEALTH CARE
Committee on Practice and Ambulatory Medicine

Each child and family is unique; therefore these Recommendations for Preventive Pediatric Health Care are designed for the care of children who are receiving competent parenting, have no manifestations of any important health problems, and are growing and developing in satisfactory fashion. **Additional visits may become necessary** if circumstances suggest variations from normal. These guidelines represent a consensus by the Committee on Practice and Ambulatory Medicine in consultation with the membership of the American Academy of Pediatrics through the Chapter Presidents. The Committee emphasizes the great importance of continuity of care in comprehensive health supervision and the need to avoid fragmentation of care.

A **prenatal visit** by the parents for anticipatory guidance and pertinent medical history is strongly recommended.

Health supervision should begin with medical care of the newborn in the hospital.

		INFANCY						EARLY CHILDHOOD					LATE CHILDHOOD					ADOLESCENCE[1]			
AGE[2]	By 1 mo.	2 mos.	4 mos.	6 mos.	9 mos.	12 mos.	15 mos.	18 mos.	24 mos.	3 yrs.	4 yrs.	5 yrs.	6 yrs.	8 yrs.	10 yrs.	12 yrs.	14 yrs.	16 yrs.	18 yrs.	20+ yrs.
HISTORY Initial/Interval	●	●	●	●	●	●	●	●	●	●	●	●	●	●	●	●	●	●	●	●
MEASUREMENTS Height and Weight	●	●	●	●	●	●	●	●	●	●	●	●	●	●	●	●	●	●	●	●
Head Circumference	●	●	●	●	●	●														
Blood Pressure									●	●	●	●	●	●	●	●	●	●	●	●
SENSORY SCREENING Vision	S	S	S	S	S	S	S	S	S	S	O	O	O	O	S	O	O	S	O	O
Hearing	S	S	S	S	S	S	S	S	S	S	O	O	S[3]	S[3]	S[3]	O	S	S	O	S
DEVEL./BEHAV.[4] ASSESSMENT	●	●	●	●	●	●	●	●	●	●	●	●	●	●	●	●	●	●	●	●
PHYSICAL EXAMINATION[5]	●	●	●	●	●	●	●	●	●	●	●	●	●	●	●	●	●	●	●	●
PROCEDURES[6] Hered./Metabolic[7] Screening	●																			
Immunization[8]		●	●	●			●	●	●			●					●			
Tuberculin Test[9]						●←			●										●	
Hematocrit or Hemoglobin[10]				●					●					●					●	
Urinalysis[11]				●					●										●	
ANTICIPATORY[12] GUIDANCE	●	●	●	●	●	●	●	●	●	●	●	●	●	●	●	●	●	●	●	●
INITIAL DENTAL[13] REFERRAL									●											

1. Adolescent related issues (e.g., psychosocial, emotional, substance usage, and reproductive health) may necessitate more frequent health supervision.
2. If a child comes under care for the first time at any point on the schedule, or if any items are not accomplished at the suggested age, the schedule should be brought up to date at the earliest possible time.
3. At these points, history may suffice: if problem suggested, a standard testing method should be employed.
4. By history and appropriate physical examination: if suspicious, by specific objective developmental testing.
5. At each visit, a complete physical examination is essential, with infant totally unclothed, older child undressed and suitably draped.
6. These may be modified, depending upon entry point into schedule and individual need.
7. Metabolic screening (e.g., thyroid, PKU, galactosemia) should be done according to state law.
8. Schedule(s) per Report of Committee on Infectious Disease, 1986 *Red Book*.

9. For low risk groups, the Committee on Infectious Diseases recommends the following options: ① no routine testing or ② testing at three times—infancy, preschool, and adolescence. For high risk groups, annual TB skin testing is recommended.
10. Present medical evidence suggests the need for reevaluation of the frequency and timing of hemoglobin or hematocrit tests. One determination is therefore suggested during each time period. Performance of additional tests is left to the individual practice experience.
11. Present medical evidence suggests the need for reevaluation of the frequency and timing of urinalyses. One determination is therefore suggested during each time period. Performance of additional tests is left to the individual practice experience.
12. Appropriate discussion and counselling should be an integral part of each visit for care.
13. Subsequent examinations as prescribed by dentist.

N.B. **Special chemical, immunologic, and endocrine testing** are usually carried out upon specific indications. Testing other than newborn (e.g., inborn errors of metabolism, sickle disease, lead) are discretionary with the physician.

Key: ● =to be performed; S=subjective, by history; O=objective, by a standard testing method.   September 1987

STAFF HEALTH APPRAISAL

Child Day Care Centers ● Group Day Care Homes ● Family Day Care Homes

THIS SECTION TO BE COMPLETED BY THE EMPLOYEE
NAME AND ADDRESS OF INDIVIDUAL EXAMINED

NAME OF EMPLOYER	EMPLOYER'S TELEPHONE NO.

EMPLOYER'S ADDRESS

PURPOSE OF EXAMINATION   TYPE OF ACTIVITY IN DAY CARE (Check all applicable)

☐ INITIAL EMPLOYMENT   ☐ CARING FOR CHILDREN   ☐ DESK WORK   ☐ FACILITY MAINTENANCE

☐ ANNUAL RE-EXAMINATION   ☐ FOOD PREPARATION   ☐ DRIVER OF VEHICLE

THIS SECTION TO BE COMPLETED BY HEALTH PROFESSIONAL WHO DOES HEALTH APPRAISING

PART I - As shown by physical examination, does the individual have:	YES	NO		YES	NO
1. At least 20/40 combined vision, corrected by glasses, if needed?			5. Normal respiratory system?		
2. Normal hearing?			6. Normal skin?		
3. Normal blood pressure?			7. Normal neuro musculoskeletal systems?		
4. Normal cardiovascular system?			8. Normal endocrine system?		

EXPLAIN ALL "NO" RESPONSES ON REVERSE OF FORM, GIVING PLAN FOR FOLLOW-UP

PART II - Does this individual have any of the following medical problems:	YES	NO		YES	NO
9. History of myocardial infarction, angina pectoris, coronary insufficiency?			13. Inadequate immune status (Td, measles, mumps, rubella)?		
10. History of epilepsy?			14. Need for more frequent health visits or sick days than average for age?		
11. Diabetes?			15. Current drug or alcohol dependency?		
12. Thyroid or other metabolic disorders?			16. Disabling emotional disorder?		
17. Other special medical problem or chronic disease which requires restriction of activity, medication or which might affect his/her work role? If so, specify on reverse of form.					

EXPLAIN ALL "YES" RESPONSES ON REVERSE OF FORM, GIVING PLAN FOR FOLLOW-UP, IF ANY

18. Does this individual have any special medical problems which might interfere with the health of the children or which might prohibit the individual from providing adequate care for the children? If yes, explain on reverse of form.		

PART III - REQUIRED TEST FOR TUBERCULOSIS TUBERCULIN SKIN TEST BY **EITHER** INTRACUTANEOUS MAMTOUX TWO STEP METHOD OR PERCUTANEOUS MULTIPLE PUNCTURE METHOD

PHYSICIANS REPORT OF TUBERCULIN TEST RESULTS

19. INTRACUTANEOUS MANTOUX TEST METHOD	REPORT OF FIRST TEST	REPORT OF SECOND TEST IF NONSIGNIFICANT ON FIRST TEST 1 TO 3 WEEKS LATER
Name of antigen used and manufacture.		
Lot number.		
Dose of purified protein derivative.		
Date on which test was applied.		
Date on which test read.		
Measurement of Widest Diameter of induration in millimeters.		

If Positive:

DATE OF REPORT OF 14 x 17 CHEST X-RAY (attach copy of report)	OTHER STUDIES DONE TO RULE OUT TUBERCULOSIS DISEASE

CY 322 - 9/86

20. PERCUTANEOUS MULTIPLE PUNCTURE TEST METHOD

NAME OF PRODUCT USED AND MANUFACTURER	LOT NUMBER

DATE ON WHICH TEST WAS APPLIED	DATE ON WHICH TEST READ

DESCRIPTION OF REACTION*

If Vesticulated:

DATE AND REPORT OF 14 x 17 CHEST X-RAY (attach copy of report)	OTHER STUDIES DONE TO RULE OUT TUBERCULOSIS DISEASE

*NOTE: ANY DURATION WITHOUT VESICULATION MUST BE RETESTED USING THE MANTOUX METHOD.

IF SIGNIFICANT REACTION WAS REPORTED, THE PHYSICIAN REPORT MUST STATE THAT APPLICANT IS FREE FROM CURRENT TUBERCULOSIS DISEASE OR IS UNDER ADEQUATE CHEMOTHERAPY FOR TUBERCULOSIS DISEASE.

REFERRED FOR PREVENTIVE ANTI-TUBERCULOSIS CHEMOTHERAPY? (✓)   ☐ YES   ☐ NO

_____   _____
Physician Signature   *Physician Name (Print)*

_____   _____
Physician Address   *Date*

PATIENT AUTHORIZATION

The statements and answers as recorded above are full, complete and true to the best of my knowledge and belief. Unless prohibited by law, I authorize the physician or other person to disclose any knowledge or information pertaining to my health. I understand that any false or misleading statements may cause termination of my employment.

_____   _____
Patient Signature   *Date*

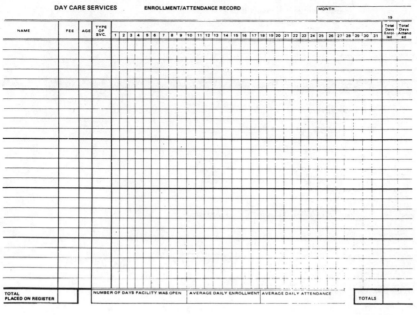

DAY CARE SERVICES   **ENROLLMENT/ATTENDANCE RECORD**   MONTH

19

NAME	FEE	AGE	TYPE OF SVC.	1	2	3	4	5	6	7	8	9	10	11	12	13	14	15	16	17	18	19	20	21	22	23	24	25	26	27	28	29	30	31	Total Days Enrolled	Total Days Attended

TOTAL PLACED ON REGISTER — **NUMBER OF DAYS FACILITY WAS OPEN** — **AVERAGE DAILY ENROLLMENT** — **AVERAGE DAILY ATTENDANCE** — **TOTALS**

PL 29A · 8-81

APPLICATION FOR CHILD ABUSE HISTORY
(Pursuant to Child Care Employment)

INSTRUCTIONS: Complete Section I of the application. Enclose check or money order for $10.00 payable to Department of Public Welfare. Send to Department of Public Welfare, P.O. Box 8170, Harrisburg, PA 17105-8170.

Applications received without fee will not be processed.

No fee required for CWEP participants.

DPW USE
DATE RECEIVED BY CHILDLINE

SECTION I - APPLICANT IDENTIFICATION

NAME OF APPLICANT (Last, First, Middle)	AGE	SEX ☐ Male ☐ Female	SOCIAL SECURITY NO.

CURRENT ADDRESS (Street, Apt., Box No., City, State, Zip Code)

OTHER NAME'S USED BY APPLICANT SINCE 1975 (Last, First, Middle)

1.	2.	3.

CHECK ONE BLOCK ONLY

☐ I am requesting a clearance for purposes of employment

☐ I am requesting a voluntary certification/biennial recertification and have enclosed copies of the Pennsylvania State Police and FBI (out-of-state applicants only) clearances

☐ I am a CWEP program participant	SIGNATURE OF CONFIRMING CAO OFFICIAL	DATE	TELEPHONE NO.

FORMER ADDRESSES OF APPLICANT SINCE 1975 (Street, Apt., Box No., City, State, Zip Code)

1.

2.

3.

4.

5.

MEMBERS OF APPLICANT'S HOUSEHOLD

NAME	RELATIONSHIP	SEX	AGE
1.			
2.			
3.			
4.			
5.			

I certify that the above information is accurate.

APPLICANT SIGNATURE	DATE

SECTION II - RESULTS OF HISTORY CHECK

☐ Applicant is not listed in our files as a perpetrator of child abuse.

☐ Applicant is listed in our files as a perpetrator of child abuse.

REPORTS IDENTIFIED

	STATUS	DATE OF INCIDENT		STATUS	DATE OF INCIDENT
1			4		
2			5		
3			6		

SIGNATURE OF VERIFIER	DATE	SIGNATURE VERIFIERS SUPERVISOR

APPLICATION

SECTION III - VOLUNTARY CERTIFICATION RECERTIFICATION

To Whom it May Concern:

_____ has requested a certification which includes a clearance of his/her name against the child abuse and criminal history files.

The results of the child abuse record clearance are listed in Section II on the reverse side. The results of the criminal history clearance is(are) listed below. Out-of-state residents must have criminal history clearance from both the Pennsylvania State Police and the FBI. The voluntary certification

It is the responsibility of parents and guardians to review this information to determine the suitability of the applicant as a substitute caregiver.

Pennsylvania State Police Clearance

- [ ] No records exist. Report attached.

- [ ] Convictions are on file which would prohibit hire in a child care position pursuant to the Child Protective Services Law II P.S. §2223.1(e). Report attached.

- [ ] Record exists, but convictions are not indicated which would prohibit employment in a child care position pursuant to the Child Protective Services Law II P.S. §2223.1(e). Report attached.

FBI Clearance

- [ ] No records exist. Report attached.

- [ ] Convictions are on file which would prohibit hire in a child care position pursuant to the Child Protective Services Law II P.S. §2223.1(e). Report attached.

- [ ] Record exists, but convictions are not indicated which would prohibit employment in a child care position pursuant to the Child Protective Services Law II P.S. §2223.1(e). Report attached.

- [ ] No clearance required.

_____   _____
SIGNATURE OF VERIFIER   DATE

_____   _____
SIGNATURE OF VERIFIERS SUPERVISOR   DATE

CY 113 - 11/85

SP 4 - 164 (2-88)

FOR CENTRAL REPOSITORY USE ONLY
(LEAVE BLANK)

PENNSYLVANIA STATE POLICE
REQUEST FOR CRIMINAL HISTORY RECORD INFORMATION
(SEE REVERSE SIDE FOR INSTRUCTIONS)

TYPE OR PRINT ONLY

PART I   TO BE COMPLETED BY REQUESTER

DATE OF REQUEST

NAME   (Last)   (First)   (Middle)

MAIDEN NAME AND/OR ALIASES   SOCIAL SECURITY NO.   DATE OF BIRTH   SEX   RACE

REQUESTER IDENTIFICATION

☐ CRIMINAL JUSTICE AGENCY - FEE EXEMPT   ☐ NONCRIMINAL JUSTICE AGENCY - FEE EXEMPT

☐ INDIVIDUAL - NONCRIMINAL JUSTICE AGENCY - $10 FEE ENCLOSED

REASON FOR REQUEST

☐ CRIMINAL INVESTIGATION   ☐ INDIVIDUAL ACCESS AND REVIEW BY SUBJECT OF RECORD OR LEGAL REPRESENTATIVE

☐ CRIMINAL JUSTICE EMPLOYMENT   ☐ NONCRIMINAL JUSTICE EMPLOYMENT

☐ COURT REQUEST ON PRIOR ARD   ☐ OTHER (Specify) _____

PART II   TO BE COMPLETED BY CRIMINAL JUSTICE AGENCIES ONLY

INFORMATION REQUESTED   SID NO. (If available)   OTN OR OCA NO. (If available)

☐ FINGERPRINTS
☐ RAP SHEET   ☐ PHOTO   ☐ PRIOR ARD

PART III   FOR CENTRAL REPOSITORY USE ONLY   (LEAVE BLANK)

INFORMATION DISSEMINATED   SID NO.

☐ NO RECORD OR NO RECORD THAT MEETS DISSEMINATION CRITERIA

☐ RAP SHEET   ☐ FINGERPRINTS   ☐ PHOTO   INQUIRY BY   DISSEMINATION BY

THE INFORMATION FURNISHED BY THE CENTRAL REPOSITORY IS SOLELY BASED ON THE
FOLLOWING IDENTIFIERS THAT MATCH THOSE FURNISHED BY THE REQUESTER:

☐ SID NO.   ☐ DATE OF BIRTH   ☐ RACE

☐ OTN/OCA NO.   ☐ MAIDEN NAME   ☐ SEX
                                                               Director, Central Repository
☐ NAME   ☐ SOCIAL SECURITY NO. ☐ ALIAS

Response based on comparison of requester furnished information and/or fingerprints against a name index and/or fingerprints contained in
the files of the Pennsylvania State Police Central Repository only, and does not preclude the existence of other criminal records which may
be contained in the repositories of other local, state or federal criminal justice agencies.

PART IV   TO BE COMPLETED BY REQUESTER

NAME OF INDIVIDUAL
MAKING REQUEST _____

REQUEST TO BE MAILED TO: LIST TELEPHONE NO. TO BE USED IN
NAME   CASE OF PROBLEM
                                                               INCLUDE AREA CODE
ADDRESS

CITY   STATE   ZIP CODE

INSTRUCTIONS FOR COMPLETION OF REQUEST FOR
CRIMINAL HISTORY RECORD INFORMATION

PARTS I AND IV
TYPE OR PRINT LEGIBLY WITH BALL - POINT PEN.
PARTS I AND IV ARE TO BE COMPLETED BY THE REQUESTER ON EACH AND EVERY INDIVIDUAL THEY
DESIRE TO HAVE CRIMINAL HISTORY RECORD INFORMATION ON.

AFTER COMPLETION, FORWARD BOTH COPIES WITH THE CARBON INTACT TO:

DIRECTOR, RECORDS AND IDENTIFICATION DIVISION
1800 ELMERTON AVENUE, ATTN: CENTRAL REPOSITORY,
HARRISBURG, PA. 17110.

NONCRIMINAL JUSTICE AGENCIES AND INDIVIDUALS MUST
INCLUDE A CHECK OR MONEY ORDER (NON REFUNDABLE) IN
THE AMOUNT OF $10.00 PAYABLE TO "COMMONWEALTH OF
PENNSYLVANIA" FOR EACH REQUEST.

NOTE: NONCRIMINAL JUSTICE AGENCIES AND INDIVIDUALS
WILL ONLY RECEIVE A COPY OF THE "RAP SHEET"
IF ANY RECORD IS IN FILE.

PART II

PART II IS TO BE COMPLETED BY A CRIMINAL JUSTICE AGENCY THAT REQUESTS CRIMINAL HISTORY
RECORD INFORMATION ON AN INDIVIDUAL.

PART III

PART III IS TO BE COMPLETED BY A DESIGNATED EMPLOYEE OR OFFICER OF THE PENNSYLVANIA
STATE POLICE, CENTRAL REPOSITORY.

INSTRUCTIONS FOR COMPLETION OF APPLICATION FOR
CERTIFICATE OF COMPLIANCE FOR A FACILITY OR AGENCY, PW 633

1. **NAME, ADDRESS, AND PHONE NUMBER OF PHYSICAL SITE OF AGENCY/FACILITY:** Indicate name, address, and phone number of a physical facility or agency where the services will be provided. If the application is for renewal, the name and address of the facility or agency should be the same as on previous application unless name is changed.

2. **NAME, ADDRESS, AND PHONE NUMBER OF LEGAL ENTITY:** Indicate name of legal entity, for example, the person, partnership, association, organization, corporation or governmental body responsible for the operation of the facility or agency. Indicate the address and telephone number of the principal office or sponsoring agency.

3. **PURPOSE OF APPLICATION:** Check if application is for a new facility or for a renewal of a current Certificate of Compliance.

4. **COUNTY:** Indicate the name of the County in which facility or agency is located.

5. **NAME OF RESPONSIBLE PERSON (OPERATOR):** Indicate the full name and title of the person who is responsible for the daily operation of the facility or agency.

6. **CURRENT CERTIFICATE EXPIRES:** Indicate date current certificate expires, if this application is for renewal.

7. **CURRENT CERTIFICATE NUMBER:** Indicate current certificate number, if this application is for renewal.

8. **TYPE OF FACILITY OR AGENCY:** Example of Type of Facilities or Agencies--

    Mental Health Facilities: Private Psychiatric Hospital, Psychiatric Outpatient Clinic, Partial Hospitalization, Community Residential Rehabilitation Service.

    Mental Retardation Facilities: Community Residential MR Large Facility, Community Residential MR Agency, Intermediate Care Facility/Mental Retardation (ICF/MR).

    Children, Youth and Families Facilities: Day Care Center, Group Day Care Home, Juvenile Detention Center, Residential Child Care Facility, County Children and Youth Agency, Private Children and Youth Agency, Foster Family Care Agency Services, Adoption, Maternity Home, Training Schools, Child Protective Services.

    Adult Facilities: Personal Care Boarding Home, Adult Day Care Center, Vocational Rehabilitation Facility.

9. **PROFIT:** Operating with the expectation of providing a financial benefit to someone or something other than the facility or agency itself. The focus is upon the ultimate aim of the enterprise, not the financial results of any particular period of operation. The focus is also upon the particular premises involved and not the legal entity which operates the facility or agency. A non-profit legal entity may be considered as operating a facility or agency for profit if the particular premises involved provides a financial benefit to the parent legal entity. Any legal entity not possessing a certificate of tax exempt status from the Internal Revenue Service will be considered operating for profit unless it provides satisfactory proof otherwise.

    NONPROFIT: Operating other than for profit. Copy of tax exempt certificate should be submitted with the initial application.

10. **TYPE OF OWNERSHIP:** Fill in proper type of ownership.

11. **PRIOR LICENSE STATUS:** Complete and explain any YES responses on separate sheet.

12. Please answer YES or NO and explain any YES responses on a separate sheet.

13. **CURRENT STATUS OF LEGAL ENTITY, OWNER OR OPERATOR:** Complete and explain any YES responses on separate sheet.

ATTACHMENTS: Attach Articles of Incorporation, State Fictitious Name Approval.

DECLARATION: The declaration must be signed by the legal entity. If the legal entity is a partnership, association, or organization, the person authorized to sign such documents must sign. Where the legal entity is a corporation, the signature must be of a corporate officer. Type or print name and title of person signing.

PW 633 4/86